Praise for *Yearning*

"This book, told in the voice of a strong yet vulnerable child—and then as a mother, fiercely protecting her children from the same fate—is insightful and compelling in its account of the survival of the spirit."

Joanne Bodin, PhD, Author

"…her life, beautifully written, without self-pity or sentimentality, is an excellent read…an uplifting glimpse into what makes a survivor."

Judy Ducharme,
University of New Mexico librarian (retired)

"Yearning is a personal account of a child, and then a young woman, who faces a sorrowful life with courage, in a country that was also coming of age. It is a story for those who remember that time and for young people who might wonder about it."

John Thomas, Writer and Editor

"Sally Cisney Mann tells a powerful, moving, and unforgettable story of tragedy and hope, loss and love, suffering and triumph. Hers is a life shaped by sweeping events—economic and social dislocation from the Great Depression, World War II, and the war in Southeast Asia. All students of "war and family" should read this work, as well as those interested in the social history of women in America and in how we construct our individual identities when the world seems unwilling to cooperate. Her truly remarkable account, at once personal and universal, details her quest for stability—and for family. Readers will shed tears at all she endured, and they'll be 'in her corner' as she struggles to prevail over heartache."

Donald J. Mrozek
Professor and Director of Graduate Studies,
Department of History, Kansas State University
Author of *Air Power and the Ground War in Vietnam*

Yearning

A Memoir

Sally Cisney Mann

To St. Christopher's,

Thank you for the happy
five and a half years of my
child hood with you.

Sally C. Mann

Outskirts Press, Inc.
Denver, Colorado

In memory of my foster mother, Jean Forrest:
You taught me the meaning of family love.

ACKNOWLEDGEMENTS

For believing I had a story worth telling and in my ability to tell it, I thank Don Mrozek. He followed the project from its beginning, as an autobiography, to its completion as a memoir.

Thanks to Sean Murphy, New Mexico author and instructor, for his inspiration and guidance.

I thank my editor, Frank Zoretich, for weeding out and strengthening my writing, word by word, line by line. His honesty and expertise offered challenges that made for some long, tough writing days.

For their never-ending support, encouragement, and feedback over the years, I thank Judy Ducharme, Joanne Bodin, and John Thomas, my critiquers and friends.

For his encouragement and understanding, and for the thirty-five incredible years we've shared, I thank my husband, Greg.

And finally, I thank my wonderful family for being just that...*my family!*

*At the innermost core of all loneliness is a deep and power-
ful yearning for union with one's lost self.*

Brendan Francis

PROLOGUE

There were seven of us in the Waiting Wives Group at Moody Air Force Base in Valdosta, Georgia, each waiting for her pilot/husband to return from his tour of duty in Vietnam. Each month we met for a potluck supper at one home or another. We talked about how our children were coping with absent fathers, how we were keeping ourselves busy, and what we'd learned about the war from our husbands and the television news.

We discussed the *what ifs* over hot cheesy casseroles, fruit cobblers, and heavily frosted chocolate bundt cakes. *What if* your husband was injured? *What if* your husband's plane was shot down and he was killed? *What if* you saw a navy blue military car pull up in front of your house and watched two uniformed officers get out? "I don't think I could open the door," I said. The other women nodded in understanding, with humorless smiles. We discussed these possibilities in a surprisingly casual tone, never actually considering they might happen to us. Some men didn't come home, but ours would.

* * * * *

On February 18, 1969, the official navy blue car stopped outside my home. Whit and Nick, my three- and

1

four-year-old sons, were playing at a neighbor's house on our cul-de-sac. I was in the kitchen heating Beanie Weenies and cutting up fruit for the boys' dinner. From the kitchen window, I saw the car pull up to our front curb and stop, but it never crossed my mind that *the* dreaded scene was about to unfold. When I opened the door, the somber faces on the two men who stood there triggered a momentary paralysis. They introduced themselves, but I stood mute. I recognized one officer as a base chaplain. I didn't know the other one. I saw their lips moving but heard no sound.

"Mrs. Brucher? Do you mind if we come in and talk to you?" I finally heard one of them say. They moved closer to the door, but I abruptly blocked their way, holding my arms straight out in front of me and backing them down the steps. They asked if my children were inside, perhaps assuming I was trying to protect them from the news. Although that wasn't the case, I knew if they entered my home I would have to accept their information. They were going to destroy my world, and I wanted them to get in their car and leave. Wrong address, wrong family, wrong news. I had succeeded in backing them out to the middle of the front yard. I couldn't look at them. I was trembling uncontrollably and shaking my head in vehement denial of the news I suspected they came to deliver.

My next-door-neighbors, Claire and Will Dennison, hurried toward us, asking the officers what this was about. I clung to Claire, desperately begging her to make them leave. Instead, she and Will listened as the chaplain said, "We have news of Captain Brucher."

Claire had to support and steer me as she and Will walked the officers and me toward their house. Inside their living room, I perched on the front edge of the chair cushion as though ready to flee. Because the officers knew Will was a colonel and a squadron commander at Moody Air

Force Base, they spoke directly to him. I couldn't follow the conversation; my brain refused to process the words until I heard… "Missing in Action."

I was instantly alert. *John isn't dead; he's alive and missing. They don't know him, how clever he is. He will survive…he will escape…he will come home.*

The officers told us that John's F-105 jet fighter was hit by enemy fire at dusk while on an armed reconnaissance mission. He ejected and his parachute landed him in a tree just over the North Vietnam border into Laos. The forward air controller kept radio contact with him, and John reported he was okay except for a dislocated shoulder that prevented him from reaching his knife to cut himself free. Because it would be dark before they could get a search-and-rescue aircraft in, they told him to take cover as best he could and they would be there to get him at first light.

I knew that early evening in Georgia meant it was dawn in Vietnam. There could be news at any moment!

After giving the information, the officers asked if I would be all right, nodded to the Dennisons, and left. Claire went to our neighbor's to retrieve the boys and asked us to stay for dinner. I remember nothing of the meal or what we talked about at the table. Will mixed a couple of strong bourbon drinks for me after dinner. Claire covered us with an umbrella as she accompanied the boys and me home through an evening shower.

Whit and Nick kept looking at me, as though asking for an explanation for the evening's unusual activities and for the adults' somber mood. Though they seemed to sense that something troubling was going on, I stayed as calm as possible while following our nightly routine and getting them tucked into bed. I decided to tell them about Daddy in the morning when there might be more news, *good* news.

It was a very long night. I paced, waiting for the phone

to ring with news of John's rescue, but each agonizing hour passed without word.

As I stared out the front window, I couldn't distinguish the rain from my tears. I'd had so many losses in my life. *Please, God, keep him safe. Don't take him from me.* All my life I'd longed for a family, and now that I had created this one with John, I just couldn't bear to lose him.

PART ONE

CHAPTER ONE

The year was 1942. I was three years old.

As the taxi carrying my mother, sister, and me drove through the wide chain link gate and down the long, winding concrete drive into St. Christopher's boarding school, a new world appeared. I took it all in with both awe and anxiety.

I saw vine-covered stone buildings and towering chestnut trees shading much of the endless acres of lawn. Children were running playfully about, curiously glancing our way. As we got out of the taxi, I heard one say, "Are they new girls? She's little!"

The sound of lawn mowers, the smell of freshly cut grass, and the friendly adults who greeted us were all reassuring. This seemed like a happy place to live. I thought of running to join the children, but held fast to Mother's hand. I was afraid she would disappear if I left her for even a moment, so I stayed at her side, rolling a chestnut under my brown sandal and watching the children. As the adults talked, one of them looked down at me and smiled as she fingered my curls. Almost imperceptibly, she shook her head from side to side.

* * * * *

My experiences until then had been the walk-up apartment in Brooklyn where I lived with my mother, father, and older sister, Nan—a surprisingly simple, normal life for that summer when the Depression was easing and the Pearl Harbor attack had already plunged the U. S. into World War II.

Mother would push me in the wicker stroller down Kings Highway to grocery shop, stopping to buy a long pretzel stick for me from a street vendor. In the evenings, my father would hit a hard, round candy with a hammer to make candy splinters that Nan and I could eat without choking. Daddy would tell stories to Nan and me—our favorite was about the invention of the first cotton gin. He made it sound as interesting as Rumpelstiltskin, and spinning straw into gold. Nan would focus on the story, but I always focused on Daddy's face as we sat on his knees. When Mother was on her hands and knees scrubbing floors, I would kiss her on her bottom. "You're a good mommy," I'd say. The routine of my life had been slow and predictable.

In the weeks before Nan and I were to be admitted to the boarding school, we had walked along a cobblestone path in a park near our apartment, holding Mother's hands as she answered all our questions about St. Christopher's.

"Why do we have to live there?" I grumbled, scuffing along in my brown high-top shoes.

Mother wore her old, yet still figure-flattering suit that was cinched at the waist. Her black hat sat at an angle on her head with a curved feather that poked upward. She squatted down to draw us close and said, "You and Nan will live at the nice boarding school for a while because Daddy is sick, and Mommy has to go to work and school. After a month, St. Christopher's will allow me to visit you, and maybe Daddy can come sometimes, too."

Mother with Nan and Sally - 1942

* * * * *

Mother had received undergraduate degrees in math and physics from Cornell University and then a master's in philosophy from a small college near her home. My dad had received his law degree from Lafayette College. But their dreams of careers were crushed by the Great Depression, when the only jobs they could find were as the janitors in the walk-up apartment building where they lived, working in exchange for free rent.

Before I was quite three, my dad had begun showing unusual behavior that was often threatening toward Nan and me. He would say things to Mother such as, "Killing them will save them." He was no longer the gentle, soft-spoken "Sam" my Mother had so loved. They started to have scary arguments. Because of the changes in him, she would scream in frustration or throw an ashtray across the

9

room, and I would run and hide under my bed. At other times, Daddy seemed depressed and withdrew from all of us. It was during this time, I learned many years later, that Mother discovered she was pregnant again. She made the agonizing decision to have an illegal abortion.

Mother found employment as a geologist's assistant, but she couldn't trust Daddy to care for Nan and me. Although his condition hadn't been diagnosed, she knew he needed to be hospitalized. A friend of Mother's recommended a place for Nan and me to stay for a while.

St. Christopher's Boarding School sat on the east bank of the Hudson River in Dobbs Ferry, New York. John Wheeler and Ette Stearns had founded the school for children in need in 1881. Fees were based on the parents' income. Paying for two children would take most of Mother's salary from her new job. With Daddy's hospital bills, she would barely have enough to live on.

Nan would be starting the second grade, but I wouldn't start school for two more years. St. Christopher's only enrolled school age children, but when Mother explained her desperation, they made an exception and allowed her to enroll both of us for what we all thought would be a brief period of time.

When packing us up, Mother had explained that we would have to take care of ourselves and mind the rules at boarding school. "I expect you to be good girls," she said, as she snugged a jar of Johnson's Baby Cream between the clothes in my suitcase. I had very dry skin and Mother had discovered this was the best treatment. She told me I would be a big girl if I used it when my skin was chapped.

"I *will* be a big girl," I had promised her. But now that I was standing here on the grounds of the boarding school, in the midst of all this beautiful strangeness, I knew I didn't want to remain without her. "Can you stay, too?" I asked, squinting up at her. Her eyes looked sad as she shook her head, and I cried.

MAIN BUILDING, SAINT CHRISTOPHER'S SCHOOL, DOBBS FERRY, N.Y.

*Early Postcard of St. Christopher's Boarding School
Main Building*

On that first day at St. Christopher's, as the cottage mother helped us unpack and showed us where to keep our belongings, she saw my jar of baby cream. "You can't have this," she said. "Only the nurse can dispense such things."

"That's my *big girl cream*," I protested. She ignored my wails and proceeded to put my clothes in the cabinets. Sniffling, I wondered how I could take care of myself now, as I had promised Mother.

During the first week, I climbed over the five-foot chain link fence that surrounded the school. I walked boldly along the unfamiliar city street, looking for my family and the small apartment that had been home to me all my life. Soon a police car pulled up next to me. "Let me help you in, young lady, and I'll take you home." I climbed into the car and sat back in relief. He didn't ask where I lived. I thought that policemen knew where lost little girls lived. Alas, he took me back to St. Chris. I had been reported missing. Returning runaways to the school was a routine matter for the local police.

I repeated this adventure several times over the next few weeks. I would go searching for my family and the police would return me to St. Chris. That first month without my parents seemed to go on forever. I wondered if I would ever see them again.

During the time that Daddy was in the mental hospital and Nan and I were in boarding school, Mother worked during the day and took courses in optics at night to learn ways of developing new lenses for cameras and laboratory equipment. When she visited us one Sunday and was pushing me on a swing, she proudly told me she'd invented a new camera. She seemed lighthearted and girlish that day, as though she had shed a great weight from her shoulders. But her Wednesday afternoon visits to Daddy at the hospital always brought the enormity of her situation back into focus. He was completely out of touch during some of her visits, insisting on conducting visitor traffic-flow in the hallway or crawling on his hands and knees, stuffing bits of trash and cigarette butts in his nose. Sometimes she would scream at the staff to do something to help him.

Mother always had a happy face when she came to visit us. But, I sensed her anxiety and therefore never caused a scene when it was time for her to leave. I'd found comfort and a sense of security in the predictable routine at St. Chris. *Insecurity* is what Mother began to represent to me. I wished for both my mother *and* the security I felt at my new home.

* * * * *

The large stone buildings that housed the children were called cottages. Stearns-Wheeler Cottage housed boys and girls ages six and seven. Sparks cottage housed girls from eight to twelve, and Gould Cottage housed high school girls. There were also cottages for the older boys.

Nan was the oldest in Stearns-Wheeler Cottage, and I was the youngest. We had two cottage mothers—one supervised the girls in our half of the cottage, the other was in charge of the boys in their half. The co-ed dining room was in the middle. The girls' dormitory had single metal beds lined up against the walls, all the way around the long room. The girls' bathroom had three bathtubs and several sinks and toilets. Our cottage mother strictly enforced the routine for washing, shampooing, combing our hair, brushing our teeth, and keeping our things orderly.

On the day of our arrival, the cottage mother had taught Nan and me to make our beds, using "hospital corners" to tuck in our sheets and blankets. Every morning, I scurried around my bed to get it smoothed perfectly, and chanted, "Hurry-hurry-hurry, hurry-hurry-hurry," because I was eager to leave for breakfast with the other girls.

Saturdays were chore days. The older girls in Stearns-Wheeler got the Dutch Cleanser, mop, and other supplies out of the cleaning closet and went to work. Feeling left out, I asked the cottage mother, "What's my job?" Something age-appropriate always had to be figured out for me. The cottage mother put me in charge of cleaning the winding staircase that led from the cottage's entry up to the dormitory. I was meticulous about this job, using the hand brush to get all the dirt to one side of each step and then brushing it down to the next step, working my way backward down the staircase. I felt proud of my contribution.

Miss Maxwell, the cook, ran the kitchen and prepared basic, nutritious meals. Four to six children sat at each round table, the boys to one side of the dining room, the girls to the other. We were taught manners: "Please pass the butter!" "Don't chew with your mouth open!" "Don't talk with your mouth full!" I got the last two confused and would say, "Don't talk with your mouth open."

I had never eaten many of the foods that were served—and I disliked anything unfamiliar. The hot cereal would get my day off to a bad start, but if you didn't eat your cereal, you couldn't have buttered toast. I was frequently the only child sent to the kitchen after dinner. I'd stand over my uneaten food for hours, having missed out on the dessert of junket, pudding, Jell-O, or tapioca. I'd rearrange the food on the plate so it would look like I'd eaten some, and ask the cook, "Did I eat enough yet?" Once, I stuffed my cheeks with figs and, after being excused, spat them out in the entryway water fountain.

The shelves and cabinets in the downstairs playroom were stacked with donated toys and books. An old wooden dollhouse sat on a low table. I spent hours playing with this miniature home and its tiny inhabitants, pretending my family lived in it. I'd hold the small mommy doll close to my body and stroke her.

"After we go to bed at night, all the dolls in the playroom wake up and play with each other," a girl named Dorothea told me. "The dollhouse becomes a real home with a family. The soldier dolls march around, and Raggedy Ann and Andy are in charge." I listened, wide-eyed. "Just before we get up in the morning," she continued, "they all hurry back to the exact place we left them, so that we never know." She and I began to examine the room and the dolls very carefully each night and again each morning to see if we could find anything out of place, but the dolls were too careful. As I looked closely into their painted eyes—and as they looked back at me—I knew we shared this secret.

There was also a long table and benches in a bay window where we could color and do crafts. "Look at my picture!" I would say as I held up my crayoned scribbling for the other girls at the table to see. No one looked up.

Mrs. McCann, my first cottage mother, was one of the most patient and caring of a long procession of cottage mothers. She played the piano in the playroom and because I was the youngest she would scoot over on the piano bench allowing me to stand on the other half to style her hair in fanciful ways. She acted so pleased with the hairdos I created. "Oh, Sally, that's lovely. Thank you." The other girls would accompany her music by blowing through tissue paper wrapped around combs, simulating harmonicas. We'd become a unique family.

During the winter, the cottage mother kept a fire burning in the huge playroom fireplace and several of us would squish together on a long couch in front of it. I was comforted by the fire's warmth and stared, mesmerized, into the flickering flames. Thoughts of home and family left me feeling isolated in the midst of all that surrounded me. I yearned for my mommy to hold me.

CHAPTER TWO

The yard behind Stearns-Wheeler contained a sand pile and a play house. A sidewalk circled the cottage, and we spent hours roller-skating around and around with skate keys swinging from our shoelace necklaces.

One evening, out in the play yard after dinner—when I was four and Johnny Burton was six—Johnny said, "Let's show each other our bottoms." He suggested we hide behind the playhouse where he thought no one would see us. With my dress up and my panties down, I leaned forward to see what strange thing Johnny had on the front of his bottom—and that's when we were caught! The horror on the adults' faces frightened us badly. One of them shook a finger at us as she scolded, "You are nasty children!"

I cried in bed for several nights, praying for God to make me a good girl. I could hear the murmur of bed-to-bed conversations around the dark dormitory and thought it was about my shame. *Will anyone ever like me again?*

Almost immediately after the play house incident, I started wetting the bed. In the middle of the night I would call down the hall to the cottage mother's room. After getting me into fresh pajamas, the cottage mother would tuck me into Nan's bed. Nan, keeping her voice low, asked her, "What if the other girls make fun of me and say *pee baby* has to sleep in my bed? What if she wets my bed, too?" The cottage mother just patted Nan without saying anything. I felt sorry for my sister.

In the late afternoons, the cottage mother would hand a big wicker basket to one of us and ask us to get bread from the Main Building for the following day. "I'll go," I would offer, waving my arms and standing on my toes to look taller and be noticed. I loved to do this errand and would go merrily across campus swinging the basket. Once in a while, I encountered visitors to the school. Funding often came from these visitors, so we'd been taught to be polite and respectful and to answer any questions in a friendly way. They delighted in talking to the children. On one encounter they rewarded me with a box of chocolate candies. When I returned to the cottage and showed the candy to my cottage mother she took the box from me, saying, "Each night when you're ready for bed, but before you brush your teeth, come to my room and I'll give you one piece of the chocolate." Sometimes, after eating my treat, we'd sit on her bed and talk, or listen to "Baby Snooks" on her radio. For those few moments it felt as though she was my real mommy. I wanted to sleep in her bed and cuddle, but she said that wasn't allowed.

On one of my bread trips across campus, one of the men who mowed the grass drove his wood-paneled station wagon next to me and stopped. "Get in, little girl, and I'll take you where you're going," he said, leaning across and pushing the passenger door open. I hesitated for a moment and then obeyed. "Aren't you a cute little thing!" he said as he pinched my cheek between his thumb and forefinger hard enough to bring tears to my eyes. He drove a short distance and then stopped. He pulled me to him, pushed the skirt of my cotton dress aside, and squeezed my leg. His big hand covered my whole thigh from my knee to my cotton panties. His fingers slid under the crotch of my panties and he hurt me. Tears rolled down my cheeks as I looked up at him with my chin quivering. He drove on to the Main Building and stopped. Before letting me out, he rubbed his rough, scratchy whiskers hard against my cheek. I hated him for hurting me and was so distracted that I almost forgot to go inside the building to get the bread. I cried as I walked back to the cottage, but I didn't tell anyone about him because I felt ashamed; I sensed I shouldn't have gotten into his car.

For several nights after that, I had nightmares. The lawn mower man was tied to one of the large chestnut trees with lots of rope, and I was hitting him with my fists, pounding him over and over with all my might. I wanted to hurt him as much as he had hurt me. He was a bad man. Each night the same dream, and each night I got to hurt him more. Never again did I volunteer to get the bread from the Main Building.

On typical nights, when all the girls were ready for bed, the cottage mother came into the dormitory and read to us. Mrs. McCann read *Uncle Wiggily* stories, which were my favorites, and then we said prayers together. Eventually, another cottage mother replaced Mrs. McCann, and then another. One read to us from the Bible and told us what bad things God would do to us if we were naughty. Another one shared her lotions and polished our nails, making us feel very feminine. "I want pink!" I shouted from the foot of my bed, holding out my spread fingers. I loved the smell of her Jergens Lotion as I rubbed it on my hands. I wished she would always be our cottage mother.

If ever we broke a rule or misbehaved in any way, we would be punished. I hadn't mastered the trick of tying my shoe laces, so I was most often sitting in the naughty chair for having loose shoe strings. I could be a very sassy girl, especially if I thought I was being treated unfairly. My tongue was my weapon of choice. I would either stick it out or say one of the two bad words I knew. One of them was *bastard*, but I didn't pronounce it correctly. "You *basket*!" I would yell at anyone being mean to me. But the cottage mother always knew what I was trying to say and I would get a bar of Ivory soap in my mouth.

Hell was my other bad word. Once, when a box of donated chocolates was being passed around, I reached for the only piece wrapped in gold foil. I was told not to take that piece because it was being saved for the birthday girl. But that was the piece I wanted and it infuriated me that I couldn't have it. "Then I don't want any of that *hell candy*," I cried. More soap in my mouth.

Each evening at dusk—that last half-hour before the children were called inside the cottages—Mr. Shoemaker, the superintendent of the boarding school, walked around the grounds, assuring himself that everything was all right and ready to be closed down for the night. He walked slowly, greeted everyone he passed, and would often stop for a few minutes to watch the children play before he moved on. I loved to join him for these walks and tried to match his stride. I admired everything about him. "I hope I have feet as big as yours when I grow up," I told him. I felt guilty for wishing he was my dad. I loved my daddy, but he wasn't there and Mr. Shoemaker was.

Daddy wasn't allowed to leave the hospital to visit us very often, so whenever he did come with Mother, it was a special occasion. One summer day, when I was four years old, I was showing him how well I could swim by doing the dog paddle in the shallow pool. He walked along the side of the pool as I frantically flailed in the water, determined to impress him. "I'm so proud of you for learning to swim, Sally," he said as I climbed out of the pool. The compliment left me beaming. Daddy seemed normal again, like the old, sweet daddy he had been before getting sick. He carried me around on his shoulders while Mother held on to his arm and looked up at both of us. For that moment, all our troubles seemed to have vanished.

I learned how to pump my legs to go very high on the swings, so high that the chains I gripped went straight out from the top supporting bar of the swings. I'd stand up and pump, seeing how high I could get and how fast I could have the swing going before jumping off, yelling, "Look at meeeee!" We were all swing experts.

When we had a rain without thunder and lightning, we danced in the play yard wearing only our panties until we were chilled and covered with goose bumps.

Each day, each season, had a rhythm comforting in its predictability. Yet I always felt detached. Nan played with the older girls but as the youngest, I was alone from the beginning. I was consumed with a longing to be somebody's little girl, somebody's friend.

World War II touched our lives in many ways. We learned some military tunes and other songs of the times, and sang them around the cottage. "For it's hi hi hee in the field artillery, count off your numbers loud and strong, one, two." Some songs seemed appropriate for our situation, though we weren't aware of that: "Don't Fence Me In" and "Nobody Likes Me," a song about eating slimy, wriggling worms.

One evening, dancers came to St. Chris to entertain us in the school auditorium. One dancer had already performed when a pretty lady came on stage wearing bright red lipstick, and heavy theatrical makeup on her eyelids and lashes. Her sequined costume was glittery in the lights. As the music began, she moved into her dance routine and then, very suddenly, she stopped and appeared to be sobbing. "Is this part of the dance?" I whispered to the girl next to me, and she shrugged. Then the dancer fled the stage and didn't return. It was later explained to us that earlier in the day she'd received word her husband had been killed in the war.

On one of Mother's visits, she told me she was disappointed that I didn't write to her. "It's not important *what* you write, Sally, as long as I get letters from you." Though I had barely learned to print my name, I promised her I would try. After a few days, I got a box of stationery from the playroom cabinet and sat for a long time, pencil in hand, trying to think of something to say. As I sat, I noticed the words on the lid of the stationery box. So this was my letter to Mother:

Dear Mother,
Ingram Stationery Company
Utica, New York
24 sheets, 12 envelopes
Heavyweight Bond
Love, Sally

CHAPTER THREE

Each child at St. Chris met monthly with the school psychologist. She observed as you played with toys to see if you appeared to be troubled by anything, and she would chat with you, slipping in questions that only seemed like friendly conversation.

One day when I was playing on campus, I was told to go to the psychologist's office. I had seen her for my monthly visit just a week earlier and I knew it wasn't my turn. When I arrived, she didn't greet me with her usual smile, causing me to think I had done something wrong. Instead of heading straight for the toys, I lowered my eyes and waited. She said, "Sally, I have something sad to tell you." She waited for me to look up before she continued. "Your father died yesterday. Your mother will be coming to talk to you and Nan about it."

The psychologist kneeled down to look into my eyes. She stroked my hair as she talked to me, but I didn't hear anything more she said.

I was five years old, and I hadn't seen my daddy very often since I'd been at St. Chris. I had difficulty retrieving a clear memory of him. I walked out of the psychologist's office and crossed the campus feeling sad and confused, not understanding what *dead* meant. I only knew it must mean Daddy wouldn't be coming to see me anymore.

The news had gotten around by the time I returned to Stearns-Wheeler. The girls swarmed me, asking questions. Then another girl ran up to us and said, "Nan's crying and hiding in a closet. She won't talk to anyone because her father died." That alarmed me; Nan *never* cried. It was then I realized how broken our family was, now that our daddy had died. The family I'd hoped to return to was falling apart. There was no home to run away to anymore. Still, I didn't cry—and wondered why. I wanted my mother.

Eventually, I learned that Mother had wanted to be the one to tell us of Daddy's death, but the school insisted it would be better for the psychologist to tell us. Mother relented, but later regretted it. In the hospital, Daddy had been diagnosed with depression and schizophrenia. They had tried a new treatment on him but, instead of helping him, the still-experimental electric shock had killed him.

Daddy was gone and that impacted Mother, Nan, and me in different ways. Mother was lost and defeated, and felt unable to cope with thoughts of pulling us together again as a family. Nan mourned the loss of her mentor, her storyteller, and the parent she related to most. I lost hope that we would have a future as a family. We each grieved in our own way. Mother never talked to us about leaving St. Chris, but there was an unspoken understanding that Nan and I would continue to live there and Mother would continue to work, go to school, and visit us on Sundays.

Just when Nan was almost old enough to be moved to Sparks Cottage, an incident at our cottage brought everything at St. Chris to a halt. A new cottage mother at Stearns-Wheeler, stressed by the responsibilities of her job, had taken to sitting on a straight chair in the hallway, reading from her Bible—probably asking God for help in dealing with all these naughty rascals.

On this particular day, Nan found a kitten on campus

and brought it into the cottage. "Get that cat out!" the new cottage mother shrieked at her. The noise frightened the kitten and it sprang from Nan's arms and scampered under a couch. The cottage mother reached to a high shelf for a thin switch we had never seen before and began to strike Nan with it, while still yelling at her to get the kitten out.

Nan was the oldest girl in Stearns-Wheeler. She was looked up to and respected by the rest of us, and we were all in agreement that she had been mistreated. She had always been our leader, so we listened as she shared her plan for revenge. Her enthusiasm was contagious.

We would leave Stearns-Wheeler Cottage in small groups, as if going out to play. We would meet at Sparks Cottage, which was closed up for a few weeks because most of the Sparks girls had gone off to summer camp. The few who had not gone to camp had been sent to live with the high-school girls in Gould Cottage.

"When we're all there," she continued, "we'll try to find a way to get in." Once in, she said we were to head to the basement and stay there until dark so as to worry our new cottage mother. This was our idea of *running away*.

"Yeah, we'll make her worry, and then she'll be sorry she hurt you," one of the girls told Nan.

"We can stay there forever, and she won't know what to do," said another.

"Now she won't have anyone to be mean to," chimed a third. Not one girl hesitated to participate.

We were lucky enough to find a low window that was unlocked in the empty cottage. We climbed inside unobserved—my short legs barely making it over the window ledge—and closed the window. We headed on tiptoe for the basement.

Because of our excitement, we suddenly all had to pee. Nan designated the floor behind the furnace for this. We all took a turn, and it wasn't long before the area reeked.

We sat around for hours, leaning against the concrete walls and talking about the circumstances that had brought us to this basement. Each girl strove to make the situation sound dire to justify our actions.

"Nobody's supposed to hit you."

"We should hit her and see how she likes it."

"The poor little kitty was scared."

"She's always been mean. She's the meanest cottage mother ever."

"I never, ever liked her. I hope she goes away and never comes back."

"I wonder what she's doing now. I hope she doesn't hurt the kitty." Thinking about the poor kitty made us all fall silent.

As the hours passed, we began to get hungry. Nan appointed Grace to cautiously slip out the window and look for one of the Sparks girls and explain what was going on and to ask for an emergency food delivery from the kitchen of Gould Cottage. Our fervor spread to the Sparks girls, who became our allies. They made red Jell-O and handed it to us in jars through the window. "We didn't know how to make the Jell-O get hard, so you'll just have to drink it," one of the girls told us.

More hours passed. As boredom and discomfort set in, we began wondering if we should abandon our rebellion. Then a Sparks girl arrived with a warning: "There's a search party looking for you!" We were stunned, but became more determined than ever to stick to our plan. After all, this was a matter of being treated unfairly. Yet, we were scared to show our faces for fear of severe punishment. The Sparks girls told us that many people had joined the search: the superintendent, policemen, teachers, and people from town—men in suits and ladies in high-heeled shoes. We crouched low so they couldn't see us if they walked past Sparks and happened to look down into the basement windows. As we peered up through those windows, we could see their important-looking feet walking by, and we became even more excited, determined, and scared.

The Sparks girls were wonderful. They pretended to join in the search for us. Whenever the search party got close, they signaled us by singing, "The Bear Went Over the Mountain." Then we'd crouch even lower and try to be very still.

As the youngest, I always seemed to create new problems. "I have to do *number two*," I said as I wiggled around in an urgent dance. The girls refused to allow me to potty on the floor behind the furnace.

"It already smells too bad over there," they complained. When they felt sure the coast was clear, they boosted me out the window.

It was dusk, and I could hear the voices of searchers calling to each other, and then I saw a group of adults in the distance moving in my direction. I quickly pottied behind a bush, but as I was trying to climb back through the window, one of them spotted me.

By the time we were herded out, smelly, tired, hungry, and looking guilty, we had spent a whole day in our basement confines. We were surprised at how well everyone treated us. When questioned, several of the older girls gave the whole story about why we had run away, stressing the cottage mother's unfairness to Nan and the kitten. We were taken back to Stearns-Wheeler to be scrubbed, fed, and put to bed. In the days that followed, we heard that the cottage mother had been reprimanded. Not long after that, she was replaced with another new cottage mother.

Shortly after Nan's eighth birthday, she was moved to Sparks Cottage. Although Nan had never shown much interest in me, I missed my sister, and the other girls missed having a leader. But when we visited her at Sparks, Nan seemed indifferent toward us, as though she was embarrassed to have this flock of little kids around when she was a big kid now.

* * * * *

During one of Mother's visits, she asked if I wanted to help the war effort. I was eager to learn what I could do. "Each time I visit you, I will bring all the foil wrappers from inside my cigarette packs," she explained. "If you peel the foil from the paper backing and roll it into a ball, I will pick up the ball of foil each Sunday and bring you more wrappers." She handed me a small bag of wrappers.

I was proud to be helping America. As I sat peeling foil from backings, I sang:

"Whistle while you work.
Hitler is a jerk
Mussolini is a meanie,
Whistle while you work."

We had to keep our bathrobes and slippers at the foot of our beds so we could find them quickly if the cottage mother awakened us during the night for an air raid drill. When we had such drills, we filed downstairs and outside to an underground air raid shelter where we would all sit on long wooden benches along the walls. The shelter had only one light bulb, dangling from a wire in the ceiling, casting ominous shadows as breezes moved it. We could hear planes overhead and—not knowing they were American planes—I thought they were the enemy getting ready to bomb us. We sang all the songs we knew and swayed from side to side together.

The cottage mother once told me, "It is very difficult to awaken you, Sally. We might have to leave you behind next time." The idea of abandonment terrified me. I was sure I would be bombed in my bed while everyone else was safe in the shelter.

Each morning, we stood in a circle around the flagpole and said the Pledge of Allegiance with our hands over our hearts. I always concluded the pledge by saying, "and just us, for all." That was how I understood it, and those words were meaningful to me.

I was still at Stearns-Wheeler when the superintendent sent a messenger to each cottage with an announcement. As word arrived, it was screamed from person to person until everyone chorused with the news; "The war is over!"

On that special night, normal routine was disregarded. The children of Stearns-Wheeler were allowed to stay outside way past bedtime. This in itself was reason for a six-year-old to celebrate. The cottage mother and the cook handed out pots and pans from the kitchen. We used spoons as drumsticks to beat on the bottoms of the pots. I clapped two pot lids together as cymbals and marched around in my own parade, lifting my bony knees high. The children ran about happily, almost hysterically, and the adults danced together and laughed. As night fell, we were still outside celebrating the end of WWII.

CHAPTER FOUR

After Daddy died, Mother began taking Nan and me from the school to her tiny apartment one weekend each month. On these visits we looked through the baby scrapbooks she kept for us. We fingered our knitted baby booties that were fastened to the cover and examined the photos inside. Mother read aloud what she'd written in the scrapbooks: her impressions of us and accounts of our accomplishments.

We would get silly with each other, laughing and teasing. "Are you ticklish here, and here, and here?" Mother would ask as she tickled under our chins, at our waists, and on the bottoms of our feet. At bedtime, the three of us snuggled contentedly into Mother's narrow bed and fell asleep with our legs and arms intertwined and smiles on our faces. In my dreams, we would stay this way always— close to Mother.

* * * * *

For most Christmases, Nan and I stayed at St. Chris, but for one Christmas, Mother picked us up and took us to Grandma and Grandpa's house in Brooklyn where we spent a few days with all of Mother's family.

One evening, Grandpa Saladino played the piano and Mother's sister, our Aunt Barbara, sang *O Sole Mio*, *Chiribiribin*, and *Finiculi Finicula*. She had short, dark, wavy hair, and stood a proud five foot four next to the grand piano that held framed photos of Mother's two brothers in their military uniforms—one Army, one Navy. Aunt Barbara's voice filled the small parlor.

Uncle Bob was the youngest of my mother's siblings, already in the Navy even though he was only a teenager. He loaded Nan and me into the rumble seat of his old car early one morning before Christmas and took us to the bakery to buy doughnuts for everyone's breakfast. When we got back to the house, Nan and I shocked all the adults with our capacity for the treats we'd never had before. After consuming over a dozen doughnuts between us we slowed down, no longer worried they would be eaten by the grownups before we got our fill. "Can you believe they ate all those?" the adults asked each other. We all laughed as they poked us in our round tummies.

At Grandma's house, I did more watching than participating. I walked around, room by room, observing family members. Mother and Grandma were in the kitchen having a disagreement. Mother drummed the fingers of her left hand on the kitchen table, smoked with her right hand, and tapped her cigarette on the edge of the ashtray long after all the ashes had fallen off. I hung around watching them for awhile, pushing the swinging door to the dining room back and forth, but not really following their conversation. "But have you thought of the girls?" Grandma asked, glancing at me. I caught her glance and stopped to pay attention. I liked that she was asking about Nan and me. It told me they really were concerned about us. Maybe they'd decide we could stay at Grandma's forever. Mother looked down at the orange glow on the end of her cigarette, but didn't respond.

Grandma was English and very dignified. She was plump and had the air of a queen. Her short, wavy, pure white hair was like a glowing halo. She taught me what she learned in finishing school as a young girl living in England. "Ladies always lead with their wrists, Sally, they lead with their wrists," she said as she slowly demonstrated with one hand daintily holding a lace-trimmed hanky pulled from her apron pocket.

Late one morning, I quietly entered my Aunt Barbara's bedroom. She was primping at a vanity with a five-way mirror that allowed her to see herself at every angle. There were tiny bottles of nail polish in every imaginable color set out on a crocheted doily on the vanity top. She watched me in her mirror as I walked around her room looking at every pretty, feminine item she had, as though I was in the kingdom of a princess. I handled some of the clothes she had laid across her bed, careful not to muss them. I thought about how glamorous she was. My mother was smart, instead. I wondered which I would rather be when I grew up. I doubted I'd be either. As I left the room, Aunt Barbara smiled at me in her mirror. I gave a little wave and said, "Bye."

Grandpa and I napped together in the afternoons. Grandpa had a stocky build. He was bald, but had a thick gray mustache. He always seemed happy. He would hang his wool cardigan sweater with the crisscross leather buttons on the doorknob before we took off our shoes and curled up together on the bed. As his warm body cuddled mine, I felt contented and loved.

Grandma was a wonderful cook. At dinnertime, she removed the apron she wore most of the day and sat at one end of the table. Grandpa sliced the meat with a bone-handled carving set at the other end of the table and led the conversation. With all the adults talking, Nan and I remained quiet and *watched* the interaction.

During our holiday, Nan and I slept on a fold-up canvas cot, with our heads at opposite ends. We would press the bottoms of our feet together and bicycle our legs. Before going to bed on Christmas Eve, we each hung one of our little socks from the outer doorknob of the room where we were sleeping. In the morning, it was the first thing we saw, and we were delighted to discover that Santa Claus had left a little box of raisins in each sock. The thought that he had come so very close to where we lay sleeping gave us shivers.

When Nan and I were bundled up for our reluctant trip back to St. Chris, Grandpa slyly slipped a quarter into each of our hands, as though he wasn't supposed to. He winked, and we knew he loved us.

* * * * *

I was excited at finally becoming old enough to attend the grammar school on campus with the other children in my cottage. The school building had two floors, with one teacher in the single classroom on each floor. The ground floor was for the children at Stearns-Wheeler; the second floor was for the upper elementary children who lived in Sparks Cottage. The girls of Gould Cottage went to an off-campus high school.

I was amazed and delighted to discover a large green parrot in my classroom. It was the teacher's pet, and only the first students to finish their work were allowed to handle him and clean his cage. That was never me. I couldn't do the school work. We were taught to read phonetically, sounding out each letter until they merged into a word. After a while, according to the theory behind this method, the word would become familiar enough to recognize by sight.

34

I struggled to learn to read, but the letters always looked scrambled to me. Learning to read a single word was painfully slow and its meaning usually lost to me after the long effort to figure it out. No one else seemed to be having this problem. All the other children could do the work fast enough to be allowed to handle the parrot. "I don't know how to *do* it," I confessed to my teacher privately and desperately. I would endure many years of shame and disappointment before I understood the term "dyslexia."

I was often reprimanded. Sometimes I would be sassy, take a peek at someone's work, or not settle down when the teacher asked for order. I shuffled my brown lace-up shoes when I was called to the teacher's desk. I winced as she struck my knuckles with a ruler, or futilely tried to jump high enough to avoid the yardstick to my legs.

* * * * *

Each morning before school, late fall through winter, all the children lined up at the infirmary door so Miss Irwin, the school nurse, could give each of us a teaspoonful of cod liver oil. It was a nutritional supplement, providing "the sunshine vitamins" A and D. Some of the children gagged on the thick syrup, but I thought it was delicious. She set a tablespoon aside just for me and would sometimes give me *two* big spoonfuls. "Mmmm," I'd say, smacking my sticky lips as I walked off. It tickled her that I thought it was such a treat.

When I had the measles, I had to stay in bed at the infirmary for several days. The time dragged and I was restless. The nurse's assistant brought me paper dolls to cut out, but I found a much more interesting use for the scissors. I cut my long braids. The small, blunt scissors weren't capable of cutting all the way through my braids, so they didn't fall off. The next morning, when the caretaker took the rubber bands off the ends of my braids and combed out my hair, the cut locks fell to the bed sheets. Half of my hair was still long and came to the middle of my back, and the other half was just below my ears. "What have you done?" she scolded. "Your mother is going to be very upset, young lady."

At Mother's next visit, instead of being angry, she took me to a beauty shop to have my hair feathered into a cut of short curls. It was a whole new look for me and I was uneasy about it until mother said that the children might not recognize me. "Maybe you should fool them," she suggested. "Choose a new name, and tell them you're a new girl at St. Chris."

I was intrigued with the prospect of being a new person. "I could be called Phoebe, or Kate, or Heather," I told her.

When Mother introduced me as Heather, the girls were fooled for a brief moment, but then quickly realized it was me and admiringly touched my hair.

* * * * *

When I was seven years old, I was moved to Sparks Cottage. I was young for Sparks, but Stearns-Wheeler had become overcrowded.

Because the other girls in Sparks were eight and older, they were allowed to go as a group to the YMCA to swim after school. Because I was too young to go, I stayed behind and helped the cook prepare dinner. When the hungry girls returned, they would always share their off-campus news with the cook and me.

When I turned eight, I was finally allowed to go to the Y with the other girls. After swimming, the girls towel-dried their hair and combed it out by the wall dryers that blew hot air. Their hair was silken, shiny, and straight. Even my sister had long, naturally wavy blond hair. But mine, which had never been dried this way before, turned into a giant mass of light brown curls, as big around as a basketball. As I looked at my wild hairdo in the mirror, the girls gathered around and laughed till they cried. I realized I wasn't like the other girls. I was...funny looking. That change in my self-perception, added to my bad school performance, made my spirit slump. I thought how sad it must be for Mother to have a girl like me.

* * * * *

Some of the girls left St. Chris on the weekends to be with their families, arriving back on Sunday at dinnertime. On Sunday nights, we didn't sit down together in our cottage for a regular dinner. Instead, the cook put lots of leftovers and cold cuts out on the kitchen table so each girl could make her own meal. Being a picky eater, I told Nan, "I wish we could eat this way every night." After Sunday dinner, we all went over to the grammar school auditorium to watch *Tarzan* movies, starring Johnny Weissmuller.

On weekends when Nan and I happened to be among those leaving campus to visit family, my anticipation of the Sunday night make-your-own suppers and the *Tarzan* movies made it easier for me to say goodbye to Mother when she returned us to St. Chris.

* * * * *

By 1947, Nan and I had been at St. Chris for five years. The number of children at the school had grown and the cottages were crowded. St. Chris was seeking foster homes for those who had been there the longest. The school began a radio advertising campaign asking couples to become foster parents.

Because few families were willing to take *two* children, siblings were often separated. Nan, now twelve, received word before I did. Because she loved animals, a foster home was found for her on a farm. We had never been clinging sisters, but we *were* family, and it had always comforted me to have her nearby. Her presence gave me a glimmer of hope for an eventual reunion as a real family.

When the day came for Nan to leave, the social worker pulled up in a car. She loaded Nan's few belongings and then Nan climbed in. That seemed alarmingly final to me. Inside my head, I was yelling, *She's mine, she's mine!* But no one noticed my distress.

Nan sat tall in the back seat, facing straight forward, looking prepared for her new life. *Or is she scared? Come back, Nan! You are my family! Come back, I need you!* I stepped up on the running board of the car and held on, refusing to get down. The adults must have suffered a moment of compassion because, instead of scolding me, they bribed me. One lady said that she would tell me what my mother was going to give me for my birthday if I got down.

"What is she giving me?" I asked meekly.

"Something that ticks."

"A clock?"

"No."

"A watch?"

She nodded.

The bargain having been completed, I got down from the running board. At that moment I heard a high keening sound, like that of a wounded animal. I didn't realize right away that the sound was escaping from *me*.

As the car drove out through the chain link gate and

onto the public road, I was suddenly overcome by a warm sensation through my body. It felt as though comforting arms were enfolding me. My crying eased. At that moment I understood something I would never forget. *I am my family. Wherever I go, my family will go. I will never leave me.* Then I turned to walk back into the familiar routine of boarding school life, believing there was no one else I could lose.

CHAPTER FIVE

Several months later I learned a foster home had been found for me. I was ready. I had anticipated this news since my sister left.

I would be going to Thiells, New York, to live with a family called the Forrests. They had a son in college, a daughter in high school, and a very old grandmother who lived with them. They also had two cats and a dog. The mother was a secretary and the father owned a grocery store, so they had a lady come in to help with the cooking and the housework. I wondered if that lady would make my bed and do the chores I was used to doing. I discussed this very promising possibility with the other girls at Sparks while we were doing the dinner dishes that evening. "You're so lucky, Sally," they all said. This notion that I might be "lucky" made it easier for me to leave St. Chris.

I had my few belongings packed and ready when the day came for me to depart. I hugged everyone goodbye and then waved and threw kisses from the social worker's car and took one last look around. I wouldn't be returning to this home.

It was late summer, and a warm breeze blew in through the open window of the car. The thirty-mile drive seemed to take forever. As she drove, the social worker answered one more question about my new home and family. "What are the names of the dog and cats?"

"Mrs. Forrest told me the dog's name is Laddie, and the cats are Snowball and Blackie," she said, briefly taking her eyes off the road and smiling over at me. "They had a different dog named Laddie, but he died not very long ago. So when they found out you'd be coming, they got another dog. He's still a puppy."

There was so much to think about. I'd never had a pet. Everything would be new.

The Forrests lived out in the country. We turned off Thiells Road onto a long driveway that made a half-circle curve in front of the house. The family was waiting outside to greet us.

The social worker made the introductions, then, as the family was talking to me, she quickly unloaded my belongings and was back in her car ready to drive away. Her last words to me through the car window were, "You be a good girl."

"I will be," I assured her, trying to look confident while my chin quivered. I felt suddenly abandoned.

My foster parents were Bert and Jean Forrest. Mrs. Forrest seemed friendly and eager to make me feel at home. She kept a close eye on me, often touching my arm or shoulder, but she didn't hover. Right away I had the feeling that she would care about me more than the cottage mothers at St. Chris ever had. I instinctively stayed close to her. Mr. Forrest seemed ill at ease, as though the process of welcoming a child to his home made him feel awkward. He stepped slightly away from the group, and then rejoined us. He put his hands into his pockets and then pulled them out and folded his arms on his chest. Then he straightened his belt and put his hands back in his pockets. He glanced around at his property as though awaiting the appropriate moment to get back to some more familiar and comfortable activity. His uneasiness kept my attention.

My new sister, Nancy, was fifteen years old and kept smiling as she watched me with friendly curiosity. My new brother, Jack, had already left for the fall semester at Syracuse University. Mrs. Forrest's elderly mother, Grandma Raymond, just seemed confused by the goings on, frequently wringing her hands.

Mrs. Forrest introduced me to Laddie, who had been nuzzling against me since I'd arrived. "We got him six months ago to replace the collie we lost," she said, "but *this* pup turned out to be only *part* collie."

Once inside their home, they presented me with gifts they'd bought to welcome me: crayons and a coloring book, a story book, and a doll. The doll was stiff, and neither pretty nor cuddly. "Mr. Forrest shopped for this doll after work today," Mrs. Forrest explained. "But he didn't want to because he'd never shopped for a doll before." She gave him a mock frown for having put him in that situation.

"Would you like to call us Mom and Dad?" Mrs. Forrest asked, and I nodded. I had called all the cottage mothers *Mom*, so it seemed the natural thing to do.

They showed me around the house and we talked into the evening. "Tomorrow, when it's light out, I'll show you around the yard and help you unpack and get settled, Sally," my new mom said. "But right now I think we'd better get you ready for bed. You've had a long day."

Because Nancy was seven years older, she didn't have to go to bed when I did. We were to share a room, so a new twin bed had been set up close to Nancy's double bed. The room felt very cozy to me. Its windows had roller shades and lacy princess curtains that were tied back with wide bows. The beds were covered with pastel patchwork quilts, and there was a soft rug on the floor. But as I lay in this new bed in a strange, dark room, I felt lonely and lost.

There were no little girls lined up in beds next to mine, chattering softly. I missed their closeness. Most disconcertingly, a deafening noise was coming in through the open windows, like nothing I had ever heard before. The cacophony raised by the frogs, crickets, and katydids made me long for the familiar surroundings of the last five years. I started to cry.

Mom Forrest came in and sat on the edge of my bed. "We don't want you to be unhappy, Sally," she said as she wiped my tears. "So I want you to stop crying now and go to sleep." I nodded. I was trying with all my might to be good.

* * * * *

Louise, the lady who helped out, was preparing breakfast when I came downstairs the next morning. As I entered the kitchen, she quickly turned to greet me with a broad smile; "Well, there you are, Sally!" she said, as though I was someone wonderful. She was a small and plain-looking woman, but something shined in her that was beautiful. It made me feel good to be in her presence, as though she already knew me—and liked me.

After breakfast, Mom took me on a tour of the grounds. The Forrests had several acres of grass, flowering shrubs, tall trees, and gardens. We followed paths around low stone walls and over grassy slopes. As we walked, Mom introduced the flowers to me by name—hydrangeas, roses, daisies, lilacs, forsythia—and all the while she was cutting long stems and creating an armload bouquet. It was obvious Mom loved her flowers and enjoyed telling me about them. I listened attentively.

Mom was fair-skinned, round-faced, and rosy-cheeked. Her long blond hair was braided and wrapped around her head. She had a happy but matter-of-fact way about her. I trusted her immediately.

We passed a lily pond where frogs were sunning on the large green leaves. Mom caught one for me to hold. His soft belly fit right into the palm of my hand, and then he leapt away. Mom and I stood there for a minute, smiling at each other.

Laddie followed us, tail wagging, tongue dangling, and eyes alert.

Standing next to the pond, I gazed back at the white, two-story frame house. From that distance it looked magical, too perfect to be my new home. I pointed to it and exclaimed, "Look at the house!" as though Mom wasn't already familiar with its beauty.

We followed the driveway out to the blacktop country road. Tiny purple violets jostled for space on both sides of Thiells Road. I'd never seen such natural beauty. The day would grow hot, but in these morning hours it was mild, and there was a breeze that wafted the fragrance of the flowers all around us.

Continuing our walk, we ended up several yards behind the house where there was a clothesline and off to the right, a chicken coop. Some distance beyond the chicken coop there was a hill that met the cloud-streaked blue sky, and it looked as though the Forrests' property went on forever.

I hurried toward the chickens as they squawked and scattered in their fenced yard. Mom told me, almost casually, "These chickens are going to be your responsibility, Sally. I will show you what you need to do every morning and every evening, and then they will be in your care." My heart was beating fast. I wanted this job more than anything.

"There's a sack of chicken feed at the bottom of the basement steps," Mom said as we headed back toward the house. "There's a long handled pot in the sack that you can use to scoop up enough feed for a meal. Each morning and each evening, you are to scoop a pot of feed and take it out to the chickens, along with the day-old bread from the kitchen."

As she talked, we entered the house through the back door. Mom set the flowers on the kitchen counter, and then we went down the basement steps so she could show me the sack of feed. "Dad brings *fresh* bread home from the store every day, so you'll use the *day-old* bread to tear into little pieces to toss to the chickens. In the mornings, you will open the henhouse door so they can come out to run around their yard. In the evenings it's very important for you to make sure they're all settled into the henhouse and locked in for the night, where they'll be safe from predators."

What are predators?" I asked.

"Things that eat chickens," Mom explained. "Like the red fox Dad saw sniffing near the chicken yard several nights ago."

This was the most wonderful responsibility I had ever had. The chickens had already been fed this morning, but I would be in charge this evening, and I couldn't wait!

Through the rest of the day, the Forrests functioned as though I had always been there. I didn't know what to make of it. "Sally, would you set the table?" "Sally, would you stir this frosting?" "Sally, would you put this food in Laddie's dish?" I didn't have time to feel strange, or new, or lonesome. I was a vital member of this family.

When the hour arrived for the chickens to require my care, I scooped the grain, grabbed the day-old bread, and off I went to the coop. Once inside the gate, I tossed the grain in a sweeping arc around the yard. They came running, hungry enough to overlook that I was a stranger to them. I stood amongst them while tearing the bread into little pieces, thinking of what Mom had told me. *Bread is like dessert for the chickens. They like it as well as people like ice cream.* I watched them peck at their treat.

Later that evening, just before dark, I went back to the coop to tuck them in.

I soon learned the chickens would usually go into their house right at dusk, but there was always a straggler. I'd chase her around the pen a few times as she flapped her wings and squawked. Then she would give up and strut into the house in obvious exasperation.

The roosters always sat on the highest perches to rule the roost. The hens would settle in for the night by hunching low on their legs, which made them look very fat and peaceful. They uttered soft murmuring sounds without opening their beaks. The evenings became an important time of day for me. I felt a communion with those birds.

Only once during my year with the Forrests did I see my sister. The social worker drove Nan out to visit me. Nan was carrying a basket with a tea towel across the top. Inside were two bantam chickens—a hen and a rooster she'd brought as a gift from her foster family. They were delightful miniatures of the ones I cared for daily.

Nan's visit was friendly, but awkward. This was a setting we hadn't shared, and she was a guest. Mom Forrest tried to make the visit as nice as possible. She set a little table in the yard, under the trees, so Nan and I could lunch alone. We didn't talk for a while, until finally I asked, "Do you like your foster home, Nan?"

She frowned and shook her head.

"Aren't they nice to you?" I asked.

"They make me kill the chickens to eat for dinner." I

was aghast! *We don't kill our chickens!* But then I began to wonder where we *do* get the chicken we eat. *It must come from Dad's store*, I decided. But I was distracted from that topic as Nan went on to talk about her friends at her foster home.

Looking at Nan, I realized how tall she had grown. She was no longer the chatty, in-charge, confident "Nanny Goat" she had been at St. Chris. She didn't meet my eyes when she talked, and I sensed her sadness. She seemed to have grown larger on the outside and somehow smaller on the inside.

When Nan was ready to leave, we shared a quick hug, but I didn't know what to say to her. I missed the old Nan.

* * * * *

The bantam chicken and rooster that Nan had brought were very funny. Despite their size, they ruled the roost in every respect. I'd never seen such bossiness! At night they sat on the highest perch, screeching at those who dared to challenge their authority.

Several weeks later, when I discovered the bantam hen was missing, I was told she had died of cancer. And the following week, when the rooster went missing, the explanation I was given was that he had managed to squeeze through the chicken-wire fencing and a fox got him. Although I was saddened to lose the special gifts from my sister, the henhouse did seem calmer, and there were suddenly more eggs to gather.

* * * * *

When I'd arrived at the foster home, only two weeks of summer remained before school started. During that time, I met my foster cousins. One of them, Ann Raymond, was my age and, like me, would be starting third grade. I asked Ann what school would be like. She told me about the different subjects, including spelling. I asked her what words we would have to spell. "We'll have to spell words like *animal*," she said, nonchalantly. I didn't know how to spell *animal*. It seemed like a very difficult word. I began to feel apprehensive, especially since I'd never had much success with school at St. Chris.

My new school was in the nearby town of Havastraw, because Thiells was not large enough to have its own school. In the mornings, my foster sister Nancy and I would wait at the bus stop on Thiells Road, just down the street from our house. The neighbor's cat wove between our legs purring as other children gradually joined us there. When we arrived at school that first day, I wondered why Ann wasn't in my class. I found out later that she was in an advanced third grade.

My teacher's name was Mrs. Blatt. She had the children introduce themselves to the rest of the class. I noticed that there were many "colored children" in my class. This was a curiosity to me. There had only been one black child at St. Chris, and she had been fairly new so I hadn't known her well.

In the days that followed, Mrs. Blatt had us lined up in five rows of desks, ordered according to her judgment of our varying academic abilities. The brightest students, all girls, were in a row of desks along the windows. I was in the last row on the other side of the room, near the door. She had quickly discovered I couldn't read.

Mrs. Blatt divided the class into several reading groups and would work with one group at a time, but I wasn't in any of them. Instead, she would call me up to her desk to work with me alone, after working with the groups and giving them a written assignment. I wanted to be good, to please my teacher and my foster parents, but I just couldn't figure out the jumbled, scrambled words I saw. Once again, I felt completely defeated.

Dyslexia, a learning disorder, wasn't known to the educational community at the time, nor would it be for many years. My foster parents and my teacher were in agreement: "She's not working up to her potential," "She hasn't applied herself," "She needs more direction," or "Her ability is questionable."

Most school days started out well. Nancy and I enjoyed talking with the neighbor children at the bus stop. After the bus dropped us off at the school grounds, we had plenty of time to sit in groups on the sidewalk and play jacks until the bell rang. I loved playing jacks, and also pick-up sticks, and I was very good at both games. I'd start each day in good spirits, but I would soon be dragging emotionally.

At home, Mom sat with some of my school papers in front of her and said, "I'm very disappointed in you, Sally. You're not putting the effort into your school work that I hoped you would." I could understand her disappointment. I was disappointed, too. If I could read, I would. If I could *fly*, I would. Both seemed equally impossible.

In the classroom, I became friends with Willy Mack, a very kind Negro boy whose desk was behind mine. When our class picture was taken, I was eager to carry it home and show Mom my new friend. I thought his picture was wonderful because the flash of the camera had caused his dark skin to shine, and with his big smile, he seemed to glow. I was surprised by the startled expression on Mom's face when I pointed him out to her in the photo. She didn't say anything to explain her reaction, but I did have some understanding of prejudice from conversations I'd overheard. I never mentioned my friend to her again.

When report cards came out, I was so ashamed of my grades that I didn't take mine home. "Oh, I forgot and left it at school," I explained when Mom asked to see it.

"You're not telling me the truth, Sally," Mom said sternly, "and your punishment will have to be that we don't take you to the circus." Although I'd never been to a circus, Nancy had told me about balloons, animals doing tricks, high wire acts, cotton candy and hot dogs, and crowds of people cheering. It had been playing in my imagination for weeks. I cried for hours, but we still didn't go to the circus.

My mother and Mom Forrest made arrangements for me to take piano lessons. Mother would pay, and Mom Forrest would see to it that I got to my lessons and that I practiced on the piano in the living room every day.

At my first lesson, the teacher said, "It will be easy for you to remember the names of the spaces, Sally, because they spell a word, F-A-C-E. What does that spell?" I couldn't tell her what it spelled. Suddenly, I just wanted to go home and never take another piano lesson. My face flushed with humiliation. I felt she couldn't want to teach such a dumb girl, but that she had to because she was Mom's friend. I knew F-A-C-E was a word I should know, a word anyone my age should know.

The lessons continued. After several months, I managed to play "Twinkle, Twinkle, Little Star," "My Country 'tis of Thee," "Yankee Doodle," and "Jesus Loves Me," some with one hand and some with both hands. When the Methodist Church we attended had its children's talent night, I played several songs. The applause I received was no less than you'd expect for a child prodigy. I stood and gave a quick bow, feeling for the first time that I was making my foster family proud.

* * * * *

Mom was a spiritual person and was active in the church. She also wrote poetry, gardened, baked, and worked full time as a secretary at the Letchworth Village Mental Hospital not far from home. Mom seemed powerful to me. She seemed to have her own communication with God. With her, I felt secure and loved. I wanted to be like her.

As Mom and I were standing out by the road one evening waiting for Dad to get home, she was slowly pulling petals from daisies and softly reciting, "He loves me, he loves me not." She told me that when she and Dad married, he had wanted a house, so she saw to it that they got one. Then, he wanted children, and she gave him two. When he wanted a store, she saw to it that he got a grocery. This amazed me, and I realized that Mom was the one to go to if I ever really wanted something. She would ask God, and He would get it especially for her.

The Methodist Church frequently had social get-togethers on the weekends. At one of them, I met Martha, a girl my age who had nine sisters. Their dad had left them when the last baby wasn't a boy.

Martha and her family lived in a large, decrepit house. The church helped them financially. When I went to play at her house one day, she shared a beauty tip while she was changing her baby sister's diaper. "If you take a diaper wet with urine and rub it on your face, it will get rid of your freckles," she said, demonstrating by rubbing her freckled face with the urine-soaked diaper. I didn't try it because I didn't have freckles.

She and I each had one of the new Sparkle Plenty dolls, designed after a character in the Dick Tracy comic strip. It was the best doll a girl could possibly have. It had short, curly blond hair. Its skin was soft and lifelike, just like a real baby. The dolls came with a hairnet, booties, brush and comb, baby bottle, and a three-outfit wardrobe.

One day, after we'd played happily with our dolls for hours at my house, Martha's mother came to pick her up, bringing each of us a piece of candy. Martha dropped her candy wrapper on the ground. "We don't do that in this nice yard," her mother scolded. "You pick that up." I hung my head in embarrassment for my friend, but I was proud I had such a nice yard.

On other summer days, golden-furred Laddie would sidle up to me as we followed Lucille, the housekeeper, around the house and yard while she did her work. As she hung clothes and linens out on the line to dry, I'd bombard her with questions: "What do animals think about?" "Do they wish they could talk?" "Have you been to a lot of places in the world?" "Have you been to Holland?" I asked her if she knew how to spell the word *pneumonia*, which I thought was so impossibly difficult I couldn't imagine ever being able to spell it. She always responded with patience and assured me that such things concerned her, too. But she confessed she didn't always have the answers.

When I'd arrived at my foster home I was quite slender, due to my pickiness with food and the controlled size of portions at St. Chris. But at the Forrest's there were no restrictions on food. I was introduced to white bread with Karo syrup poured over it as a snack. I always had the choice of either clear or brown Karo syrup. Often, while Lucille worked, I would sit at the small table in the kitchen listening to the radio and eating syrup on bread. At the evening meal, there was usually cake for dessert. I gained forty pounds in less than a year. Now I was a hefty 100-pound nine-year-old.

I was very unhappy with myself—for my poor school performance, for becoming fat, and because I didn't know where I really belonged in this world.

One evening, after Mom and Dad got home from work we had a quick dinner and drove into the downtown part of Havastraw. Although I was familiar with the school grounds in Havastraw, I had never been to the shopping area before. I was very excited.

As we walked along the sidewalk, Mom saw a couple of her friends. "Well, hello Jean, and who is this?" they asked, smiling at me and then looking to Mom. I wanted to hear who I was. *I'm your daughter! Tell them I'm your daughter!* "This is Sally," is all she said.

We went into a stationery store and it was amazing beyond words. There were shelves of neatly stacked papers and cards—everything you could possibly imagine. I wanted to say to someone, *Look at this!* I walked past each different display, but didn't see anyone to say it to—Mom was busy with a purchase. The most wonderful thing I saw was tracing paper. You could put this thin, almost transparent paper on top of any picture and trace it. How I would love to have some! I dashed to Mom to tell her of my discovery, but she shushed me while the salesclerk was talking to her. I realize now that she couldn't have been at all aware of my wonderment of what was ordinary to her, or of how limited my experiences had been before coming to live with her.

It was getting dark when we got in the car to go home. I was very quiet, stunned to think of how many things there were in the world that I hadn't known about.

* * * * *

Grandma Raymond, Mom Forrest's mother, did things I thought were silly, like putting her dress on backward or wearing her slip on top of her dress. I was shamefully impatient with her. Sometimes I would even tease her, and then she'd chase me with a broom as fast as she was able to move. "You wicked child!" she would say. But we really did care about each other and when we were at peace, she told me about growing up in "Ioway" (Iowa). I'd sit next to her as she reminisced, trying to imagine her as a young girl. At school, a classmate had shown me how to give a butterfly kiss by fluttering your eyelashes against someone's cheek. When I asked Grandma if I could give her a butterfly kiss, she was apprehensive, remembering other tricks I'd played, but she finally agreed. As I moved close, I could see her tense. When I got my face against her cheek and fluttered my eyelashes, she seemed pleasantly relieved and surprised at the gentleness of my "kiss."

Because Nancy was seven years older, she had her own friends and would frequently spend time with them away from the house. Occasionally she would include me in an activity with her friends or take me to one of their homes, where I would sit quietly, listening to them talk about boys and plans for their futures. One time, Nancy walked with me to a small store, about a mile from home, where she bought me a comic book and a bag of penny candies. Then we went across the street to the post office to pick up the day's mail before going home. It wasn't the treats that made me feel happy as I walked along with her, but that I felt she liked me.

One of Nancy's friends lived nearby, and her family also took in foster children. But those children were retarded and weren't being cared for with kindness. I would sit in a glider swing with them in their backyard and smell that they had soiled themselves. They looked miserable. Their punishment for not using the toilet was to stay in their soiled clothing for hours. Nancy's friend was not troubled by this. "Next time they'll learn," she'd casually say. It made me sad to see children treated this way, so I didn't like to go there.

Their home was a small farm, with pigs, horses, a cow, geese, and many dogs and cats. One day, I followed Nancy and her friend into the fenced area for the geese. I'd never seen a goose before and had no reason to think they were any less friendly than my chickens. As I approached a goose, it shot its long neck forward and let out a loud honk. Frightened, I stepped back quickly as it started coming at me in a running waddle. I fled in a circle around the pen, but the goose stayed so close on my heels that I couldn't pause to unlatch the gate. Soon, other geese, all honking, joined the chase. I was screaming for help and running as fast as I could, to the utter amusement of the two older girls. Nancy finally stopped laughing long enough to open the gate for me. I never went near the geese again.

* * * * *

My foster brother, Jack, was home from college only for Christmas and summer vacations. He was tall and handsome and didn't seem to mind having me as his shadow. He had a magical way of turning a conversation into a game. "What does that have to do with the price of eggs?" was his response to many things I brought up. Then the challenge was to make a connection between what I was saying and the price of eggs. He laughed at my ingenuity, and quick, but complicated responses. He used words like *witchmacoo* and *humdinger*.

When he arrived home for Christmas with a present for me, it became a game that lasted until my bedtime on Christmas Eve for me to guess what it was. He gave me hints: "It can talk." "You can help it talk." "It will make you happy." I followed him around begging for more hints. When Christmas morning came, my gift was a set of Uncle Remus records. I played them on the old Victrola on the sun porch, cranking the handle to wind it up whenever the voices started to slow. I learned all the songs on it and sang along. It was the perfect gift.

CHAPTER SIX

I learned a lesson from Mom one day, through a simple episode. It has stayed with me and kept me strong through difficult times in my life.

Laddie was my constant companion. We each had enough puppy in us to be good buddies. Because Grandma Raymond got many things mixed up and often didn't remember what people told her, she frequently created troublesome situations. Mom had told her not to give Laddie the day-old bread to eat, but occasionally she did it anyway. Mom said this might be why Laddie threw up on the living room rug one day. His vomit was full of long, skinny, wriggling worms. I was thoroughly disgusted, but I couldn't take my eyes from the horror of it. Mom quickly got a dust pan and some cloths and squatted to clean up the awful mess.

"How can you *do* that?" I asked incredulously, as worms dangled from the edge of the dust pan.

Mom stopped, stood up, and looked me straight in the eyes. "We do what must be done, Sally," she said sternly, making each word staccato for emphasis. She stared at me until she was sure I understood what she had said. There was no further conversation.

My mother offered similar lessons on her Sunday visits to my foster home. On one visit, as we were walking through the quiet Theills neighborhood, she said, "Life is like a card game." She was looking straight ahead and it was almost as though she was talking to herself. "You are dealt certain cards, and those are what you must play the game with." She paused, but then looked down at me and added, "Life deals you certain experiences, some are happy and some are difficult. You can't trade them in. You must go about your life working with all you are dealt in the best way you possibly can. That is your *lot in life*. That determines your character."

* * * * *

Late in the school year, during my stay with the Forrests, Mother decided she wanted to unite her family by taking Nan and me out of our foster homes and moving us to Virginia. She had been offered a job as a physicist with the Interior Department in Washington, D.C.

The Forrests were alarmed, though they didn't let on to me what was going on. They told Mother, "The move will uproot Sally again from a place where she is settled in and loved. Taking her away from our home could be emotionally damaging to her. Please reconsider. It wouldn't be in her best interest."

Without explaining the reasons to me, Mom arranged to have me tested by the lead psychologist at the Letchworth Village Mental Hospital, where she worked. He was to spend an entire afternoon with me to get a complete psychological evaluation by administering a battery of tests to determine my intelligence quotient and my emotional stability. Mom felt sure the test results would confirm my need to stay in her home.

When the day of testing arrived, I was told only that I would get to "play games" with a doctor Mom knew at work. Dad Forrest picked me up at school. I was in high spirits and told him excitedly, "I got an A on an arithmetic test, Dad—my first A!"

The tall, middle-aged doctor reminded me of Mr. Shoemaker, the nice superintendent at St. Chris. He introduced himself and shook my hand. He motioned me toward a small chair across from him and made casual conversation until I seemed relaxed and comfortable. He was completely nonjudgmental and nodded and smiled at everything I did and said.

"Name as many birds as you can, Sally," the doctor said, leaning back in his chair. Living with the Forrests, I was familiar with many birds and flowers, so I went to work, naming all I knew. His eyebrows rose at the ongoing list. "That's very impressive, Sally."

He asked me to draw a picture of a man. "What kind of man should I draw?"

"Any kind of man you want to," he said

On a large, blank piece of paper, I drew a farmer in blue overalls. His hair stuck out from under his hat and he had a big smile on his face.

Then I took an ink blot test, and that really freed me to use my imagination—there was no right or wrong.

I enjoyed my day of testing—the games and puzzles and other fun activities. I did the best I could and earned praise. Fortunately, I didn't have to read anything.

I later learned that the results of the testing showed I was a well-adjusted child. In the ink blot test, I'd seen no people, only animals. I saw two rabbits in rocking chairs, two birds flying toward each other—interpretations revealing I had more trust in animals than in people. My IQ was well above average, causing more curiosity about my inability to read. Because the testing indicated that I wouldn't be emotionally harmed by leaving the Forrests, they had to

61

accept that I would be moving to Virginia with my mother at the end of the school year.

At Mother's next visit, she told me, "I want you and Nan to come live with me so we can be a family again. Would you like that, Sally?" For so many years I'd longed to hear this, but now I had mixed feelings. I wondered what Mom Forrest would think. Mom had become my *mom*. Her home had become my home.

"We'll move to Virginia," Mother said, smiling. "You'll like Virginia; it's such a pretty state. I've accepted a job in Washington, D.C., and that's just a short way from Virginia. What do you think?"

"That sounds nice," I said as I nodded my head and smiled. Because she was so enthusiastic and hopeful, I didn't want to hurt her feelings, but I was filled with nervous butterflies: fear and sadness mixed together. I loved my mother, but mostly on Sundays, the day she had always visited me over the last six-and-a-half years. *That* was her day.

Looking back, I realize the gravity of the decision Mother had made in taking the job at the Interior Department. All those years she'd been content to be a visitor in her children's lives. Now she either had to take us with her or not see us anymore.

At the end of the school year, Mrs. Blatt told me I hadn't passed third grade. "I have already discussed this with the Forrests," she said, "and they'll talk to you about what needs to be done when you get home." Then she sent me along with my report card in hand to catch the school bus. Word must have gotten around; no one would sit with me. The other children sat at a distance, whispering to each other—I was certain—the news of my failure. I dreaded having to face the Forrests.

Mom didn't say anything when I first arrived home, but her disappointment was obvious in her demeanor. She didn't look at me and I couldn't look at her.

While she was preparing dinner in the kitchen she told me that I would be privately tutored for six weeks and then tested to see if I could qualify for fourth grade before leaving to live with my mother.

To get to the tutor's house, I would have to ride a city bus. "Please don't make me go!" I begged. "I'm scared. What if I get off the bus at the wrong stop and get lost and you can't find me?" Mom told me I had no choice and assured me that I wouldn't get lost. I finally agreed to ride the bus, secretly accepting it as punishment for doing badly in school.

The tutor was a woman, older than Mom, who had wavy hair that was just starting to gray. We developed a friendly relationship. When I used her upstairs bathroom, I took time to tour the bedrooms. I looked at family photos on the dressers and bedside tables—smiling faces, arms around each other, children sitting on parents' laps. I felt a mixture of envy and curiosity at being in a family home where people so obviously cared about each other. I'd experienced something of that at the Forrests, though I knew I wasn't *really* a part of it. Would my new home with Mother feel as loving as the tutor's? I doubted it. I'd never felt very important to Mother.

What the tutor tried to teach me wasn't anything like what was being taught in school. But I passed the test for fourth grade. I suspected, however, that I was allowed to pass only because I'd be leaving anyway.

I was nine years old when the time came for me to leave the Forrests. Because we'd become very close, it was difficult for Mom to let me go. We sat together on the couch in the living room and talked quietly about how we would miss each other. Mom patted my hand as I made promises to write "all the time." I doubt she believed me.

She probably thought I would quickly forget my year with them and she would never hear from me. Instead, I wrote to her monthly, and sometimes more often, for over thirty-five years. I looked forward to her letters with news of my extended foster family. She filled the card or sheet of stationary with her handwriting, curving her sentences around from the bottom of the page and up the side margin, filling every tiny space, as though she had so much to tell me that she could barely fit it all in.

I kept her current on how things were going in my new life. I sent her pictures of me in the nylon-net formal I wore to my first dance. I sent her photos of my pets and friends. I told her about my boyfriends. I sent her announcements of my high school and college graduations. She met my husband through pictures, and my children as each of them arrived. She shared my grief when my husband's plane was shot down in Vietnam. We shared our lives with each other, and I loved her more with each passing year.

But we didn't know this on that day of parting. I had the excitement of the adventure ahead. Mom had only the sorrow of our goodbye.

She handed me a small gift box. "This is for you, Sally." I opened it and found a sterling silver pin—a galloping horse. Mom pinned it to my dress and said softly, "If you ever feel lonely and want to come back to us, just pin this horse on your clothes and close your eyes—you'll see me then with my arms open wide—and come galloping back."

She couldn't bring herself to drive me to the Greyhound bus station for the long trip that would take me to my mother. She asked Nancy to take me and told her to buy me anything I wanted.

While Nancy and I waited at the bus station, I didn't talk. I was feeling abandoned again. I remembered what

Mother had told me about learning to deal with one's lot in life.

Nancy asked sympathetically, "Is there anything I can buy for you, Sally?" I looked around and then pointed to a rack of brightly swirled lollipops that were bigger than my opened hand.

I climbed the metal steps of the bus, clutching my lollipop. I sat by a window and looked out at Nancy. *Please come get me. Don't let me go. I want to go back home with you.* But the doors of the bus closed and I waved a slow goodbye as it pulled away from the station.

I was traveling into the unknown. *I am my family. I will never leave me.*

CHAPTER SEVEN

I rode with Mother and Nan on the city bus from Washington, D.C. to the stop closest to our new home in Arlington. It was dark out, and the city was alight with colorful signs, flashing as though in celebration. I'd never been in a big city, and in other circumstances it might have been thrilling, but in my weary state I felt resentful of the gaiety.

When the bus stopped in our neighborhood, we still had to walk several blocks to the duplex Mother had rented. Nan and I carried small suitcases. The rest was being sent. We were oddly silent, each of us having our own thoughts about this new life. I was mourning the loss of the foster family I loved. I always knew my mother and sister were my real family, but they were new to me, again.

Our house was on a long curved street of duplexes that all looked alike. Mother said, "Because our house is on the curve, it's the one that peeks out at you, so you'll never go into the wrong house by mistake." That made me smile.

The home was small and plain, with very little yard. The furniture was unfamiliar and I wondered if Mother had owned it before we moved.

It was quickly apparent that this was a neighborhood of young parents and babies. Mothers walked up and down the sidewalk pushing strollers and carriages. I asked Mother about a woman who looked funny because she was so skinny but had a big belly, and Mother told me she was pregnant. I'd never seen a pregnant woman before.

Nan and I were old enough at nine and thirteen that Mother felt she could leave us alone while she was at work. Because she didn't have a car, she was picked up each morning by a co-worker and transported across Memorial Bridge to the Interior Department. I realized this was a time of transition for her, too.

For days I sat by the window in hopes of spotting a potential friend, but saw no one my age—just young mothers and babies. There was no one with whom I could pass the long hours while Mother was at work. Nan met a girl her age who lived nearby. Mother had instructed Nan not to leave me alone, but one afternoon my sister took off to visit her new friend. After Nan was out the door, I decided to follow her and shadowed her to the end of the block, hanging back so she wouldn't see me. Minutes after Nan went inside this girl's apartment, I knocked on the door. When Nan's friend answered, I told her I was Nan's sister. "Oh, hi, come on in," she said, holding a lighted cigarette. She was well developed for thirteen and had messy blond hair. She and Nan were both smoking cigarettes. Mother smoked, but I'd never seen Nan smoke before.

"What did you do, follow me?" Nan asked, obviously peeved. "Go home and stay home," she ordered, pushing me out the door.

Sitting by the window once again, feeling bored, I considered putting on my little sterling silver horse Mom Forrest had given me, closing my eyes, and galloping back home to her. I wanted to gallop back, but I knew if I did I would never want to open my eyes and lose her again. I wondered who was taking care of the chickens and whether Laddie was puzzled about where I'd gone and was looking for me. I wondered if there was a hole in my foster family where I had been.

When Nan arrived home later that afternoon, she didn't talk to me except to say, "Baby! Jerk!" as she passed me.

Before Mother got home that evening, I had decided that I would put my life in Mother's hands. I would lean on her, trust her, and love her—because I needed her.

When Mother finally arrived, I announced that Nan had left me alone and gone to a girl's house to smoke. Nan glared at me with hatred in her narrowed eyes. Mother looked at her for an explanation. "I wasn't gone for long, she's just being a baby," Nan said, before huffing off. Our antagonism began at that point and never stopped.

Each day, Mother would ask me, "Have you seen Nan smoking today? Do you know if she has cigarettes?" Nan had never been a protective big sister, not even at St. Chris, though I always felt comfort in knowing part of my family was close by. Now I didn't know where my loyalty lay. Nan accused me of being a "dirty tattle-tale baby" for snooping for cigarettes in her purse and reporting to Mother.

Mother must have begun to realize then that dealing with us might be more difficult than she'd anticipated. We were no longer tiny girls with tiny problems.

School had always been a humiliating experience for me, and in spite of my new clothes and new, colorful school supplies, Hume Elementary School was no less disappointing. By fourth grade, teachers expected to be able to give assignments to a class and have the students quietly do the work. I could read at first or second grade level now, but not well enough to read through a complete assignment. When school proved to be a disaster for me again, I lost interest in everything. I became sullen and moody at home and at school. "I can't do it and I won't do it!" I would yell at Mother in frustration.

Mother soon realized our neighborhood of very young families wasn't a good setting for Nan or me. On the weekends, a real estate agent began showing us single-family houses in other parts of Arlington. One had a television set, which I'd only heard about and never seen before. "If we buy your house, will the television be ours, too?" I asked the lady who owned the house.

She looked at Mother, raising her eyebrows and smiling, as if asking whether including the television would cinch the sale. "That's quite possible," the woman said to me in a sing-song voice.

Mother wanted to find a house we could afford in a neighborhood with children close to our ages. One day, we were looking at a house for the second time. It was empty and clean, unlike the first time we'd seen it. Mother announced, "This will be our new home."

It was a narrow, two-story, four-room house—two bedrooms, a kitchen and a living room—on a small triangular lot with lots of shrubbery, at the corner of 19th and Quesada Streets. I went upstairs to the bedroom that Nan and I were to share. I lay down on the sun-bathed oak floor, basking in the warmth with my eyes closed and my arms outstretched. It was my private acceptance of this house as our family home.

Mother made a ceremony of introducing us to the house, making each room seem welcoming and enticing in some way. "Isn't this kitchen cheery!" she said. "There's even room for a small table. As we walked through the living room, she said, "We can make the screened porch into a sunroom where we can have some of our meals and you can even sleep out here in the warmer months." The people who'd owned the house before us had used the screened porch for storage. It had been piled high with boxes when it was first shown to us. After we moved in, Mother went to work scrubbing the screens and hand-sewing a brightly striped cover for a twin daybed and a matching cover for my grandfather's steamer trunk that had come with him from Italy when he was a teenager. A card table and chairs were the final touch.

Nan quickly made friends at her school, and I made many friends in the neighborhood. Quesada was a dead-end street with lots of children, including three little girls about my age who lived right next door.

The friction between Nan and me continued. I kept tattling on her: about her cigarettes, about her having a boy in our house while Mother was at work, about her not coming home after school as she was supposed to. Nan came after me with fists. Once, after she'd pummeled me to her satisfaction, she steamed off, saying, "Stay out of my things, and quit telling on me, you little brat." I retaliated by tying her nylon stockings in knots, knowing she wouldn't know I'd done so until she'd be rushing to dress for church on Sunday.

With so much dissension between Nan and me, it was clear that the sleeping arrangement wasn't working. Mother decided to share the larger bedroom with Nan and move me into the smaller bedroom. It wasn't sunny, but I liked having my own space for the first time. How peaceful it was to not share a room with someone who was always angry with me.

Soon after we moved in, Mother told me that although she worked very hard, we didn't have much money. The house had cost her $10,000, and she was struggling to put some money into a savings account. "You'll have to understand that we can't afford to buy candy, cookies, and cake, Sally," she said. "When you want something sweet, you'll have to eat fruit. It will help a lot if you don't complain

71

about this." I was flattered that she had confided in me about her finances. No one had ever talked to me about money before. Little did I know that fruit was *more* expensive and that she was doing this to help me lose the forty pounds I had gained while living with the Forrests. The weight came off slowly, without my even realizing it.

When we moved into this house, I transferred from Hume Elementary School to Charles Stewart Elementary. The school building was newer, with lots of glass allowing sunlight in. Everyone seemed happy and welcoming. I worked hard on the assignments and tried to keep my deficiencies a secret. My reading skills improved, which helped all other areas of my school work. I made friends and even joined a Girl Scout troop. I felt more at peace with myself and my life. I sang the popular tunes of that era on the mile-and-a-half walk to and from school. "I'm Looking Over a Four Leaf Clover," "Nickelodeon," "Cross Over the Bridge." I loved the Johnny Ray songs: "Letter of Goodbye" and "The Little White Cloud That Cried." Singing seemed to help me heal from having to leave my foster home, from being an academic embarrassment in school, from being fat, and from living with a sister I was betraying and who therefore didn't like me.

Nan's foster home hadn't offered the serene farm life she'd anticipated when she left St. Chris. There were chickens, but she'd had to kill them for food. She had her own room, but it was a hot attic room where she was isolated from the rest of the family. She got severe impetigo on her legs, but received no medical treatment. I wasn't yet aware of all those things, but I did know she wasn't happy in her foster home.

Mother could see Nan was having a difficult time adjusting to our being together again, so she got her an Irish setter puppy. "This is Nan's puppy because she's the big

72

sister," she said, without revealing the part about Nan having had a rougher time in foster care. Nan named the puppy Princess Penelope and called her Penny. The puppy's antics lightened the mood of the family. She kept us entertained and sometimes embarrassed us. Penny played one of her funniest tricks on my sister.

At fifteen, Nan wasn't developing in the bust line as much as she wished. She solved what she considered to be her flat-chestedness by buying foam rubber forms that fit in her bra. One day, when changing clothes, Nan left these falsies on the floor. Penny, in her playfulness, grabbed one in her mouth, ran down the stairs, pushed open the screen door, and raced out through the front yard and into the street. Nan chased her outside, yelling, "Mom, Mom!" Mother and I couldn't help but laugh when we saw how Penny was taunting her. The whole neighborhood knew this was Nan's dog, and what it was that Penny had in her mouth. Penny took a get-ready-to-run stance and whenever Nan made a move toward her, Penny loped away. Lifting her head and shaking the foam falsie in her jaws, she seemed almost to be laughing at Nan. Then Penny ran down the street and out of sight. It was hours before she returned home, mouth empty. "I'm never leaving this house again! You can't make me!" Nan yelled as she stomped upstairs. She stayed in the house for a few days until her embarrassment subsided.

Penny grew lean and tall. She was a neighborhood dog, but she had an allegiance to our family that seemed to be what held us together during this adjustment period.

Every day, when I walked home from school, Penny was waiting for me a couple of blocks from home, sitting at the top of 19th Street hill. One day, when I had a sports event after school, I got a ride home with the parents of a friend. It wasn't until dinner time that we noticed Penny was missing. "I bet she's still at the top of the hill, waiting for me," I said. I ran out into the night, and sure enough, there she was at her usual post, looking confused that I was coming from the wrong direction. She wagged her tail as I hugged her and we went home together for dinner.

Penny was a purebred Irish setter, and Mother had said she wanted purebred puppies so that we could sell them. It was a problem when Penny went into heat because we'd never been able to keep her contained in the yard. I offered to walk Penny on a leash one afternoon, but by the time I got to the end of our street, we were swarmed by other dogs that were after her. Mother had warned me to keep all dogs away, but there were so many and they were so persistent! All I could do was to lift Penny up in my arms, leaning backward to keep my balance with the big load. "Get dooown!" I screamed at the more aggressive dogs that were jumping up on me. It was a struggle to carry Penny the full block home while being besieged by her would-be suitors. The next day, Mother arranged to have Penny bred with another family's male Irish setter. In exchange, the other family would get their pick of the litter.

When the time arrived for the puppies to be born, we watched as one potato-sized puppy after another slid out and was cleaned by Penny, who knew exactly what to do. It was late at night by the time all eleven were born and suckling on their worn out mother. "What a good girl you are," I told Penny, stroking her head. She was too exhausted to lift her head, but her eyes followed me and I could see a very slight wag of her tail.

When the puppies were eight weeks old, we sold all except one. Because he had a bent tail—the last inch went sideways—nobody picked him. I named this puppy Mine. Mine and I spent our summer days in constant togetherness. I carried him on walks and to my friends' homes. He slept on my bed every night.

One day, Mother said, "Someone is coming to see the puppy and I don't want you to make a scene, Sally."

"No." I pleaded, "He's mine. You know he's mine." A lady and little girl arrived and decided they wanted him. Frantic, I was hiding in the front bushes, wailing loudly as they carried him past me to get to their car.

"Why is she crying?" the girl asked her mother.

"You hush now and come along," the mother said.

I was inconsolable for days. How could Mother have let someone come and take Mine away when she knew how much I loved him.

The following month, someone in Mother's office had kittens to give away. She brought one home. It was tiny and golden. "This kitten is Sally's," she informed us, trying to make it seem that everything was now fair. "You'll be responsible for caring for your own pet, Sally." With Penny and Dolly, our family was complete.

I was a girlfriend type of girl who needed friends to share news with, be secretive with, and just be with. I played with the girls next door, but within that first year they moved away and a young, newly married couple moved into their house. They didn't know I slept on the screened porch, and so they didn't lower their bedroom shade or close their window at night. I couldn't see any actual bedtime activity because I was on the first floor, and their bedroom was on their second floor. I could, however, hear them—and it intrigued me. Lying in bed, I would watch their window until I fell asleep.

Sometimes I played with Lucy, who lived half a block from us, but we didn't match up. She was clingy—simply always there—and I got tired of her. I tried being bossy and rude to keep her away, but she was forever standing on my front stoop, pleading, "Why can't you come out and play?"

Her parents owned and operated a bar in nearby West-over Village shopping center. They both smoked non-stop and their home was thick with a cloud of smoke that left a nasty yellow residue on every surface. Because of the smoke and the stink, all the neighborhood children avoided going there. But Lucy's clever parents soon found a way to make their house a popular place; they bought the first tele-vision set in the neighborhood. Every day at the same time, all of us children showed up at the Caulder home to watch The Howdy Doody Show. Often, the ten or more of us huddled in front of the TV and sang along with the show's theme music. When the show was over, we were herded outside. A few of us usually stayed to play in her yard. For a short time, Lucy was almost a celebrity. But over the summer, other families got television sets and Lucy's popu-larity faded.

A military family, the Wardens, moved in across the street from us. The father worked at the Pentagon and the mother was a housewife. I wished my mother was a housewife. She was the only mother in the neighborhood who had a job away from home.

Their oldest child, Patty, was eleven, also. We were to start seventh grade at Swanson Junior High School that fall and we became inseparable friends. She had a nine-year-old sister and a five-year-old brother. The family reminded me of the Forrests. Patty's mother exercised control in a strict but caring way. I loved being at their house, observ-ing how things worked. The children had respect for the parents, never dreaming of disobeying. In our house, Nan was always breaking rules, I was always crying, and Mother was always yelling. In the Wardens' house, there was no chaos, no upset.

I learned how to study from Patty, and I became more enthusiastic about school, spending whatever time it took to do well on an assignment. I learned to always ask for extra credit work and to make study time a priority. My new teachers and friends weren't aware of my limitations, and now perhaps they would never have to know.

"I want you to sign up for a college prep course of study," Mother said when I was choosing my classes for ninth grade. I was flabbergasted that she thought I was smart enough to go to college, but I signed up for the required courses. The foreign language I chose was French, even though I had enough difficulty reading English. I got through two years of French by asking for extra credit work from Madame St. Cyr. I wrote poems in English and then translated them into French. They didn't rhyme in French, but she was pleased with my effort and passed me with a grade of C.

In home economics class, something happened that greatly boosted my self-confidence. As we were discussing ways to improve ourselves, I said, "I wish I wasn't so fat." The teacher and students looked puzzled.

"Why do you think you're fat, Sally?" the teacher asked. She had me stand in front of a full length mirror to make me realize I was no longer fat. The weight had come off so slowly that my self-image hadn't changed. All seemed right in my world now that I was getting Bs and Cs in school, had lost enough weight to require a new wardrobe, and had many friends.

I started participating in after-school sports because Patty Warden did. We tried broad jumping, high jumping, volleyball, and basketball. I was more athletic than I'd ever imagined and did well in everything I tried. Patty's dad built a high-jump set in their backyard so she and I could practice. It had an adjustable bar that could be raised so we could challenge ourselves to jump higher. I was often at Patty's house, either playing board games and drinking juice or playing outdoor games after dinner.

Patty and her sister both had curly, bright-red hair, much curlier and less manageable even than mine. "I hate my curly hair," Patty often said, and that made me feel she was a true friend. Whenever we discussed our hair problems, we ran our fingers through our curls as though that alone would straighten them.

Patty and I took dance lessons one evening a week at the Junior Recreation Center (JRC) in preparation for the occasional evening dances at Swanson Junior High. We dressed in taffeta, velvet, or lace for these junior high dances. Patty and I would stand off to one side of the gym floor with our friends, hoping someone would ask us to dance. We complimented each other on our dresses. My hand-me-down purple taffeta dress rustled as I walked, inspiring compliments from the other girls. One of them had a flower pinned to her dress. "My mom did that so I would smell pretty," she said.

Our parents had issued strict instructions to never go outside the school building at any time during a dance. "The not-so-nice girls are out there smoking with the not-so-nice boys," they said, adding a warning about how difficult it would be to recover from getting a bad reputation.

Warren Beatty, who would become a famous actor, was two grades above me when I first started going to these school dances. He was suave on the dance floor, kissing the neck of a woman who seemed much older—maybe even high school age. He talked about wanting to be a master of ceremonies when he grew up. I thought he was just a show-offy rich kid with unrealistic aspirations. I guess I was wrong.

One night, after telling Mother and Nan that I hadn't been asked to dance very much, Nan stepped into the role of the sister I had always wanted her to be and gave me two wonderful suggestions. "Wear a bright dress so that you stand out, Sally, and never stand with a group of girls. Boys that age are shy. It's difficult enough for them to approach one girl by herself. They almost never approach a group of girls."

Mother shopped with me and bought me a bright red dress with a full skirt to wear to the next school dance. I stood alone at the dance, trying not to look bored. I missed my friends, and they looked over at me, wondering why I wasn't standing with them. But when I got home that night I excitedly reported to my mother and sister, "I was asked to dance every single dance!"

Whenever Nan was expecting the arrival of a boy picking her up for a date, she would insist that Mother and I dress up, that Mother not quiz him, and that I keep my trap shut. If I peeked through the living room curtains to see if he had arrived yet, Nan would shriek bloody murder at me. After Nan and her date left, Mother and I would sit there, all dressed up with nothing to do. We had some of our best talks on those evenings. Mother explained words to me that I'd heard, such as *whore* and *queer*. She told me what it was like when Nan and I were born, how sick she'd been both times with breast infections. She talked to me again about *one's lot in life*. And she surprised me with this advice: "If you're ever with a boy and want to make love with him, don't demean yourself and cheapen the act by doing it in the back seat of a car. You should at least get out of the car and lie under the stars."

Nan left for college when I was twelve and she was sixteen. She had attended summer school each summer, which gave her enough credits to graduate early. Our relationship had improved the year before she left, so I was sad to see her leave, although it consoled me to inherit all her baby-sitting jobs. The house seemed dull without Nan to stir things up.

The summer before high school started, my friend Patty Warden's father was transferred to the state of Washington. We promised to write, but we never did. After Patty moved away with her family, I became friends with Wanda Gleason, who lived a block-and-a-half from my house. Wanda had always gone to a private school, so I only knew her from the neighborhood. She was an only child who lived in a large house with an emotionally cold father and a mother disfigured by a disease that had caused parts of her body to enlarge—her face was distorted with extra flesh, her nose was unnaturally large, and her fingers all looked like thumbs. Wanda was extremely embarrassed by her mother's appearance.

One day at her house, Wanda and I were looking through some of her family's old photo albums. I was astounded to see what a pretty, slender woman her mother had been. "She was beautiful!" I exclaimed. Wanda only nodded.

"I want to talk to Wanda about her menstrual period and boyfriends," her mother once told me, "but when I try, Wanda screams at me and runs from the room." I liked Wanda's mother but I didn't know how to help in her effort to be close to her daughter.

When talking to Wanda on the phone one evening, I told her, "I'll give you a quarter if you go into the living room, give your dad a kiss on the cheek and tell him you love him." She said she would when we hung up, and later I paid her. I wondered if she really had. I wished I had a dad to say that to. After begging her father for years, Wanda's dad finally relented and allowed her to attend public school for her junior and senior years.

Wanda and I didn't have classes together in high school. I would usually visit her at her home after school. I looked with fascination in her dresser drawers filled with pretty jewelry, all still in gift boxes. She had beautiful dolls that had come in doll suitcases with complete wardrobes. Though I was beyond the doll-playing age, I envied her possessions. When I was mad at my mother, I would escape to Wanda's house to complain. We were each other's confidantes those last two years before leaving for different colleges.

When Wanda was in college, her father committed suicide; her mother died a few years after Wanda graduated. And many years later, I learned that Wanda took her own life at the age of sixty-one. An old high school acquaintance found my name in Wanda's address book and called to tell me the sad news. Though we lived two thousand miles apart, Wanda and I had kept in touch at Christmastime over the years.

* * * * *

When I was fourteen, and Nan had been in college for two years, Mother decided to sell the Quesada Street house and move us to an apartment. I was to start high school that fall and Mother thought it would be a good time to make the transition from the upkeep of a house to the ease of an apartment. When she first mentioned it, I immediately protested. This was the home I'd needed for so many years, and it represented security for me. "*This* is our home. I won't go!" But no amount of crying or arguing could dissuade Mother.

The Buckingham Apartments were touted as "garden apartments." Behind them there was a grassy area with trees, shrubs, and an occasional bench. There were squirrels and birds and walking paths. Young mothers walked their babies in strollers and met at the benches to talk. But from the street, the apartments were two-story brick buildings, almost institutional-looking, with no charm. I didn't want my friends to know I lived there and I didn't want to go to the high school that the kids living in my new neighborhood attended. I never made the change of address on my high school records, so there was no school bus for me to ride. I had to walk a mile-and-a-half each way for school, lugging my heavy textbooks.

With Nan in college, just Mother and I shared this two-bedroom second-story apartment. As always, Mother managed to give touches of warmth to the decor. She put potted philodendrons on the window sills. She had our furniture reupholstered and had summer slipcovers made. She hung a small framed print of "Whistler's Mother" above the table in the small dinette off the kitchen, and hung other prints from the National Art Gallery on the apartment walls. She bought our first television set—I think to soothe my misgivings about the move.

* * * * *

I would do anything to please Mother, to ensure she would keep me and perhaps even love me. "May I fix you a nice cup of tea?" I'd ask her in the evenings. And she'd ask me to massage her feet with cream after her hard day at work.

But seeking her approval made me more vulnerable to her sarcasm and ridicule. If we were in the tiny kitchen at the same time, and she stepped on my foot, she'd say, "Get your big clodhoppers out of the way." My feet had grown faster than the rest of me, and at size nine were the largest in the family. If I ever sat down while Mother was still busy, she'd say, "You're nothing but a good-for-nothing lazy lummox." I learned not to sit until Mother was ready to sit.

I asked her once if she loved me. She replied, "That's something you should know without having to ask." But she never said she loved me, so I never really knew. She wasn't a hugging, kissing kind of Mother who said, "I love you so much," or "I'm very proud of you," as I dearly wished she would. So all through high school I continued to do the things, join the groups, and be the kind person I thought would make her proud.

CHAPTER EIGHT

High school sororities were popular in 1953 when I was a sophomore at Washington-Lee High School. Some sororities were looking for girls from wealthy families; others wanted girls with sophistication, beauty, popularity, or brains. I fit into none of those categories, but was still able to find a niche in Kappa Delta Phi. They wanted girls who were likely to be fun and enthusiastic, regardless of social or academic standing.

The initiation phase was called Hell Week. Mother worked my hair into fifty braids for the first event which was to take place on the streets of downtown Washington, D.C. We recruits, wearing mismatched, baggy clothing, sold squares of toilet paper to passers-by for a penny a sheet and scrubbed the sidewalk with toothbrushes. A small crowd gathered around us, chuckling.

Then we were taken to the sorority president's house and fed raw oysters and a dish of lard with raw peanuts and cayenne pepper on top. We each had to eat a raw onion covered with Tabasco sauce and drink a glass of vinegar. There were wastebaskets in front of us to use as "vomit buckets," and they got plenty of use. We recited the sorority rules and sang the sorority songs we'd memorized. After bending over for a few good whacks on the behind with the sorority paddle, we were pronounced new members.

Each summer, the sororities and fraternities of Washington-Lee High School went to the beach at Ocean City, Maryland for a week. Kappa Delta Phi was the only sorority that stayed at the beach for *two* weeks. We saved our money for months. I ironed shirts at the home of one of my sorority sisters, Anna, whose mother had nine children. I baby-sat for neighbors and got an after-school job working at Hecht's department store. Mother still didn't have a car, so I walked to and from the store. I couldn't start my homework until getting back from Hecht's at 9:30. I stashed away everything I earned. I'd do almost anything to earn the money to go to the beach.

One parent chaperoned each cottage, or was supposed to. We preferred a parent who was likely to be a loose enforcer of rules, a chaperone who would read, go to the beach, and turn in early—one who was never concerned with curfews or even with the whereabouts of any of the fifteen or so girls in our cottage.

My first summer at the beach was between my sophomore and junior year. Everyone felt totally free. Evening walks on the boardwalk inspired couples to cling to each other in the sheer joy of romance and freedom, as they watched the moon's reflection on the night-blue waters of the Atlantic. Drinking parties on the beach later at night sometimes resulted in a girl losing her virginity on the warm sands of the dunes—beyond the firelight, but still close enough to hear the guitar music.

Kappa Delta Phi spent the first week like the other sororities, partying with the fraternity guys and tanning for endless hours in the hot sun. We used baby oil for tanning lotion, and many girls suffered from sunburns by the end of the day. "Get me a stick of cold butter!" wailed Jeanette. "This burn is killing me!" She and the others swathed themselves in butter, hoping for relief. My olive skin became darkly tanned and my light-brown hair, streaked with shades of blond from the sun, remained tightly curled because of the seaside humidity.

One night I went on a blind date with a geeky, pimply, skinny, fraternity guy who immediately tried to make moves on me. "Stop that!" I insisted.

"You're just wasting my time." He sounded totally annoyed. "What do you think I asked you out for?"

"I want to go back to my cottage right now!" I said, shoving him and his hands away.

My date returned me to the cottage, bemoaning the fact that he had lost so much of his evening. My roommate at the cottage was my friend, Suz. She also reported a bad experience and was glad to see me back at the cottage early. "I can't stand the stupid jerks that don't even know your name, barely look at you, and want to get right to third base," she said.

"They don't care who we are; they only want one thing," I added. We both laughed at the idiocy of boys who thought they could sweet-talk through our defenses.

The second week, after the other sororities and fraternities returned home, we spent most of our time with the lifeguards. "These college guys are sooo much more mature," one sister swooned. We had them over to our cottage, just half a block off the beach, and cooked skillets of fried chicken or soup pots of spaghetti. The presence of these well-built, darkly-tanned "hunks" in our cottage made us feel we had celebrities in our midst. We couldn't take our eyes off them. They enjoyed hanging out with us and being fed.

Each girl laid claim to her own lifeguard. Mine was Mike, nicknamed "Saddlebags." My nickname had become "Blushing Violet." I was fifteen and Mike was eighteen, though he told the older sorority sisters he was twenty-one.

He taught me to kiss: "Don't pucker up like a little girl, just slightly part your lips, like this." His gentle kisses made my heart pound. Mike was a master of romance without being at all aggressive. We walked on the beach hand in hand. I visited him at his lifeguard station during the day, and he either hung out at the cottage or took me to the movies in the evening. At the end of that week, our summer love simply faded. I never saw Mike again, but I've held onto the sweet memories.

* * * * *

When we lived on Quesada Street, we'd attended the Lutheran Church because it was within walking distance. I sang in the choir and Mother taught Sunday school. I knew Mother's religious beliefs differed from the Lutheran's, and so I asked her one day, "How can you teach things you don't believe?"

"They trust me to teach *their* religious beliefs," Mother replied, "and that's what I do."

When we moved to the Buckingham Apartments, a new Unitarian church was being built just two blocks away. Mother and Dad had been Unitarians and were married in the Unitarian Church in Brooklyn. Mother and I joined this new church and attended regularly.

The minister's sermons were exceptionally meaningful to me and I rarely found my mind drifting. One Sunday the sermon was called, "Liberalism, Agnosticism, and Atheism," and clearly defined the differences. This church challenged long-accepted traditional beliefs that I, too, had often questioned. I was learning how to sort through religious beliefs, to see what I could accept. This was my break from traditional religion and the beginning of a search for my own truths.

The church's youth group was called Liberal Religious Youth, or LRY. They were the greatest bunch of kids I'd ever been involved with. We had bake sales, newspaper drives, car washes, dances, guest speakers from other religious organizations, and group discussions and debates. These teenagers weren't necessarily from wealthy families, but most were from intellectual, well-educated families. We questioned, challenged, and searched for information on the meaning of life.

Sometimes we challenged too fervently. One Sunday evening, a Catholic priest was our guest speaker and we went into attack mode, challenging the beliefs of the Catholic Church. "How do you know the Bible is the word of God?" "Doesn't prophet mean poet, and the Bible is creative prose?" "Why do you continue to prove your point by saying the Bible says it's so?" "Since the Bible has been rewritten over the years, wouldn't the meaning also have changed?"

Our over-aggressive questioning embarrassed our group sponsor. After the priest left, he scolded us, saying, "We will no longer have guest speakers if you can't show them the proper respect. Just because a person's beliefs are different from yours doesn't mean they're wrong. Everyone's beliefs deserve consideration and respect." This was as important as any lesson I have ever learned.

Later that same summer, I spent a week at Murray Grove, a Unitarian camp in New Jersey. At candlelight services we praised nature, the innate goodness of humankind, and the liberal, open spirit within us. We also had two weeks of fun.

Through the Unitarian Church, I met some older teens who were in a hostel group. They had purchased an old hearse to transport themselves and their bikes to Canada for a cycling tour the previous summer. They'd used public restrooms to wash themselves and a few pieces of laundry. They'd tied their wet clothing—including bras and panties—to the back of their bikes to dry in the breeze as they rode.

I didn't have a bike of my own when I joined, but one of the girls in the group had an extra to loan me. The first trip I took with them was to the Blue Ridge Mountains in Virginia. The hills were a real challenge for me. I was lagging behind on one hill, puffing hard and berating myself for slowing the group down, when I felt a hand on my lower back. Todd Crane was pushing me up the hill as he pedaled his bike beside me. "Thanks a lot," I gasped. Had he not helped me, I would have had to get off my bike and push it up the hill. That night, we stayed at a hostel; the whole group of us sprawled on top of our sleeping bags on the floor. I lay on my tummy, aching all over and with my legs cramping into painful knots. When I moaned as an especially painful one attacked my thigh, Todd came over to my sleeping bag and massaged my calves and thighs until I dozed off.

The next day, as we were riding down a long steep hill, my front tire blew out, swerving my bike into a stretch of grapefruit-size rocks on the shoulder of the road. I was thrown over the handlebars and scraped along the rocks. I lay there, not moving or making a sound, wondering if I was alive. When the others sat me up, I discovered I was badly bruised and scratched. My face and hands were bloody and my top front teeth had cut through my lower lip. My light-blue sleeveless shirt was shredded down the front.

"Are you all right, Sally?" someone asked.

"I think so." I didn't know for sure. I looked at the bike—the front wheel was no longer a circle. "I'm so sorry, Norma," I said, beginning to cry. "I've ruined your bike."

"Don't worry about that," she replied. "It's just an old one we never used anyway. I should have had my dad check the tires before giving it to you."

All six of my companions, including twenty-six-year-old Cal, our chaperone, rode along slowly next to me as I pushed the misshapen bike. We found an area nearby to camp, in some trees just off the road. By mid-afternoon, my right wrist was swollen and sore. "It really hurts and I can't bend it," I told Cal as he checked it.

"We're going to have to find a doctor," he said. He gave the group instructions on setting up for the night, then loaded me onto the back of his bike to take me into the nearest little town. On its main street, we saw a doctor's sign in the front yard of a residential home with two front doors. Cal knocked on the one that said "Dr. John Brigham" and waited.

"Yes, may I help you?" asked the grey-haired man who opened the door. He looked at my bruised and swollen face, then down at the wrist I supported with my other hand. Cal explained that I'd had a bicycling accident.

"Please, come in," Dr. Brigham said. He x-rayed my wrist and showed us the fracture on the screen. Then he cleaned my arm and dabbed at several places on my face with a swab.

"I think this will work just fine," he said, placing a formed metal plate under my wrist and the palm of my hand. "This will hold the ulna in the proper position as it heals." Then he built a plaster cast around the form. "You'll have to keep this on for two months, and then see your own doctor to have it removed." He gave me his business card and asked that I send the metal form back to him when the cast came off.

Cal and I rode back to camp, where everyone comforted me and said they would sign my cast when we got back

91

home. I had disrupted the whole day's ride, so they were all eager to get more riding in even though it was almost dark. They left me at the campsite with a butcher knife to protect myself, saying they would be back in an hour or so, and off they went on their lighted bikes. I hunkered down in the dark, hoping no one would come by before they returned. All my life I seemed to be the youngest in any group and always the one causing problems.

We were gone only for a three-day weekend. When we returned home, Mother was shocked at the sight of me. I'd never been injured before. Cal filled Mother in on what the doctor had said.

I was filthy, bloody, and my hair was an unbelievable rat's nest. Mother helped me bathe, as I couldn't use my right hand without getting the cast wet. She gently worked all the tangles from my hair as she shampooed it. "You are surely a disaster, Sally, but we'll get you all cleaned up." Mother had never been so gentle and concerned about me. She almost seemed to be proud of me.

By the time I was clean, in fresh pajamas, and in bed, I was completely exhausted. I slept for sixteen straight hours.

Other trips with this group weren't as traumatic. After several trips, I'd developed terrific leg muscles. One evening, some of my school friends came over to our apartment, bringing a 45 record player and an assortment of records so we could dance. The guy I was dancing with was very tall, so I was on my tip-toes, which caused the muscles in my calves to bulge. I wasn't aware of it until another boy yelled, "My God, you've got legs like a football player!" I didn't know whether to feel embarrassed or proud. It didn't seem very feminine, but I was able to keep up with my cycling group, and that was more important to me.

* * * * *

During my high school years, I was attractive, but not stunning. I was friendly, but not outgoing. I was neither disliked nor popular. I was an average student, getting mostly C's, and even that was an effort. I was constantly challenging myself to read better and faster. Still, none of my friends knew of my reading problems. The challenge remained a private one. At sixteen, I still had never read a book for pleasure.

I was in a college preparatory program and thought I wanted to be a nurse. Mother approved. "They look so perky in their white hats," she said, "and their starched white dresses look so crisp." I planned on applying to the College of William and Mary in Williamsburg, Virginia.

In my junior year, I joined the Nurses' Club at school, and was encouraged to do volunteer work at Arlington Hospital. I went there once a week and read to the children in the burn unit. It was a wrenching task. The sheets on their beds were pinned up above their naked bodies to allow air in and keep the cloth from sticking to their healing skin. They lay flat on their backs listening intently to the stories I read, but never smiling. When I arrived home feeling depleted, I told Mother, "Their burned skin smells so bad and they just lie there looking as though they're half melted, so sad and helpless."

Mother brought a typewriter home from work one day to complete some reports that were due. She didn't take it back the following day, so when I got home from school I set it on the floor in the middle of the living room in our second-story apartment. Then I sat and hen-pecked:

As I look through the window
The sky through the trees
Is like heaven and paradise
Mixed with a breeze.

Next, I wrote:

Acknowledge what ye read,
For I write with heartfelt sincerity,
Not with fleshly wisdom,
But by the grace of God.

I proceeded to write poems about being a nurse, falling in love, poems of religion and death—some morbid, some humorous. My alarm clock died and I mourned for it, missing its ticking. In one poem, my grandmother was an angel in heaven. In another, I was to give birth to Jesus' brother through an immaculate conception. Poems became my diary, the way I expressed myself.

* * * * *

In Mr. Courville's civics class when I was a junior, the topic turned to integration of the races, which was a hot issue in 1954. The consensus of the teacher and the students who spoke up in class seemed to be that the races should be kept separate. I have always had a strong sense of right and wrong, and this was one topic I felt most strongly about. I raised my hand and when I was called on, stood up next to my desk to address the class. I didn't lean on the desk. I didn't look around. I simply stood tall and spoke. It was as though I had stepped out of my shy self. My voice was full of conviction as I said, "Skin color has nothing to do with the character of a person. Personality, intelligence, morals, and ethics are things to be judged by, not something as superficial as skin color. If we can't see past the color of one's skin, then perhaps we should all intermarry and have a lovely mulatto-colored skin without lying in the sun for hours. If we just value and respect each other, it will solve the whole racial problem and bring peace to our country."

Suddenly aware of what I'd done, I slid down into my desk chair, wondering how I'd gotten that nerve. I kept my eyes down. The whole class fell silent, waiting for the teacher to respond. After a long pause, Mr. Courville said, "Let's move ahead with the assignment at the end of chapter 8." My hands shook as I turned the pages.

I felt nervous in the hallway after class, but nothing was ever said to me.

* * * * *

After my junior year, I found a summer job as a program director at an elementary school playground that was just a few blocks from my home. My co-director organized the sports; I did the crafts, table games, and Kool-Aid parties.

I loved being outdoors with children all day and having the responsibility of keeping them entertained and busy. Two little girls followed me and copied everything I did. Rachel and Rebecca were twins and part of a group of ten-year-old girls who lived near the school and came to the playground every day of the summer. They were my shadows and my helpers and they clung to me. "I hope I grow up to be like you," they purred. "Do you have a boyfriend?" "You're so pretty." They stroked my ponytail, leaned their heads against my arms, and as I gave them each a squeeze, I felt a flood of sweet contentment at being adored by these little girls. They helped the younger children as we made Easter bonnets from paper plates and crepe paper streamers. We made lanyards from gymp to put our house keys on and wear around our necks. We had coloring contests, circle games, and song fests.

This job paid very well, and by the end of the summer I had turned six hundred dollars over to Mother to put away toward college.

* * * * *

I had loved to sing from the time I was a three-year-old, warbling the "Hallelujah Chorus" while gargling with salt water for a sore throat. I sang in church choirs and I joined musical groups each year of high school. By the twelfth grade I wanted to be in the esteemed Washington-Lee High School Choir. They wore choir robes and sang at many prestigious events in Washington, D.C. During the individual try-outs my nervousness caused my first-soprano voice to rise especially high. Though I didn't have a strong solo voice, I sang on key and knew how to blend my voice with a group. "I made it!" I shrieked to Mother that night.

"Good for you!" she said, sharing my enthusiasm.

Choir was one of our electives, and each day in class, "Miss B," our talented, no-nonsense director, put us through an hour of voice exercises, teaching us to breathe from our diaphragms.

Wearing our navy blue robes with large white collars, we filed into our places on temporary bleachers for a performance at the Tomb of the Unknown Soldier, where we sang the "Battle Hymn of the Republic" for President Eisenhower. We also sang in the National Cathedral in Washington, D.C., the walls echoing our voices as the sunlight streamed through the high stained glass windows. Recordings of our concerts were sent to schools overseas. Music was the happiest part of my high school experience. Mother never attended these performances. I never pushed her to; I just accepted her absence as I had accepted her leaving Nan and me in boarding school and foster care for so long. I believed she was doing the best she could. But I always pretended I saw her in the audience at every event and that she was bursting with pride.

* * * * *

During my senior year of high school, I was elected president of Kappa Delta Phi sorority. At the first meeting I presided over, I suggested changing Hell Week, with its humiliating tasks and torturous spankings with the sorority paddle, to "Help Week." "The new pledges will be required to help out neighbors in need and volunteer at different hospitals and charitable organizations around the city, and then report back to the group," I explained. They all supported the idea. My confidence was soaring.

* * * * *

Early in my senior year, I saw a notice posted on the hallway bulletin board announcing that applications were being accepted for a two-week student exchange trip to Greeley, Colorado. The next night, while I was studying with my friend Gail at her house, she asked, "Are you applying for the exchange trip?"

"No, I don't have anything that would qualify me."

"Yes you do, Sally. Let's apply together," Gail encouraged. "What activities are you in?"

"I'm in the choir, and I was in the chorus for three

97

years, and some other junk, but nothing important."

Gail was very involved in school activities and seemed to know how to use them to her best advantage. She instructed me: "Here's what you're going to say on your application: 'I have always been very involved in the music programs in school, and I'm currently in the Washington-Lee Choir. I would like the opportunity to visit a school in another state to compare the music programs.'"

"Do you think that would be enough?" I asked.

"I know it would. I'll get the applications tomorrow."

I was mildly excited, still not believing I had a chance of being selected.

We worked on the wording of our applications at Gail's house the next evening until we thought they were good enough to turn in. Within two weeks, thirty students were selected for the exchange program from our senior class of over six hundred.

"Oh my gosh!" I screamed to Mother. "I can't believe it! I'm going to Colorado! We even got to look through the applications from the Greeley, Colorado students and choose the home where we wanted to stay. I chose Carol Bidmore. She lives on a 7,000-acre ranch."

I gave Mother all the details and told her what I'd need to do and buy to prepare for the trip. I told her that Carol Bidmore would be coming from Colorado to live with us after the Washington-Lee group returned home. Mother couldn't get a word in as I bounced around the house as though I was on a pogo stick.

"What do you think it will be like Out West?" I asked Gail. No answer was necessary; our imaginations took over. Gail and I hugged and danced around, but she seemed more excited by my enthusiasm than she was about being selected herself. Gail always behaved more sedately than me.

The application from Carol Bidmore in Colorado said that she was a member of FHA. "That's Future Homemakers of America," the trip coordinator explained. "They do sewing, cooking, and other domestic activities, and awards are given to those who do the best work."

That April, thirty students from Washington-Lee High School boarded the train bound for Greeley, filling one of the cars. We shared all of our vivid television knowledge of Wild West gunfights on dirt streets, horses being tied to hitching posts outside of stores, and cattle being herded through the main streets of town.

What we saw as we stepped off the train in Colorado was a quiet farming and ranching community with wide open spaces. A breeze carried the sounds and smells of livestock. Men wore cowboy boots, tall wide-brimmed hats, and belts with large buckles. I immediately loved Greeley. It lacked sophistication, but seemed wholesome and natural, with a pureness and freshness that was exhilarating.

During our stay in Greeley, we attended classes that we'd said in our applications particularly interested us, went on sight-seeing bus trips to Denver with our Greeley counterparts, and toured the campus of Colorado State College in Greeley (now known as the University of Northern Colorado) where we bought CSC tee-shirts in the college book store. The two weeks flew by, and before I knew it, we were on the train heading home again, each of us wearing a new cowboy hat the Greeley students gave us as a farewell gift.

The day after I arrived home, I sat Mother down and said as calmly as I could, "Mother, I know I said I was going to apply to William and Mary to study nursing, but I've changed my mind. I want to go to Colorado State College. I want to be a teacher. Please let me. Pleeeease."

Mother supported my decision. She knew that enthusiasm could contribute to success. The college accepted me as a probationary student because my high school grades weren't as high as required. This meant that administrators would review my grades after the first academic quarter and decide if I could stay. I knew I could do it. I would work harder than I'd ever worked.

CHAPTER NINE

In 1956, my last summer before leaving for college, I was hired as playground director again. My co-director that summer was David, who seemed introverted. He barely spoke to me unless he needed my help in organizing an activity. I didn't know if he was unfriendly or just shy.

Over the years, I'd become quite slim. I'd let my hair grow long, controlling the curls by pulling them back in a ponytail. The long hours in the sun darkened my olive skin, making my pale green eyes stand out. Now, for the first time in my life, I felt pretty.

One day, early in the summer, a very good looking friend of David's came to the playground. His name was Sean and he hung around chatting with David and me for hours. Sean soon began arriving regularly, after getting off work, to spend the rest of the afternoon with us.

Once, when I wore a purple-and-white-checkered sundress—it tied on the shoulders, fit snugly in the bodice, and had a flared skirt—I noticed that Sean's eyes always seemed to be following me. It made me feel a little self-conscious, yet flattered. He was muscular, had a blond flat-top, blue eyes that had a suggestive twinkle, and a smile so alluring that I almost blushed when I looked at him.

He took me out on dates to wonderful places I'd never

been before, and he always wore the most fashionably
trendy casual clothes. We went to plays and art galleries.
We went hiking and fishing. We took drives in his little red
Nash Healey, with the top down, into the Blue Ridge
Mountains, stopping at small shops to browse.

He took me to a basement-level pizza restaurant in
Washington, D. C. It had red-and-white checkered table-
cloths and was dimly lit by candles stuck in Chianti bottles
with different colors of candle wax dripping down the
sides. The pizzas, thick with melted cheese and herb-laden
tomato sauce, were carried to diners' tables by waiters who
were dressed in black slacks and white shirts, lending an air
of formality.

Sean and I existed in our own world that summer, just
the two of us sharing intimacy I had never felt before.
There was no past or future, only the present. I was seventeen and Sean was my first love. I'd had boyfriends and I'd
dated a lot, but I was *in love* with Christopher Sean Martin
III.

By the end of the summer, we both knew we had something special. He'd pick me up each day after I'd finished
my playground duties and we'd talk endlessly about getting
married and having children. We even named our future
son. Sean had been known as "Bear" when he was playing
football in high school, so our son (Christopher Sean Martin IV) would be nicknamed "Bruin."

Mother and Sean had become close over the summer.
When he got off work he would usually go to our apartment and wait there for me to get home and then have dinner with us. Mother and Sean arm-wrestled, played cards,
talked about his future plans, and told jokes. It was as
though he was her son. It made times when the three of us
were together lots of fun.

One night after a date, Sean pulled into a parking space

near my apartment and left the car running. Heavy rain drumming down on the car competed with the rock-and-roll tunes Sean was playing on the car radio. The windshield wipers were thumping quietly back and forth. Sean pulled me close to kiss me and started to slide his hand under my dress and up my leg, but I resisted him. I always resisted because I was afraid that his first intimate touch would make me want more. I didn't want to be just *another girl he'd had sex with*, like all the girls he'd told me about. Our relationship had to be more than that. And I wasn't about to give my heart and body to a man for the first time while rock-and-roll was playing. I wondered what would happen if he changed the radio station to romantic music. If "When I Fall in Love" came on the radio, would I let him touch me *then*? Would I want to go all the way with him? But I never suggested he change the station; I was afraid romantic music would melt my resolve.

"When you love someone, you want to *make* love with them," Sean said as persuasively as he could for the umpteenth time.

"I just want to wait until we're married," I whispered into his ear as he held me.

I knew he'd had sex regularly with his previous girlfriend. But I wanted our relationship to endure and our lovemaking to be worth waiting for. The windshield wipers continued to thump, and I interpreted the beat: *not-yet, not-yet, not-yet.*

Our families both had memberships at the same pool. Sean and I went there on weekends all summer long, that summer before I left for college. We'd stand in the water, facing each other, holding hands and talking for hours at a time.

At home, Mother told me that she and Sean's mom wondered what we could possibly talk about for that long.

Even I couldn't always recall what we'd talked about. Just being with him seemed to make hours disappear.

Sean, two years older than me and a former high school football player, had received a full athletic scholarship to the University of Virginia. But while playing in one of the last games in his senior year of high school, he'd suffered an injured kidney and it had to be removed. As a result, he'd lost the scholarship and was now taking a year off, working in a men's clothing shop to earn money so he could attend the university on a paying basis in the fall.

In late August, we went our separate ways, but still as sweethearts. We carried each other's framed photos with us as a symbol of the tie that would hold us together even though there were so many miles between us. Our parting was bittersweet. My longing to go off to college in Colorado meant leaving the man with whom I planned on sharing the future, but I was convinced that choosing one didn't mean losing the other.

Mother and I shopped for my college clothes, and she spared no expense. For the first time in my life I owned an enviable wardrobe. I had ruffled pink nylon baby-doll pajamas, a kelly-green velvet party dress studded with rhinestones, a red wool pea coat, and several pleated wool skirts to wear with sweaters to classes. My favorite was a hooded raincoat from Lord & Taylor in Washington, D.C. It was tan on the outside, with a red plaid lining inside and it flared out from the shoulders. I could hardly wait for it to rain so I could wear it. Unbelievably, it cost a hundred dollars—a far cry from the hand-me-down or handmade clothes I'd worn in high school.

My life was going in so many wonderful directions, and it *seemed* that Mother shared my excitement. I hadn't thought about Mother being alone or how her life might otherwise change. Perhaps *she* hadn't thought about that yet, either. Or, perhaps she was anticipating new freedoms as much as I was.

Since Gail and I had both been exchange students and were both going to CSC in the fall, she assumed we would be roommates. Mother, however, convinced me that would be a bad idea. "Gail has a strong, confident, and assertive nature and you need space to be yourself, to grow," she said. "If you room together, you won't become your own person." That advice seemed ironic to me, since mother was such a strong-willed and assertive person. I anguished over telling Gail in a way that wouldn't be hurtful.

"I think that we should room with other people in college and that way meet new friends," I began, as we filled out our admission forms, including dorm requests. "But I still want us to be really good friends. Don't you think that's a good idea?"

Gail's surprise and disappointment showed on her face, but all she said was, "Okay." Our friendship was never the same after that.

When I received my acceptance letter from CSC, I learned I would be living in Snyder Hall. Soon to follow was a letter and photograph from one of my assigned roommates, Deborah Hatchell from Spearfish, South Dakota. The third roommate would be Sachi Kai from Hawaii.

CHAPTER TEN

Gail and I arrived in Greeley after sunset. We took a
taxi from the train station to the campus. Our
trunks, too large to fit in the taxi, would be delivered separately. I had loaded my Grandfather Saladino's
steamer trunk—that had come over with him from Italy
when he was a teenager—with clothing along with other
items I thought I might want, including an assortment of
my favorite stuffed animals and—for further sentimental
comfort—the album I'd put together of family photographs.

The taxi driver delivered Gail to her dorm, and then
asked me, "Which dorm, ma'am?"

"Snyder Hall, please."

When I entered through the large wooden front doors
and into the formal entry hall lit by sparkling chandeliers, it
was like stepping into another world. I felt like Alice in
Wonderland. It seemed especially strange that no one was
in sight. After waiting several minutes for someone to greet
me and help me find my room, I peeked down the first-
floor hallway and saw a girl coming out of one of the
rooms. "Excuse me," I called. "I just arrived and I don't
know where to go. Can you help me?" The girl looked like
an upper classman or grad student. She hurried toward me
and introduced herself as the dorm assistant. She took me
to a podium-type desk and flipped through stapled pages to

find my name and room number.

"Most of the students arrived earlier in the day and are already in their rooms unpacking and visiting with their roommates," she said.

As I climbed the winding staircase to my room on the second floor, I hesitated halfway up, and leaned on the railing. I was having a flashback to being a three-year-old at St. Christopher Boarding School when my job was cleaning the staircase in Stearns-Wheeler Cottage. Both then and now I was on my own in a new environment. Fourteen years had passed, which seemed a lifetime. But at that moment it also seemed as though no time had passed at all. I felt small and vulnerable.

My room was at the end of the hall, on the right. Deborah rushed out to greet me and pulled me into the room. "This is ours!" she squealed. "I'm so glad you're here." Pointing to the beds, she added, "We can shop for matching bedspreads and things to decorate the walls, and my folks are still here, so they'll pay for some stuff." Her enthusiasm was contagious. It was a small room with one small closet, and I wondered how it would hold the belongings of all three girls.

Almost an hour later, Sachi arrived, making our trio complete. We had a group hug and then looked each other over. Deborah seemed bubbly, vibrant, and full of plans. Sachi was more reserved, even seeming shy. Deborah told me later that I impressed her as being citified and sophisticated. *Me, sophisticated?* It was Sachi's first time away from her home in Hawaii and she seemed uncomfortable in her new surroundings. Smiling, she listened as Deborah and I chattered. When there was a pause, she said, "I have something for you in my suitcase." She heaved a bag almost as big as her petite self onto the bed, unlatched it, and pulled out two long muumuus. Deborah and I were thrilled with these dresses and held them up to us. But—how awkward! We'd neglected to bring gifts to share. So we switched the conversation to choosing beds. Deborah said she'd already chosen the lower bunk, if that was all right. Sachi chose the bed that came out of a wall. I was left with the top bunk, the one I wanted, anyway. The high bed would provide me a bit of privacy for reading mail and studying—and no one could use it as a couch to flop on.

The following morning we started unpacking before going off as a group to registration. We made instant friends with other new students while waiting in long lines.

Afterward, I followed the campus paths lined with low shrubs and wandered across the manicured lawns. All the towering trees shading the campus once again reminded me of St. Chris, and I felt the nudge of little Sally inside of me. The campus seemed so vast; I wondered how I'd ever find my way to classes. I felt insecure and alone, but I would not have chosen to be anywhere else.

Beanie caps were distributed to the freshmen at registration and we were required to wear them. Whenever an upperclassman said, "Button Frosh," you had to put one finger on the button at the top of the cap, curtsy, and obey any reasonable command. It seemed stupid and embarrassing at first, but was actually a good way to get acquainted. I was flattered when upper class guys paid so much attention to me.

"Button Frosh," a boy sitting on a low wall called out as I passed. I stopped and curtsied. "Where are you from?" he asked.

"Arlington, Virginia."

He was surprised that I was from a state so far away. Several other guys had gathered by then. They continued to ask questions: "Which dorm do you live in?" What's your major?" "Do you need any help finding your way around?"

By the end of the day I had accepted several dates. One of the guys who asked me out was the president of Tau Kappa Epsilon fraternity. I later learned TKE was one of the best fraternities on campus. This was nerve-wracking in a good way. Everything seemed to be happening so fast. I already had a nervous stomach from worrying about how I would find enough time to study so I could keep my grades up and get off probation.

* * * * *

As weeks passed, Sachi seemed increasingly intro-verted and unhappy. She told us she missed her boyfriend, left behind in Hawaii. She was always either writing letters to him or reading letters from him. The foods that were served in the dining hall weren't what Sachi was accus-tomed to and in just a matter of weeks it was obvious that she had gained a lot of weight. Her clothes no longer fit, making her even more miserable. By the time Sachi de-cided to withdraw from school—at the end of the first quarter—and return to her home in Hawaii, she was about twice the size she'd been when she arrived.

Sachi, Deb and I shared a long group hug, as we had when we first met. We all got teary-eyed and Deb and I wished Sachi happiness.

"I'll miss you so much, but I know you'll be happier at home near your family and boyfriend," I told her. Sachi nodded and smiled through her tears.

Everyone living in Snyder Hall knew everyone else in the three-story dorm, but Deb and I became especially friendly with all the girls on the second floor. At the end of the quarter, we were allowed to shift rooms and room-mates. Because we'd lost Sachi, Deb and I wanted to move in with the girls across the hall. There were four of them, but two were moving out. This was a much larger room, and it was at the front of the dorm so you could look out and see any activity in the courtyard below.

Danielle Matthews from Castle Rock, Colorado, and Lillian Porter from Sturgis, South Dakota were our new roommates. The four of us became close and remained roommates and best friends for the four years until graduation.

Each of us added something unique to the mix. Lilly was maternal and instructed us all, through example, on manners and appropriate behavior. Deborah was the planner, organizer, and cheerleader. Dani had a mystique about her, with her long, shiny auburn hair, her pseudo-accent and pseudo-sophistication. She and Deb smoked cigarettes.

I seemed to gain something from each of them. At the time, I wasn't sure what I contributed to the group. But after years of reflection, I now think it must have been my insecurity and naiveté that called out to them for their guidance and encouragement.

Deb was brilliant and taught me how to study more effectively. Lilly made sure I stayed grounded despite all the attention from boys I was receiving on campus. "The taller the willow grows, the lower it bends, Sally," she'd say to remind me to stay humble and not be self-absorbed. Dani encouraged me to open up and relax with boys—to have fun.

My roommates were my family in college. We teased each other about our shortcomings in a kind way and corrected each other's table manners and English. We encouraged and motivated each other. We remembered each other in some small way on every holiday or special occasion. On Valentine's Day it might be a book of stamps, or on a birthday it might be a potted plant.

When "care packages" arrived from Lilly and Deb's

moms, there was always something for each of the room-mates, as though we were sisters. Dani and I were pleased to have these "adopted" moms think of us.

The four of us shared clothes, studied together, and held regular "round robin" sessions to discuss things that were bothering us. We remained calm and vented our concerns gently.

"When you borrow my sweaters you don't fold them carefully, and there are always wrinkles when I want to wear them."

"When you come in after a date, you let the door slam and it wakes me up."

"You have too many lights on when you're up late studying."

"You bring friends in the room when you know I'm studying for a test."

That was one of my complaints. There were no study rooms in the dorm and I needed to get away to concentrate on my studies. My first quarter's grades had been good enough to get me off probation, but I was still anxious about keeping my grades up.

When I turned eighteen, my roommates and other girls on Snyder's second floor threw a party for me. I'd just come out of the shower room and was walking down the hallway in my bathrobe when a girl in the room across the hall from mine called for me to step inside. I entered and saw ten girls all dressed in their best clothes. They yelled, "HAPPY BIRTHDAY!" It was a complete surprise. I started to cry and laugh at the same time. It was the second time I'd had a birthday party. The first time was when I'd turned nine and was living with my foster family.

Deb's mom had sent a birthday cake packed in popcorn. Each girl had splurged with her meager spending money and gotten me a gift. My roommates had chipped in to get me a tan cardigan sweater, which I kept for forty years before letting it go into the Goodwill donation bag.

It was too expensive for me to fly home on holidays, except for Christmas. Dani didn't have a close relationship with her family and so she didn't go home either. The two of us switched off going to Lilly and Deb's homes for all other holidays and school breaks, where we were made to feel part of the family. Deb's mom made us all matching pajamas, and Lilly's parents took us to Mount Rushmore where we ate buffalo burgers.

* * * * *

My roommates had no notion I'd coped with dyslexia all my life. They probably didn't know much about learning disabilities, anyway. Determined to keep my secret from them, I often hid in the hallway phone booth, where I'd sit on the floor reading and underlining by the dim light, leaning my head back against the booth from time to time, to let it all sink in. Few calls came into the dorm late at night, so it was a long time before I was discovered. Some evenings, I'd walk to the library and climb the metal stairs to the highest stack where I'd discovered a window seat with frosted glass far to the back. In the warm weather, I often studied under a tree in a remote area of the campus.

In class, I always sat in the front row, taking the best notes I could. When I got back to the dorm, I typed up the notes—a slow process for me because I was only a two-finger typist. As test time approached, I re-read my typed class notes and the portions of my textbooks that I'd underlined in red. My method of study took an inordinate amount of time, but it worked for me, and I was able to maintain a B average. I think now that other parts of my brain were slowly beginning to compensate for the part that caused my dyslexia, because I was able to read and comprehend much better than ever before. Once off probation status, I was able to relax a little. I had the study routine down and was able to balance my social and academic activities.

A degree in elementary education required many psychology classes. It was a subject I loved and I did well in all of them.

Between classes one morning, I walked into Brew-Inn, the campus café, to get coffee and a Heath candy bar when some guy in my psychology class yelled out to me from the back of the room, "Sally, did you see the posted grades from the last test?"

"No," I called back to him. "I don't think they've been posted yet."

"Yes, they have, and you got the highest grade." I was embarrassed that he would tease me so loudly in a public place, so I didn't say anything more. He came over to my table and asked if we could study together for the next test, and I tentatively agreed.

I rushed from Brew-Inn to the classroom and checked the posted grades. I *had* gotten the highest A. *How can that be? It must be a mistake.* But when I got back to my dorm room, I found that almost everything I'd underlined in the text had turned out to be a question on the test. That felt eerie. It was as though I'd had some premonition.

One of my psychology classes met five days a week. After I climbed three flights of stairs in the psychology building, I'd see my professor waiting outside his classroom. He'd follow me inside, even though I was never the last student to arrive. The other students started to tease me, saying that Dr. Gibbons had a crush on me, and that I was likely to get an A in the class. I really wanted an A, but I was mortified to have a teacher pay so much personal attention to me.

Dr. Gibbons was a good-looking twenty-six year-old with a PhD in psychology. He announced to all his students that if anyone was having problems or just felt the need to talk, he would be glad to schedule private counseling for them during his office hours, which he posted on the chalkboard. Others in my class dared me to make an appointment to talk about something, anything, with him.

"I'm not going to do that," I told them. "It would be embarrassing." Also, I didn't want to talk about my past or my problems with anyone, especially this handsome teacher.

Dr. Gibbon's interest in me had seemed to intensify after I turned in a poem I'd written early in the quarter to fulfill a weekend assignment. He'd asked us to write a few lines on "Who Am I?" Here's what I gave him:

I am a drive of ambition to reach a goal,
A mass, a mind, a heart, a soul.
Born to live and meet my needs,
Striving onward to new creeds.
Sensitive to joy and woe,
From dust to dust, I come and go.

Dr. Gibbons had collected our writings, but made no comments about them. From then on, however, he often seemed to hover over my desk. I found that unsettling because I was still very insecure about my work. In high school, I had worn my hair down and used it to screen my work so that no one could see how badly I was doing. But in college I wore my hair in a ponytail, losing that privacy.

At the end of the quarter, I got a B for the class. Feigning sadness, I told my roommates, "I guess his crush wasn't big enough."

A week after that class ended, I was in my dorm room

when I heard the familiar hallway yell, "Phone call for Sally." I went to the hall phone booth carrying the textbook I'd been reading.

The caller said, "This is Tim Gibbons. I was wondering if you would like to go out to dinner with me some night." I was flabbergasted. I wished I could just hand the phone to someone else.

"Yes," I replied. "I'd love to."

"How about this Saturday? I can pick you up at six and we can drive into Denver to have dinner at the Brown Palace Hotel."

"That will be fine."

"Good, I'll see you then. I look forward to an evening with you."

I ran to tell my roommates.

"My psychology professor is taking me to dinner….in Denver!" I said, but in the anxious way that meant: *help me, what'll I do*? They just stared at me with their mouths open.

The news spread like wildfire. By 6 p.m. that Saturday, every girl in the dorm was hanging out of the windows as he approached the entrance. As we walked out together, my face was burning because I knew all eyes were on us.

The hour's drive to Denver seemed much longer than ever before. He kept asking questions that he hoped would start a conversation, but didn't succeed in getting me to respond beyond a few polite words.

"How did you hurt your hand, Sally?" he asked at one point.

"I slipped on the ice on the way to class," I said, touching the scabbed area on the back of my right hand. I suddenly felt like a stupid little kid playing dress up with this man. I had on a dark-red knit sweater-suit, black suede heels, and a matching purse—another outfit Mother had splurged on.

116

Throughout the expensive candlelit dinner, I struggled to get past the awkwardness and relax. That seemed easier to do when I was chewing and unable to talk, so I tried to keep food in my mouth.

On the way home, my anxiety peaked when Tim said, "I bet you're tired, Sally. Why don't you put your head on my shoulder?"

I sat up straight in a pretense of wide-eyed perkiness. "Oh, I'm fine," I said. "I'm not tired."

To my relief, Tim never asked me out on another date. I found out that he had become the house father for the TKE fraternity house. I was told he offered this advice to any TKEs who had a date with me: "You behave yourself. She's very young and inexperienced. You be respectful of that." The guys got so fed up with him for always watching over me that one night they waited for him to go to sleep in his Murphy bed, and then lifted his bed up into the closet with him in it, and closed the closet doors.

Early in the second quarter, there was a flu epidemic and many girls in the dorm were getting sick. An announcement posted on the front door said: "Any student who feels flu symptoms coming on is to report to the front desk to have her temperature taken."

When I came back from classes one afternoon, dragging and weak, I went to the front desk and told the student on duty that I felt sick. She stuck a thermometer in my mouth, then checked it after a moment and told me my temperature was normal. My symptoms, she said, were probably just the result of my imagination—a sympathetic response to so many of the other girls falling ill.

I went up to my room, put on my pajamas, and got in bed. Within a couple of hours I developed a croupy cough. Between coughing fits I gasped for air. My alarmed roommates called the dorm mother, a young graduate student, who took one look at me and called the doctor.

The doctor arrived within the hour and checked me over. "You need to be in the hospital, young lady," he said. "I'm going to call an ambulance to transport you."

When he and the dorm mother left my bedside, I croaked to my roommates, "I need some cute pajamas, some really cute ones. I can't go to the hospital in these." I got up and changed into a pair of Lilly's jammies that were navy blue flannel and had white polar bears all over them.

At the hospital, they put me in an oxygen tent. By morning my temperature was 105. I didn't have enough strength to sit up. I couldn't eat solid food, so they gave me milkshakes with a straw. "You've never tasted such disgusting milkshakes!" I reported to my roommates. "They must have put medicine in them." As soon as I was able to get to the bathroom on my own, I poured each milkshake down the toilet.

I was in the hospital for six days with bronchial pneumonia. Mother said I must have gotten sick because I had become so thin. I weighed 109 pounds and was five feet, six inches tall. She gave me an ultimatum: "You get back up to 120 pounds or else you're not going back to school after the Christmas holidays." I couldn't let *that* happen, so I started eating everything in sight. I began going to the dining hall for breakfast, which I had always skipped. I ate two desserts at dinner. My roommates bought bags of candy bars for me. No matter how hard I tried, I couldn't get above 116. But after Christmas, Mother let me return to school. She knew I'd made an effort to meet her weight requirement.

* * * * *

There were times in college when I felt a strange, intense sadness. Sometimes, when alone in my dorm room, I would suddenly feel alone in the world and would break out in wrenching sobs. Once, Lilly came into the dorm room when I wasn't expecting her and caught me in this state. "What's wrong, Sally?" she asked, with deep concern in her voice.

"I don't know," I said, shaking my head between sobs.

"Don't you want to go out on your date tonight?" she asked, searching for an explanation.

"I do want to. I've been looking forward to my date with Eric all week. I don't know why I'm crying," I said, feeling ashamed and embarrassed for my unexplained behavior. There seemed to be a deep well of sadness inside of me that just erupted from time to time. When I tried to examine it in quiet moments, I thought perhaps it came from being in an institution again, boarded up with girls my age, just as at St. Chris.

In a drawer I kept the sterling silver pin of a galloping horse that Mom Forrest had given me. I had never once put it on since leaving my foster home, though I had wanted to so many times. I longed to see Mom's open arms when I closed my eyes, to cry to her and laugh with her, but the thought of having her gone again when I opened my eyes, pushed the temptation from my mind.

CHAPTER ELEVEN

After completing my freshman year at Colorado State, I went back to Virginia for the summer and back to my job as playground director. Sean and I resumed our relationship, spending long weekend hours at the pool and in the mountains, talking and dreaming. Saying goodbye again, at the end of the summer, was even more difficult. "Promise you'll write every day," I whispered into his ear as we clung to each other. Although we'd made serious plans for our future, we agreed to continue to date others at our separate colleges. Neither of us felt threatened by that.

When I returned home for Christmas break, Sean surprised me with a beautiful, Tiffany-set diamond engagement ring. I walked through that holiday smiling dreamily and holding my left hand before my face, admiring the ring and letting the sunlight catch its facets.

As the holiday break was nearing its end, I decided not to go back to college. I wanted to be with Sean. I applied for teaching positions at nursery schools in Charlottesville, where Sean was enrolled at the University of Virginia. It all seemed so perfect. Sean would get his bachelor's degree, I would be working with children, and we would be together. Mother was even excited about the plan, because she had come to love Sean.

During the full month I waited for replies from the nursery schools in Charlottesville, I often thought wistfully of my roommates in Colorado carrying on without me.

Sean came over to the apartment one day while Mother was at work. I was in good spirits but Sean wasn't talking much, nor smiling. He seemed depressed. I tried to cheer him. I stood behind the large blue ottoman he was sitting on in the living room and wrapped my arms around his neck. He gave no reply when I asked what was on his mind. I bent to rest my cheek on his blond crew-cut and then kissed the top of his head, squeezing him tighter. He pulled me around to sit down beside him and looked at me briefly and bleakly, before turning his face away, saying, "I've been dating this girl at school. She called last night. She's pregnant."

As he continued, he stared out the front window, refusing to look back at me. I was shocked. I couldn't talk, or think, or even breathe.

"I think that the only right thing to do is to marry her," he concluded. "I'm really sorry, Sally."

I waited for him to tap my nose with his finger and tell me he was teasing. After several minutes of silence, with tears running down my face, I slowly removed the beautiful diamond ring from my finger and handed it to him. Then I ran to my room, curled up on my bed, and sobbed into my pillow.

Sean followed me to my room and sat on the edge of my bed. He started to pull me to him, but then let go and turned away.

"Should I call your mother, Sally?"

I managed to nod.

He helped me up and supported me as we walked to the hallway phone. He dialed Mother's work number and when she answered he told her, "Sally has something she wants to say to you."

He handed me the phone. I held it to my ear, but I couldn't talk. My mouth tried, but there was no voice in me, just tears. Sean took the phone back and said, "I think you should come home," and hung up.

When Mother arrived home forty-five minutes later, Sean met her in the living room at the front door. I could hear them talking, but couldn't make out the words until Mother's voice rose in anger. "I want you to leave," she said. "You are never welcome here again. I never want to see your face."

When she came into my room I knew he was gone. I hadn't even heard the front door close.

"When I got the call, I thought you two had either broken up, or shared..." she paused, "your first love-making experience."

Mother washed my face, which was her way of consoling me. "Let's get you freshened up." That's all that was said, but she had pain in her voice. Sean had already seemed like part of our family, like a son to Mother. I appreciated her loyalty.

The very next day I received word from a nursery school in Charlottesville that they wanted to hire me as co-director of the school. "Could you come as soon as possible?" they asked. But I knew I'd lost the future I had planned with Sean. Of course I wouldn't take a job now, in the city where Sean was going to school

Within minutes of that call, Mother was on the phone to the Dean of Women Students at Colorado State College. She explained what had happened, and told her I was on the way back to school. She requested that the dean get me registered for the appropriate classes, and also asked her to arrange to have one of my roommates, or someone else I knew, meet me at the airport in Denver.

All three of my roommates met me at the airport. They were respectful of my state of mind and didn't pry. "Are you okay?" they asked, holding on to me, and then just left it at that. They talked about what was going on around the campus and in the dorm, to bring me up to date on news and to keep the conversation away from anything upsetting.

"We should do something fun next weekend," Deb said.

"Not me," Dani said. I'll be dead in accounting if I don't cram for the test."

So you'll risk, what, getting an A-minus?" That was Lilly.

As I listened to them during the drive back to the campus, I started to relax. They were tactfully ignoring me. Adrift in the flow of chatter, I leaned my head against the car's window. I must have napped, because the drive seemed only half as long as usual.

The vacancy in our room hadn't been filled during my one-month absence, so I moved right in and carried on as though I'd never been gone. Other dorm friends called out, "Welcome back, Sally."

I walked the campus in a daze for more than a month, attending all my classes, fulfilling all assignments, and performing normal tasks, but I felt hollow inside. I didn't smile or confide in anyone. Slowly, however, I came out of the fog and started feeling almost okay again.

For the remainder of the school year, I kept to a strict daily routine of classes and study, and as my grades improved, my confidence returned.

* * * * *

The following summer, I dreaded seeing Sean at the neighborhood pool. At Mother's suggestion, I invited other boys I knew to go to the pool with me. She said doing so would show Sean—or any members of his family who might be there—that I had moved on. One day, when I walked out of the girls' changing area, I saw Sean sitting in a lounge chair on the other side of the pool with his sunglasses on. I couldn't tell if his eyes were open or shut, but he didn't seem to be with anyone. I awkwardly avoided crossing paths with him. I didn't stay for long and when I was leaving, I passed Sean's mother who was just heading for the refreshment area. She reached out to me and said, "You were the best thing that ever happened to Sean, Sally." I paused briefly, placed my hand over hers and smiled before moving on.

I called Sean's mother later that week, when I thought Sean would be at work, to ask if I could come over to return my framed photo of Sean. It had won a dorm contest for "Best Looking Boyfriend." While I was with his mother, I asked for the framed photo Sean had of me. She made a disappointed-looking frown, but retrieved it from his room and handed it to me. I didn't ask any questions. We hugged as I was leaving.

After that summer, Mother moved to Santa Monica, California, so I was able to visit her without worrying about an encounter with Sean. I never saw him again.

* * * * *

In the fall of my junior year I was nominated for Homecoming Queen. Although I didn't win, it was fun to be a candidate. We all received big golden mums that we wore on our coats as we rode in convertibles in the homecoming parade.

I was also invited to be a charter member of Angel Flight, a sister organization to ROTC. We eighteen "angels" were trained to march in parades with the ROTC and we wore uniforms like the cadets, but with skirts. The ROTC boys nominated me for Military Ball Queen. I wore a long, pale-pink, nylon-net formal to the ball—and was crowned queen!

Even more unbelievably, later in my junior year, the TKE fraternity nominated me as a contestant for Miss Colorado State College. I'd felt like such a funny looking girl from the time I was in boarding school and the wall dryers at the YMCA had blown my hair into a massive ball of curls that made the older girls laugh. It was a negative self-image that was confirmed when I gained forty pounds in one year at my foster home, ballooning into a fat nine-year-old.

"I don't think I'm pretty enough or poised enough, and I sure don't have a talent to perform for the Miss CSC contest," I told my roommates. They encouraged me to recite some of my original poems for the "talent" part of the competition. I rehearsed in front of a mirror, trying to seem expressive but not overdone in my recitation, to stand tall but not be stiff.

When the big night arrived, my roommates were all a-jitter, and I was a wreck. I had borrowed an ultra feminine white lace formal from a friend. I tied my ponytail with a white lace ribbon. I wore a light shade of pink lipstick but—as usual—no other makeup.

I wanted to win, but I didn't think I had a chance. I thought I knew who would win. Laurel was a lovely and graceful drama student who did a dramatic reading to display her talent. She was my choice.

The auditorium was packed, including all the people standing in the back and along the side aisles.

The bathing suit competition was first. I wore black spike heels with my black bathing suit. I hated being so scantily dressed in front of so many people. My legs trembled as I walked in spotlights along the specially-built high runway that took me right out into the audience of college students and townspeople. The responsive applause was very supportive, but I couldn't wait to get into more clothes.

The talent competition came next. I was afraid I would forget the words of the poems I had chosen to recite and end up standing there mutely. I met the eyes of a student I knew in the audience, and by pretending I was reciting just to her, I made it safely through the poems.

I was much more comfortable when we paraded in formal gowns. After that, the five other contestants and I stood in a small half circle behind the microphone, stepping forward one at a time to answer questions read by the president of the student body. None of us knew the questions in advance, and a couple of the girls who went before me got tripped up. But my confidence rose because I knew from experience that I could usually express my opinion spontaneously on anything—even into a microphone to a large audience.

The question I was asked: "Do you think a college education is as important for girls as it is for boys, and why?" I knew at once *what* I wanted to say, but took a moment to decide *how* best to express my answer.

"I definitely feel that a college education is as important for girls as it is for boys," I began. "Even if a girl decides not to have a career, but to stay home and raise children, she would be a better person, a better wife, and a better parent, having first been educated. She would be enriched and find life more meaningful. She would have a broader sense of herself and therefore feel more fulfilled. Then, if she chose, she could develop a career later."

Before I could step away from the microphone, I was asked how I'd come to start writing poetry. "I was inspired by my foster mother who still writes poetry," I responded.

After the question phase was over, the candidates

moved into a larger semi-circle on stage. Someone appeared from back stage to hand the white envelope with the winner's name inside to the student body president. He tore the envelope open. I kept glancing at Laurel, intending to catch her reaction when her name was read. The announcement of the winner didn't register at first because I was expecting to hear Laurel's name. I actually thought I *did* hear him say her name. Then I saw several smiling people hurrying toward *me*. They carried a rhinestone crown, a long purple velvet robe, a large golden trophy cup, and two dozen red roses. I was the new Miss Colorado State College!

Miss Colorado State College – 1959

I tried not to screw up my face and bawl, but I couldn't contain the tears. As the previous year's winner placed the crown on my head, she whispered loudly enough for me to hear over the applause, "You will always remember this moment."

Laurel was the first one of the other contestants to reach me, and she gave me the warmest, longest hug. She seemed truly happy for me. Then the other contestants hugged me, too. The music played and, with the velvet robe trailing behind me, I walked as though on a cloud down the runway into a standing ovation. "Thank you, thank you so much," I said through my tears to all of them.

Mother wasn't there. She had never found it necessary to give a reason why she couldn't attend events, however important they might be to me. She visited me only twice during my four years at Colorado State College. The second time was on my graduation day. The first time was during the winter of my junior year.

When she arrived that winter, I was eager to share everything about my college life with her. I wanted her to see me in the surroundings that had helped make me happy and confident. When I heard the call that Mother had arrived at my dorm, I flew down the stairs and hugged her. My friends stood about, knowing this was not the ordinary parental visit. Mother had never been like other mothers, but I was used to that—and used to overlooking it.

I introduced her to everyone before she even had a chance to take her coat off. She showed no enthusiasm, not even noticeable interest in my friends. She was simply polite and formal.

One of my wishes was for her to be good to my roommates. This might be Mother's only opportunity to reciprocate some of the kindness and generosity my roommates' parents had shown me. I awkwardly tried to express this to her when we were alone.

"It's made me feel so good when Deb and Lilly's parents sent packages that included gifts and food for me, and when they welcomed me into their homes," I said. "I hope we can do something for them while you're here."

Since Mother didn't respond, I didn't think she understood. But that night she took all four of us out to dinner. We sat at a round table in a very nice but casual restaurant where we all tried to fill her in on highlights of our years in college. She seemed restless, inattentive—almost annoyed. She couldn't seem to share my joy, my new self-confidence, or my friends.

She had never been a warm mother, one who expressed her pride and love in ways I longed for, but she had been there for me many times with wise advice and she had supported me financially.

By the end of her three-day visit, Mother still seemed aloof and distant. I wondered what I could have done differently. How had she hoped this visit would go? Perhaps, at home, *she* now felt as lonely as I did as a little girl. Coming to my school and meeting my friends—how lively we four were together!—might have made her feel even lonelier.

CHAPTER TWELVE

I n my junior year of college, I became a member of the Alpha Phi sorority. My three roommates were already members, but still lived in the dorm room we shared. They wanted to move from the dorm to the sorority house, and wanted me to pledge the sorority and move with them. I didn't want to lose my friends—my college family—so I joined. Now we were truly the sisters we had always felt ourselves to be. We shared a room again, this time with two sets of bunk beds. Ours was a small family within the larger sorority family.

I soon learned that a visit to the sorority's kitchen was a uniquely pleasant experience. The minute Cook saw you, she would sit you down at a small table, put a piece of freshly baked pie or a bowl of homemade soup in front of you and offer advice while continuing to prepare dinner. "You must listen to the universe!" she might insist, a wry smile creasing her round face. "I only wash my hair when there's a full moon. No other time is safe." Her oily hair, drawn tightly back into a bun at the back of her head, served as evidence there'd been no full moon for the past couple of weeks. We all loved Cook and the meals she made for us. We noticed that on winter days she always arrived in an ancient thread-bare coat, so for Christmas we all chipped in and bought her a new wool one. She modeled it, spinning in circles and laughing.

There was always someone to study with at the sorority house, even in the bathroom—one girl might be soaking in the tub while another sat on the closed lid of the toilet going over study notes with her. The senior girls had already had some of the courses we were now taking, so their coaching was especially helpful. We could always take our personal problems to older, wiser sisters who took the role of advisor as seriously as a mother might.

"After our last date he said he'd call, but he hasn't," a sister confided to a small group in the living room. "And now Jane says she saw him on campus with Janet Mueller!"

"Maybe they were having a conversation about classes and he's just been too busy to call yet," counseled one of the girls. "Give it another weekend. Let us know how it goes."

In countless ways, I was delighted to discover, the sorority served as a support group—a devoted family—for each of its members. Everyone in the sorority seemed eager to help each of the others succeed academically as well as socially.

Even years later, when I was thirty-two and going through one of the most difficult times in my life, I fell back on my regional Alpha Phi alumni group for support.

* * * * *

When I won the Miss CSC contest I was awarded $100 for clothes and I automatically became the representative from my school for the Miss Colorado contest to be held in Denver that summer. After my junior year, Mother and I shopped for clothes in Santa Monica that would be appropriate for the events of the weeklong pageant.

I got time off from my summer job at a daycare center

and flew to the Denver airport where a sorority sister met me and took me to the pageant hotel. "Good luck, Sally," she said as she hugged me. "I know you'll do great, win or not." I sat in the lobby and watched as the other candidates arrived, each of them lovelier than the one before. Their graceful movements, flowing hair, and slender figures amazed me. I kept thinking: What am *I* doing here?

Because we'd been told we would be judged on grace and manners from the moment we arrived at the hotel—judges could be anywhere—I thought everyone I came in contact with was a secret judge: the taxi driver, the doorman, the chaperone on our floor. I could never relax. I was so intimidated that a touch of paranoia set in. When I sat next to a gray-haired man—a judge?—at a formal dinner for the contestants, I was thankful for the drilling my college roommates and I had given each other on table manners.

When my sorority sister's mother delivered the gown I was to borrow again for this contest—freshly dry cleaned and covered in plastic—I realized that, although it was lovely and demure, it wasn't as elegant as the gowns to be worn by other girls in the pageant. Some of their dresses could have been flaunted by movie stars at Academy Awards ceremonies.

Everywhere we went, cameras flashed. "It's the most wonderful experience of my life," I heard one contestant gush to a reporter. "I'm making so many close new friendships." *Unbelievable! How is that possible during a traumatic, nerve-wracking, and emotional week when we're all competing against each other?* I steered clear of the press.

The big night arrived, along with flowers, telegrams, and phone calls wishing me luck. I just wanted the pageant to be over, but felt an obligation to do my best in representing my school.

Each contestant was escorted on stage by an Air Force Academy cadet in formal uniform. The cadets, who had happily volunteered for this duty, then stood at attention behind us. My escort was John Brucher. Tall and slender, with a blond flat-top haircut and piercing blue eyes, he had a cocky way about him that made me smile.

"You're going to win," he whispered.

And the winner of Miss Congeniality was…not me.

Again, he whispered, "You're going to win."

After each runner-up was announced…no again.

When the new Miss Colorado, Marlinda Mason, was crowned, I felt anguish at letting him down. But after the contest, John asked if he could keep in touch with me.

We exchanged a couple of letters that summer, and after I returned to school for my senior year we dated a couple of times. There was nothing particularly memorable about those dates. John was attentive in a formal, "spit-shined way." We discussed his classes, his grades, and his plan to attend pilot training after graduation.

"What are *your* plans?" he asked. His mood was friendly and politely inquisitive, but his blue eyes always looked intense.

"I'll teach school somewhere when I graduate, I'm not sure where."

I spent the fall semester of my senior year student-teaching at an elementary school in Greeley, just a mile from the campus. This requirement was worth a full quarter's credit. An "A" would raise my overall grade point average and help me secure a good job after graduation.

The supervising teacher of the first grade class, Mrs. Regan, spent the first week co-teaching with me, and I thought that would continue; I would observe her techniques in the classroom and then, at times, she would observe me teach and offer suggestions. But after those first

134

few of days she left me entirely alone with the first-graders for the rest of the quarter. I don't know where she went or what she did. I made lesson plans on the weekends and carried through with the lessons the best I could, but I wished she was there to coach and show me ways I could improve. I did receive fifteen credit hours of "A" in student-teaching. I took it as my reward for allowing Mrs. Regan to take those months off. I've always wondered whether the principal was aware of her absence.

Toward the end of my senior year, recruiters from different school districts around the country came to CSC to interview graduating students for teaching jobs. I got offers from Colorado, California, and even Alaska—which gave me a feeling of freedom and control over my life. Never having lived anywhere west of Colorado, except for a summer in Santa Monica, I accepted a first-grade teaching position with the Santa Monica Unified School District. I would live with Mother and share expenses until I saved enough money to afford my own place. My salary would be $4,500 a year, more money than I thought teachers earned. I was flying high.

* * * * *

Graduation day arrived. Mother made her second trip to my college in the four years I'd been there. The evening before graduation, when we were sitting alone in a quiet corner of the sorority house living room, with no ceremony she handed me a small gift box. I opened it to find a watch to replace the one she'd given me for high school graduation, which I was still wearing. "Thanks, Mom," I said as I gave her a hug. I reached under my chair for the gift I'd ordered for her a month in advance: a twelve-inch-square navy blue leather manicure case with a zipper all the way

135

around it and her initials embossed on the front in gold. I told her it was a thank you for allowing me to go to the school of my choice, for buying my beautiful college wardrobe, and for paying for most of my four years of college.

None of my friends had gotten their parents a gift. When I told them *I* had, they asked, "How come?" I just shrugged. I somehow knew it was the thing to do. But when Mother opened the package and saw the manicure case, she acted as though the gift was merely something to be expected.

"Nice," was all she said, pushing it to the side of the over-stuffed chair. I wanted to reach for it, unzip it, and show her each tool—but I didn't.

I always tried to please Mother, yet never seemed to hit the mark. Her coming to my college graduation meant more to me than any gift she could have brought.

Saying goodbye to college friends was sad, yet exciting. "I'm going to miss you so much," we said over and over as we hugged each other, wrapping our arms around the full graduation robes and knocking hats askew. Some parents asked anyone standing nearby to take photos of them with their kids. Mother looked ill-at-ease throughout this event.

"Good luck with your job in California," Deb called to me as she was leaving with her parents. "And write!"

We were all eager to embark on our new lives. The four roommates had agreed to meet at the top of the Empire State Building in New York City ten years from graduation day, and every ten years after that. It never happened, but we *have* kept in touch as the decades rolled on.

* * * * *

Mother and I moved into a two-bedroom apartment in Westwood Village—a neighborhood wrapped around the

University of California and bordering Santa Monica. The Village had a quaint collegiate feel to it. Baskin Robbins, with its 31 ice cream flavors, was a new shop just down the street and a good place to meet people and hang out, as I sometimes did. Someone would always sit at my table and strike up a conversation, asking if I was a student at UCLA, surprised to learn I was a teacher in nearby Santa Monica.

Sharing an apartment with Mother was frustrating. I didn't feel the new freedom I had anticipated. Although we each paid half the costs of food, utilities, and rent, she was still the mother and made the rules. Once, I set the ironing board up in front of the TV. "Since when do we set up the ironing board in the living room and make it look like a work area, Sally?" she asked in a soft, incredulous voice, as though I'd lost my mind. When I had a date, she would insist that I stay in the bedroom so she could "get acquainted" with him. Not until she called me could I make my "grand entrance." That seemed so high schoolish to me.

Because I wouldn't receive a paycheck until the school year began, by the end of the summer I was behind on my share of the expenses. I needed transportation, but couldn't afford a new car. I suggested to Mother that she buy a new car and sell me her old two-tone blue Studebaker. She said I should take the city bus to my job until I'd saved enough money to afford a new car. But after mulling the idea over for a while and talking to people at her job, Mother decided she *did* like the idea of getting a new car for herself, and sold me her old one at the going rate.

When I put my purse and school papers on the passenger seat that first day, I just sat in the Studebaker for a minute—savoring the feeling of being a true professional—before driving off to my new school.

Late that summer, my college roommate, Lilly, had accepted a third-grade teaching position at a different school in Santa Monica. Lilly hadn't had time to find a place to live, so she'd moved in with us, temporarily.

Lilly and I enjoyed hanging out at the apartment complex's large pool with the other young adult residents. Someone was always having a weekend party and playing loud music. Groups of partiers moved from one apartment to another with drinks in hand. But Lilly and I both felt constrained by Mother's authoritarian attitude: "You need to do some house cleaning before you head off today." "You girls left a mess in the kitchen." "Let's turn off the TV and call it a day." Lilly said we should move out and get our own apartment. I wanted to do this very much, but I was afraid to approach Mother with the idea. I didn't know how to do it tactfully enough to not provoke her.

When I finally emboldened myself to tell her, Mother responded stiffly, "I don't like the noise from the pool anyway, so I'm going to get my own place and you and Lilly can stay here."

Lilly and I knew we must suppress our excitement until we were alone. I felt guilty about being so happy.

Mother relocated to a quieter area of Santa Monica where she'd found a "garden apartment" that was closer to her job at the Lear Jet Corporation.

How giddy Lilly and I felt when we were alone in the apartment for the first time! We were two new elementary school teachers with our own cars and our own apartment. It was too wonderful to believe. But down deep I worried that Mother's departure hadn't gone as peacefully as it seemed. I feared she felt I had been disloyal.

We had Mother to dinner sometimes and I called her frequently, but still my uneasiness persisted. Then Mother called to invite us to her apartment for dinner the following Wednesday night. I hoped the invitation was the beginning of a new and more relaxed relationship with her. But on the designated day, my principal assigned me to after-school bus duty, making me late getting home. Lilly got back from her school even later. We arrived at Mother's almost a full hour past the appointed time. When Mother saw us through the open sliding glass door, she exploded. Before we could enter she slammed the door so hard I thought it would shatter. "You callous, ungrateful, good-for-nothings!" she yelled at us through the glass. She scared Lilly almost as much as she scared me. Lilly had never seen a *mother* behave like that. She started to step forward to make an effort to explain and apologize—to try to reason with Mother—but she decided against it when she saw my panic.

After watching her through the glass for several minutes as she screamed in fury, raising her fisted hands at us, we turned and slowly walked away.

The first time I called her after that incident, she told me I had been "unforgivably inconsiderate," for wanting to live separately and choosing Lilly over her. She slammed the phone receiver down before I could respond. After that, Mother stopped talking to me. I tried calling her many times, but she would hang up as soon as she heard my voice.

* * * * *

Lincoln Elementary School was in a poor area of Santa Monica. When I began my first year of teaching, I was assigned twenty-two students, all six-year-olds in school for the first time, not having been to kindergarten.

I'd looked forward with trepidation to my first day of teaching. I had worked in the classroom ahead of time, putting up bulletin boards, sorting through materials that my Colorado student-teaching supervisor had given me to use, and stocking the room with scissors, pencils, crayons, construction paper, writing paper, and other items from the main supply closet.

The room was sunny. It had a glass door to the left of a wall of windows that looked out onto the play yard where the students would line up on the first day of classes to enter the classroom when the bell rang.

I'd received "good luck on your first day of teaching" messages from a few of the other teachers.

Everything was ready.

But my anxiety mounted as I watched the children lining up outside the door. I momentarily felt inadequate to teach a classroom of six-year-olds. I would have done almost anything not to have to open that door when the bell rang. I had to keep reminding myself that they were also new and didn't know what to expect. We would learn together.

As I opened the door, I stood before the line of students and held my hand up. They quieted long enough for me to tell them any desk they chose was fine, but to sit quietly. Then I stepped aside. They looked unsure of themselves as they moved into the room wearing their new dresses, pants and shirts, shoes, and some carrying new book bags.

It was soon apparent that my first-graders didn't know their colors, numbers, letters, letter sounds, or how to write. They didn't know to raise their hands, or even how to listen to instructions. They couldn't do an assignment alone and were dependent on me every minute of the school day. I was convinced that first grade was the most difficult grade to teach.

I came to find out that my class contained the most challenging students in any of the first-grade classes at Lincoln Elementary.

Shirley, a diabetic girl, needed snacks throughout the day. Maria was a happy little Hispanic girl whose family was so poor that she arrived at school barefoot. Freckle-faced Ken was always annoying the other little boys by touching them in their private areas. Ken's favorite target was Duane, a tall, handsome black boy. These "touches" once sent Duane into such a burst of fury that he picked up the jars of paint from the easel and threw them across the room, splattering walls and windows with primary colors.

Katie, beautiful, precocious, and totally blind reached her hand out each morning to touch what I was wearing. If there was any texture to the fabric, she would say, "You look pretty, Miss Cisney." She made my heart ache with the pleasure of knowing her.

And then there was Bobby who thought he was a record player and wanted to grow up to be an elevator. While the other children drew pictures of houses with flowers in the yard and smoke coming out of the chimneys, or sailboats in the ocean, Bobby took gleeful and intense delight in drawing the mechanical workings of elevators. When it was his turn to stand before the class and share his coloring, Bobby would point to coils and cables in his picture and explain their function. "This is the wheel that closes the elevator door."

One day, Katie waved her hand in the air for my attention. "Something's wrong with my typewriter," she said. "Some of the keys won't go down."

I immediately saw the problem: a three inch pencil stub had been pushed down into the keys of her Braille typewriter. Bobby, whose desk was right in front of hers, was fanning both of his hands in front of his face excitedly. Students sitting nearby told me Bobby had pushed the pencil stub in there. He hadn't sabotaged the typewriter to be mean, but simply because he was intrigued by the machine. I moved Bobby to another place in the room and explained the situation to Katie. She just smiled and said, "Okay, thank you." Katie seemed to understand so much more without her sight than most people who are *not* blind.

"My eyes!" Bobby screamed in reading circle one day, covering them with his hands as though someone had thrown acid at him. I rang the buzzer for the school nurse, who took him to her office. When she returned with him a few minutes later, her only statement was, "There's nothing wrong with this cherub's eyes." At the end of the school year, I learned that Bobby was to be admitted to an institution for disturbed children that summer.

My principal, Mr. Stein, was about forty-five and married, but he behaved like a macho teenager. He flirted openly with the female teachers, patting and tweaking bottoms and breasts. They just shrugged it off with a roll of their eyes, as though dealing with a difficult student. I was appalled and steered out of his path whenever possible.

One day he entered my classroom while I was using reading-instruction materials to work with my students. He'd come to tell me of a schedule change, but glanced at the children's work as he left. He didn't say anything about the worksheets then, but later, during recess in the teachers' lounge, he berated me in front of all the other teachers in the room for using what he called "out-of-date worksheets." *But I received them just a few months before, while I was student teaching!* As he ranted on, I felt my face turn a burning red. I didn't know how to respond, so I said nothing.

He visited my room again when I was using Valentine's Day as a theme for the children's work. They were to write a classmate's name on each Valentine envelope, purchase make-believe stamps with make believe money (a math lesson) and put each Valentine in a cardboard mailbox they had painted red, white, and blue. The student "mailman" made deliveries to each child's desk.

"What a total waste of time!" Mr. Stein complained later that day. "Can't you come up with something more productive than that?"

During another of his visits, I was teaching my students a lesson on telling time. They were each attaching a long and a short strip of black construction paper to the middle of a white paper plate with a brad, to make a clock. Later in the day, Mr. Stein again scolded me for wasting their time.

One day he arrived in my classroom with another man as I was reading a story to the children to calm them after their lunch recess. Both men sat on the sink counter in the back of the room, swinging their legs and talking loudly enough to be distracting. "Can't beat this for a job, huh, getting paid for sitting around listening to stories?" Mr. Stein said. They both chuckled loudly, and I lost the children's attention.

At home that night, I bawled to Lilly, "I can't take it anymore! I hate Mr. Stein and I hate California. I'm getting out of here at the end of the school year." We made an effigy of him out of newspaper, hung it from our second floor balcony railing, and burned him.

But I remembered something Mother had told me long ago: "Don't be a quitter. Always do your best with a bad situation and see it through." That's what I focused on until the end of the school year.

Mr. Stein never offered support or showed appreciation for my long hours and dedication. But when I told him I wouldn't be returning, he said, "I'm sorry to hear that. You're a good teacher, and there's no doubt in my mind that you would have made tenure."

CHAPTER THIRTEEN

After my year of teaching in California, I moved back to Colorado, where I'd been hired as a first-grade teacher in Colorado Springs. I'd written Mother a note, and followed up with a call well in advance of my departure. She had mellowed toward me over time. We were now on somewhat friendly speaking terms and she seemed okay about my move and busy with her life.

With Christie Burrs, a college sorority sister who would be teaching high school physical education, I rented a large, four bedroom house in the high-end Broadmoor area. The house was owned by wealthy snowbirds who spent their winters in Florida. It was furnished tastefully and was equipped with everything we needed, other than the linens and clothing we brought with us.

Christie and I placed an ad in the newspaper looking for two more housemates and found Luanne and Megan, who were also teachers. Each of us taught at a different school. We had just time enough to settle in before school started.

In the evenings and on weekends, we got to know each other. We shared stories of our students and schools while we did chores and prepared and ate our meals. No matter how badly our teaching day had gone, we knew we could explode with frustration when we were safely together in the evenings. Sharing our problems kept them in perspective and even made us laugh when we saw the humorous side of them.

Winters in Colorado Springs were bitterly cold and snowy. But the Broadmoor area, which sat high above the downtown part of the city, got hit especially hard. Many a morning we had to have AAA come to jump-start one or more of our cars. When school was cancelled for a snow day, no children could have been more gleeful than we four teachers. We'd cook a man-sized country breakfast for ourselves and stay in our pajamas and robes all morning, sitting by the fire and gazing through the massive living room windows at the hills of billowing snow lowering down into the city.

I was dating a couple of cadets at the Air Force Academy, but no one special had come into my life. Then one day I got a call from John Brucher, who had been my escort at the Miss Colorado contest. We'd lost touch with each other. He explained that he'd heard another cadet mention my name, so he called information to get my phone number. We chatted for a while, and then he said, "Could we get together sometime? I'd sure like to see you again."

John didn't have a car so I drove to the Academy for our first date and waited in the parking lot outside his dorm for him to arrive at the appointed time. Many guys came out to meet their dates wearing tweed and corduroy suits, looking preppy. John strode up to my car—tall, handsome, flashing a heart-breaker smile—in shiny, worn, navy pants and a white shirt with the sleeves rolled up. John drove my car around the Academy grounds and then we parked and talked the evening away.

It wasn't long before John and I were dating exclusively.

I enjoyed driving to the Academy on weekends. The

Academy site, with its forested hills and rolling acres, was a ripe setting for young love. John showed me off to his roommates and friends, though too frequently with a sexual innuendo that made me blush. "She's quite a *piece*, isn't she?" he'd say, or "That tent dress just piques the imagination, doesn't it?" They all laughed and I just figured, "Guys will be guys."

Once, when a group of cadets and their dates were having a snack at a table in Arnold Hall—the Academy's student union—John complained that the rain had gotten his shoes wet. He lifted his foot, revealing a highly polished, but very damp black shoe. "That's what happens when you don't wear rubbers," I said. Everyone at the table roared with laughter, though they knew what I'd meant. I didn't stop blushing until the conversation finally turned to something else. John seemed to like my naiveté and would wink at the other guys.

When John brought his AM/FM radio over for me to keep in my bedroom, he told me what stations he enjoyed most and that his favorite piece of music was "Rhapsody in Blue." I spent many dreamy evenings stretched out on my white satin bedspread listening to "John's music."

"I think I love him," I told my roommates.

* * * * *

John was a bookworm who always did well in school. He graduated as valedictorian from his high school in Clatskanie, Oregon, but instead of going right on to college he enlisted in the Air Force. After two years of service, his commanding officer, impressed by his high test scores, encouraged him to apply to the Air Force Academy. The Academy didn't admit him then. Instead, they sent him to preparatory school for entrance to the Academy the fol-

147

lowing year. So John began his freshman year at the Academy in 1958 and was immediately dubbed "old man" because he was three years older than the other freshmen.

He excelled in his coursework. Academics always came easily to John, so he was able to spend much of his time training and traveling with the track team. He often ran in remote areas of the campus, where deer roamed. "Running with the deer gives me a feeling of peace and freedom," John said, "and it's a great break from all the hours of studying." When I watched John run on campus I was amazed at the fluidity of his movement.

I drove to all of John's track meets and saw how demanding he was of himself. He was different from the other, more carefree track runners. When a bad run made him cranky, he'd be irritable with me, or even ignore me. There was no consoling him. I loved him, but I wished he wasn't so intense. If he didn't excel at something, he seemed to feel it reflected badly on him as a person. I thought that, over time, I could help him conquer that kind of thinking.

* * * * *

Teaching in Colorado Springs was vastly different from teaching in Santa Monica. Because I'd received my degree in Colorado, my teaching methods weren't constantly challenged, as they had been in California. I quickly made friends with the other teachers at my school and found the principal to be supportive. Having one year of teaching experience gave me confidence that I could handle a classroom of students and be an effective teacher.

"Where did all these children come from?" one teacher asked on registration day, gaping at the long lines of children and parents that wound through the halls and out into the play yard. There were more than twice as many than were expected. We didn't have enough teachers, rooms, or even desks for them all.

On the first day of classes, fifty first-graders crowded into my room, almost all of them from military families. Most of these children, unlike those in Santa Monica, *had* attended kindergarten and were familiar with classroom procedure. The mothers vied with each other to see who could be room mother, to plan parties and accompany us on field trips during the school year. I ended up with a team of three mothers.

Because of the shortage of desks, some of the students had to sit on extra chairs brought in and placed at the back of the room. The principal, Gordon Stokes, assured the teachers that arrangements would be made as quickly as possible to get the over-sized classes on split session.

After a couple of weeks, I was teaching thirty-three students in the morning from eight to one, and then another teacher took over the classroom to teach the afternoon session with different first-graders. I received full pay, but had a good part of my afternoons free—and how I enjoyed those afternoons!

Some afternoons I spent grading my students' work or preparing projects for units I was teaching—but other afternoons I spent running errands, catching up on laundry and housework, shopping for clothes, or at the beauty salon.

One of those afternoons, after I'd begun teaching a unit on our solar system, I wrote a poem to help the children identify something distinct about each planet. I put the poem to the music of "Twinkle, Twinkle Little Star," and as I sang it to my students the next day, I pointed to each planet on a large colorful wall poster.

Mercury is near the sun.
Venus is the second one.
Our planet Earth is right next door
to planet Mars, who's number four.
Jupiter's done quite a thing,
he married Saturn, see the ring.
Uranus, next, is number seven.
Neptune is the next in heaven.
Planet Pluto's very small.
Now see if you can name them all.

* * * * *

At Christmastime of 1961, John formally proposed. We were sitting in my old Studebaker at the Academy, with the engine running to stay warm. We'd talked of marriage and a future together, but when John surprised me by opening the lid of a little navy-blue velvet box it took my breath away. I stared at what was in the box, and then up at John, as he smiled broadly. He told me the miniature of the Air Force Academy class ring had a one-karat oval diamond. He said he had saved up for months so that he could order it when the Jostens dealer came to the Academy to take orders for class rings and engagement rings.

"Yes, yes, yes, I'll marry you!" I told him, and he slid the ring on my finger. The glare of light reflecting off the snow that bright winter afternoon seemed dim compared to the flash of sunshine refracting off my diamond. I squealed with excitement. This handsome man! This ring of commitment!

"I've loved my years at the Academy," he said, "but knowing we'll be together makes me happier than anything else." We decided on a June wedding, three days after John's graduation.

To announce our engagement at my school, I ordered a cake to take to the teacher's lounge. It had been decorated with a simple gold ring of frosting in the middle, my name on one side and John's on the other. As the teachers arrived in the lounge for coffee during the morning recess, they saw the cake on the table. Hugging me, they offered their congratulations.

There was much wedding hustle around the Broadmoor house. Two of my roommates, Christie and Megan, were also getting married that June. All three of us were busy making wedding plans—choosing wedding invitations, wedding gowns and bridesmaid dresses, shopping for trousseaus, and planning our receptions—while also teaching school every day. We barely had time to date our beloveds.

Of course, everything had to be new. Not one piece of old underwear was to be taken into married life. We ceremoniously burned all our old undies in the stone fireplace in our backyard, stifling our giggles to make it seem like a proper ritual. With each sip of wine, we tossed an item of underwear into the flames and made a toast.

"Here's to Megan! May she and Dave have ten beautiful children." (Megan gasped at the number.) The flames zapped her lace-edged nylon panties.

"Here's to Christie and Dan. May they ride off into the sunset on their bikes and have a whole team of children."

"May John and Sally have a squadron of marching kids."

Luanne joined us in our laughter and toasts.

As the burning and wine-drinking continued through the evening, the toasts became more outlandish.

"May Christie and Dan not leave their bedroom for the first month of their marriage."

"Here's to John teaching Sally a thing or two—or ten—in the sack!"

We were giddy with anticipation of our new lives. Visions of married bliss and happy babies filled our heads.

The local newspaper ran large engagement photographs of Christie, Megan, and me on the front page of the society section. The headline over the pictures announced in boldface type: "Three Roommates-Teachers Marry." We bought extra papers and clipped the page as a memento.

Christie and Dan were getting married in the Catholic Church on the same day that John and I were getting married in the Air Force Academy chapel. We decided to have both wedding receptions at our Broadmoor house—in different areas—after our wedding services.

Megan would already have flown home to Utah for her wedding. Luanne and her mother would be guests at both weddings, and then head back to their family home in Montana the next day.

One evening when we had our three guys over for dinner—turkey and all the trimmings—I left John and the others in the living room and went to take the turkey out of the oven. After setting the turkey on the dining room table, I walked over to the group, placed my hand on John's arm, and said, "We're ready to eat as soon as the carver carves." He pulled abruptly away from me.

John barely spoke to me for the rest of the evening. He avoided meeting my eyes and addressed his conversation to other's at the table. He left that night without saying goodbye.

I laid awake all night thinking about what had happened. Perhaps he had never carved a turkey before and felt I was putting him on the spot and humiliating him. I wished he had taken me aside and explained his feelings. I was so baffled by his extreme reaction that I wondered if I really knew him; I actually considered calling off the wedding. When I told John this on the phone the next day, he said,

"It was just a little misunderstanding. Don't overreact." I understood he must be feeling stressed because we were so busy and everything was happening so fast. I felt stressed, too.

* * * * *

Mother called to let me know that she had received the invitation, but didn't plan to attend my wedding. No explanation given—none expected. I consoled myself only slightly by remembering that she hadn't attended my sister's wedding, either. And then I felt shame that *I* hadn't attended my sister's wedding. But I'd been a teenager then, with no money, and Mother wouldn't help finance the cross-country trip.

Deborah, one of my college roommates, loaned me her wedding dress and made the necessary alterations herself. I periodically drove the fifteen minutes to her nearby town for after-school fittings. Deb would give me advice on marriage, and we'd giggle as we did while roommates. "Guys eat a lot, Sally," she told me, "so you can't get by with a salad for dinner." And, "Sometimes just cuddling in bed turns them on, so if you're not in the mood, stay on your own side."

I began to correspond with John's parents, in Oregon, whom I had never met. Our letters were friendly, but I was eager for them to like me in person. I could sense the pride they had in their son and their enthusiasm about our wedding. They were planning the rehearsal dinner, which they would be hosting at a Colorado Springs restaurant. Mrs. Brucher wrote that they were buying new clothes for the trip and that they'd placed an announcement of our marriage in their local newspaper, the "Clatskanie Chief."

My sister, Nan, would be my matron of honor. Her

husband, Bob, would walk me down the aisle. Deborah would be my only bridesmaid. John chose Carl Pearce and Larry Briggs, his best Academy friends, to be his attendants.

It wasn't until I'd sent out all of the wedding invitations that I realized I had neglected to invite my first-grade class. I took a spare invitation to the school office, had mimeographed copies made, and sent one home with each child. My students and their parents were tickled to be invited. When the children arrived at school the next day, many had small gifts—mostly useful kitchen items, including some of the newly-popular Tupperware containers.

In Colorado Springs, car dealerships gave special deals to graduating cadets. John and I pooled our money and purchased a brand-new 1962 Chevrolet Impala. I selected the color "fawn," a metallic beige, and John selected bucket seats, power steering, and automatic transmission. John wanted me to keep the car at the Broadmoor house, so I drove it back and forth to my school and to the Academy that last month before we were married. I was so nervous driving my first brand new car that I took ridiculously long to get anywhere. Parking nearly paralyzed me. I dreaded damaging our most prized possession.

It was the end of John's senior year and I was preparing to attend the Graduation Ball. For that, I wanted the most magnificent dress I'd ever owned, not something borrowed. I wanted to be extravagant.

I went to an exclusive shop in Colorado Springs called The Wild Rose. It was on the second story of a downtown building and had large display windows so people on the street could look up and see a display of elegant gowns. You had to ring a buzzer to be admitted.

Inside, however, there were no gowns in sight, which seemed odd. A fashionably dressed saleslady motioned me to a brocade settee. "And what is it we're looking for to-day?" she purred.

"I'm looking for a gown to wear to the Graduation Ball at the Air Force Academy. My fiancé is graduating."

"Oh, how nice, and what style are you looking for?" she asked.

"I don't really have a particular style in mind."

"Well, make yourself comfortable and I'll see what I can find."

The woman disappeared for a while, and then returned with several dresses. I was tempted to look at the price tags but I didn't want to seem gauche.

She held each dress out to me as though it was from a queen's wardrobe and made of spun gold. She awaited each of my murmurs of approval with a tight smile and raised eye-brows. Some of the dresses I quickly eliminated as too sophisticated. I tried on two of the others and finally selected the all white gown with a sequined fitted top and satin spaghetti straps. Its slightly gathered skirt was an iridescent taffeta that brushed the floor. The dress took my breath away. It was simple, yet elegant. Looking at myself in the mirror, I felt like Cinderella going to the ball. It cost eighty dollars and was by far the most expensive piece of clothing I had ever purchased.

When John arrived at the Broadmoor house on the night of the dance, he grinned from ear to ear when he saw me in my new dress. He was wearing his "mess dress," a military tuxedo. I'd never seen him look so handsome.

CHAPTER FOURTEEN

John's parents were due to arrive the day before his June sixth graduation and stay through to our wedding on the ninth of June. I'd only exchanged a few letters with them while planning the wedding. In one of those letters Mrs. Brucher asked if my mother could arrive early enough to attend John's graduation.

"No," I wrote, "she won't be able to come for the wedding or graduation. I wish she could." It was never mentioned again, so I assumed John had given her some background on my relationship with my mother.

I was apprehensive beyond reason about meeting John's parents for the first time. What if they thought I was an unsuitable wife for their son? When the crucial week arrived, I was recovering from a horrendous case of hives, which I hadn't suffered since times of anxiety when I was a little girl. The itchy, dime-sized red welts that had covered my body, daubed with pink calamine to quiet the itch, were almost gone. Although John's mother and father were welcoming me into their family, I stood alone. What would they think of me, this girl with no parents?

John picked me up at my school and drove me to the motel where his parents were staying. After he made the introductions and we all exchanged brief hugs, I excused myself to use their bathroom—nervousness always made me think I had to pee. Once in the bathroom, I started to tremble. As I looked in the mirror over the sink, I felt a huge sob trying to break through. I put my hand over my mouth, trying to suppress it. Then, removing my hand, I inhaled deeply and exhaled slowly, trying to calm my nerves. I stayed in the bathroom long enough to hear John's mother voice her concern about me. "John, do you think Sally is okay? Was she feeling ill?"

When I stepped out of the bathroom, pretending nothing was wrong, Mrs. Brucher hugged me again—and this time she held on to my hand and patted it reassuringly. John's parents seemed to be genuinely warm people, genuinely happy to meet me.

That evening, as we dined at a restaurant, Mrs. Brucher asked, "Sally dear, would you feel comfortable calling Martin and me Mom and Dad?"

In my life, I'd already called so many people mom and dad: my own parents, cottage mothers at St. Chris, my foster parents, and now it seemed natural to me to include John's parents, Martin and Jenne. My newest Mom and I smiled at each other across the table whenever our eyes met during the meal.

Over dinner I told them John had received his pilot training assignment just a few days earlier. I looked over at John to make sure it was okay for me to continue the story. "He drove right over to my house, trying to remain calm so I wouldn't guess the good news before he could spring it on me. He beat around the bush while I laughed at his coyness. I shouted, 'Where, where?' He grinned and said he's been assigned to train in T-37s and the new advanced T-38 jet trainer at Williams Air Force Base in Chandler, Arizona. We're so lucky he got the pilot training base of his choice, and I will be near my sister Nan and her husband and their baby daughter who live in Scottsdale, just an hour's drive away. We're thrilled!"

I went on to explain that I'd already applied for a teaching position with the Chandler schools and had received a call confirming there was a first grade position for me. "Everything seems so perfect," I told them, and we all toasted to that.

I had plenty to be happy about. I would be marrying a newly commissioned officer right out of the Air Force Academy. His parents seemed eager to welcome me into their family. We had received our first-choice assignment. I had a job waiting for me there. And we had a new Chevy Impala to transport us into our *happily ever after.*

* * * * *

On graduation day, John's parents and I were among other proud parents and fiancées watching these young officers parade by, all spit and polish. Dad Brucher had been up since dawn watching the cadets' drill on the parade grounds. When we stood for the playing of the Star-Spangled Banner, I glanced at John's parents. The pride that showed in their faces brought tears to my eyes. The staccato of the flapping and snapping flags on this sunny, windy day lent a sense of patriotism.

After listening to Vice President Lyndon Johnson give the graduation address, John and the other graduates received their diplomas and returned to their seats as second lieutenants. Then, in Academy tradition, they stood and tossed their white hats high in the air. John's parents and I jumped out of our seats, along with all the other guests at this event, cheering the graduates.

* * * * *

After two days spent packing for our honeymoon and the move to our next assignment, our wedding day arrived. That morning, I picked up Mom Brucher at the motel for our hair appointments. Meanwhile, though I didn't know it, John and one of his attendants were celebrating his last hours of bachelorhood by hitting a few bars.

We'd hoped to be married in the striking new Academy chapel, which was supposed to be completed in time for the Class of 1962's weddings. But to everyone's disappointment, some aspect of the construction didn't pass inspection, so the weddings had to be held in the less-inspiring Arnold Hall.

Arnold Hall was decorated with flowers and candles and equipped with a podium altar and, for the attendees, folding chairs. A royal-blue plush aisle-carpet ran from the podium to the bottom of a long, broad staircase that led to a room upstairs where Nan and Deb helped me into my gown and adjusted my veil. Then they left to take their positions to precede me down the staircase to the main floor.

As Wagner's Bridal March played, I slowly descended the long staircase, clinging to the arm of my sister's husband, Bob, while trying not to let my white satin heels catch on the hem of my gown. We walked to the altar where John waited, smiling at me. Bob took a seat in the front row. John seemed amazingly relaxed, loose, almost giddy. I looked at him wishing I didn't feel so nervous.

The ceremony was brief. John and I focused on the ritual rather than on each other. I didn't gaze into John's eyes and think even briefly, *my husband, my love, forever*. Almost before I knew it, we were pronounced husband and wife by a chaplain we had never met before.

As we left the podium and walked down the aisle between the two groups of guests, I noticed my little students waving shyly at me, their teacher-bride. The girls were dressed in their fanciest clothes, wearing gloves, hats, and pastel dresses flared out by crinolines. They had sweet, demure smiles and waved their white-gloved hands. The six-year-old boys—all twitchy and uncomfortable during the ceremony—wore suits and ties and looked like miniature versions of the dads who sat next to them.

John and I were pelted with rice as we left Arnold Hall arm-in-arm through an arch of sabers held by his newly commissioned fellow officers.

At our house, long tables covered with white cloths had been set up everywhere in the front yard for our catered reception dinner for sixty-five guests. During the dinner, Dad's bald head started getting sunburned, so he tied a knot in each corner of his large white dinner napkin and placed it on his head as if the napkin was a hat. Instead of looking silly, it almost seemed like an accessory to his tuxedo.

As the dinner ended and the day grew hot, we moved inside to the living room for the cutting of the cake. After another round of toasts with sparkling wine, Carl Pearce gave a short speech wishing "Bruck" and his beautiful bride a happy life together. John used his Academy saber with his name engraved on the handle to cut the three-tiered wedding cake. Then he stuck his tongue way out and licked frosting from the length of the blade. "John!" I gasped. Everyone laughed. That photo is in our wedding album.

Finally it was time for us to drive to our honeymoon hotel in Denver. I went upstairs and changed into my new traveling clothes: a yellow and white suit and a small yellow pill-box hat with a short veil that covered my forehead. When I was dressed, John joined me in the bedroom and we stepped out on the bedroom balcony where I threw my bouquet down to the reaching scramble of single women. John removed the blue garter from my leg and threw it to the single men, who didn't seem as eager.

We drove off in our beautiful new Chevy Impala, tin cans tied to the bumper clattering loudly behind us.

* * * * *

Using the three hundred dollars the Bruchers had given us for a wedding gift, we stayed in the honeymoon suite of the Denver hotel. Porters wheeled clothing racks out to our car to take our hanging clothing and luggage to our room. Neither John nor I had stayed at a fine hotel before and didn't understand the protocol or what and when to tip, so he doled out a little here and there, never knowing if it was adequate.

Our room had a high ceiling and was spacious. It had a king-size bed and separate bathrooms for the bride and groom.

For dinner, we ordered a large platter of shrimp and a bottle of Champagne from room service. As we raised our glasses to each other, John slumped against the headboard of the bed. He had been unusually quiet in the car, but I thought he was merely weary after our long, busy, and exciting day. Now he seemed groggy, maybe even ill.

"Are you okay?" I asked.

"Larry and I went to bars this morning and drank right up to the wedding," he confessed. Yet here we were, sipping more Champagne. My husband: drunk on our wedding day and on our wedding night!

As John poured himself another glassful, I went into my bathroom to shower and dress in my new nightgown and peignoir set. Its sheer fabric flowed gracefully as I made my entrance. I saw John's eyes brighten and I felt shy, wondering if he could see through both layers of nylon.

For months, John and I had read and discussed sex manuals together. He knew I was a virgin and had seemed

162

pleased about that. "I'll go as slowly as you want and be patient and understanding on our first night, Sally," he'd reassured me. Now I was eager to finally express my love for him completely.

I waited while John showered and put on the white cotton pajamas with navy blue piping that I'd bought for him to wear this night.

The lovemaking wasn't what I had dreamed it would be—what I had waited so long for. John wasn't slow and he wasn't gentle. He didn't touch me in the ways I needed to be touched or love me in the ways I longed to be loved. Afterward, he fell asleep without holding me or talking to me, and I quietly wept as he snored.

* * * * *

In the morning we set off to the 1962 World's Fair in Seattle. During the three-day drive, we argued constantly over trivial things. We barely noticed the beautiful scenery along the way. I wanted the trip to be a happy time, but as the miles went by, the antagonism grew. At a stop on the morning before we got to Seattle, we locked ourselves out of the car. Each of us blamed the other, and that set the tone for the rest of that day. I wondered if I had made a mistake and married a man I really didn't know.

We had dinner in the Space Needle restaurant that evening, after standing in line for four hours in the hot sun. I left the table to go to the restroom. When I came out, John was gone—our table was gone! For a disorienting moment, I felt the sting of abandonment, that all too familiar feeling. But I quickly realized that although the restrooms at the top of the Space Needle were stationary, the outer ring of the restaurant slowly rotated to give diners a moving 360-degree view.

We look happy in photos we took at the Fair, but we were *not* loving honeymooners. I didn't understand why. I kept wishing John would give me a jolly hug or look in my face and tell me he loved me, that he was glad I was his. I could remember feeling the same way about my mother. I had such a need for love to be expressed, to be someone's special girl.

After a couple of days at the Fair, we drove south to Spokane to visit John's brother and his wife, Craig and Fran. I didn't think our honeymoon could get worse, but the welcome mat didn't seem to be out during this visit.

There had been a boyhood competition between Craig and John, encouraged by their father, and it was still apparent. John acquiesced during the visit to keep the peace.

Since Craig and Fran hadn't been able to attend our wedding, we thought they would be interested in hearing the highlights of John's graduation, our wedding, and our trip so far. However, they seemed bored to the point of breaking in to talk between themselves.

Fran interrupted as John was talking about the graduation flyover of jets, to ask if Craig had forgotten to pick up the beer. Craig interrupted in the middle of the humorous story about Dad wearing a napkin on his head during our reception dinner to ask Fran, "Did you get back to Stan and Gail about bowling on Wednesday?"

We quickly took the hint and kept the rest of our travelogue to ourselves.

Late in the afternoon, we unloaded the luggage from our car and Craig led us to an old vacant house next door that was in extreme disrepair. "This is where you'll be staying during your visit," Craig said as he swung the door open. John didn't show surprise, but I hesitated before following him inside.

Is it filthy, or is it just that the paint is old and crumbly?

It was barren except for a bed with a stained mattress. We set our luggage down and went back over to Craig's house for supper. Fran said the leftovers she pulled from the fridge were from a meal they'd had with friends the night before: cold shrimp and some side dishes in varying amounts.

When we finished eating, John told me that he and Craig were going to a couple of bars in town. Shortly after they left, Fran yawned and said, "I'm going to turn in. Here are some sheets and pillowcases, and a flashlight so you can find your way next door." And with that she was gone.

So on the fifth night of our marriage, I sat alone and scared in the dark, empty house. While waiting for John to come back to me, I started to cry. By the time he staggered in at three in the morning, reeking of alcohol, my face was red and puffy and I had a splitting headache.

"I don't get to see my brother very often," he slurred. "Did you want him to think I'm already so pussy-whipped I can't go out with my brother for a few drinks?"

We had to put the mattress on the floor because the bed frame was so rickety we were afraid it would collapse. John fell asleep quickly. And now that he was with me, I felt safe enough to drift off, too.

During the visit, Craig wore white-gone-gray, stretched-neck undershirts as outerwear. Fran barely spoke to me, and once when she did, she said I was "...one of those Academy brides who thinks she's so perfect."

On the last day of our visit, I made myself move slowly as we packed up and loaded the car. I didn't want my eagerness to be obvious, but I couldn't pull my feet in and close the car door fast enough.

Our next stop was John's parents' house in Clatskanie, downriver from Portland, along the Columbia. John had little to say during the drive. I wondered what he was thinking. Was he glad to get away from his brother? I wanted to discuss the odd experience, maybe even laugh together about it, but I feared triggering another upset between us. Instead, I went over the visit in my mind, thinking about how my roommates would react if I were back there telling them about it. We'd all laugh at the absurdity and rudeness. As I mused about it, I turned my head and looked out the passenger window for a private smile.

When we drove up to the stately old home John's grandfather, John Henry Mustola, had built many years before, John's parents met us on the wide front porch where the American flag was breathing with a slight breeze. They greeted us enthusiastically, reaching out for hugs. As soon as we were inside they offered drinks and asked us to tell them all about our trip, "every detail," Mom said. It was such a relief to be welcomed with kindness and courtesy.

There were fresh cut flowers in the guestroom. And when I commented on the perfumed sheets, Mom laughed and said, "We're already thinking of grandchildren."

Mom was warm and chatty. In her home, I felt relaxed for the first time since the start of our honeymoon trip. She chuckled when I told her about getting locked out of our car, and my confusion upon stepping out of the restroom at the Space Needle. In sharing our mishaps with her, I was able to see things in a more humorous light.

John asked his mother to make some of his old favorite meals, and Mom set about cooking. She refused my offer to help, so I sat and visited as she prepared chicken tetrazini, fruit pies, and vegetables tossed with parmesan and almond slivers. We chatted as though we were old friends who hadn't seen each other in a long time. I knew I would love this new relationship.

The next morning, Mom said, "I want to show you off." So we walked down the dirt road that led from their house, stopping in at neighbors' houses. Each neighbor hugged me, said they'd heard so much about me, and had us sit while they brought out refreshments. They were almost like extended family of the Bruchers.

When we got back to her house, Mom gave me several empty milk cartons and directed me to a wild raspberry patch about a hundred feet behind their house. "Every quart of raspberries you pick will make a pie," she said. A couple of hours later I returned, scratched all over my arms and legs, but in wonderful spirits, with four quarts of raspberries. That evening, her still-warm pie—tart, sweet, and topped with melting vanilla ice cream, was pure heaven.

On another evening in Clatskanie, John and I went to the only place in town that served food. It was a restaurant by day and a club at night. Its owner was an old high school friend of John's who was part of a small band that played there. He saw us as soon as we walked in and, at his signal, the band stopped mid-song and switched to "Here Comes the Bride." Everyone in the place cheered when the music stopped, and we were quickly treated to drinks. I surmised that in a town this small, where everyone would know the news about everyone else, they had expected us to drop by—or maybe Mom had called ahead. I loved seeing John look so at home and relaxed with old friends.

I had rediscovered the John I knew, and I was relieved to think our marriage was back on course. We relaxed with Mom and Dad for several days before packing up and heading to our new assignment in Arizona.

CHAPTER FIFTEEN

When John and I arrived in Chandler, we discovered the small town was badly in need of rental apartments for the families of student pilots. We were running out of options by the time we stopped for a sandwich at a café on Chandler's main street. An older, dignified-looking man sitting on the stool next to me overheard our conversation and told us he owned a small but brand-new office building nearby. His insurance office was on the ground level, but there were two fully furnished efficiency apartments over the office. "My son is living in one of the apartments," he said, "but you're welcome to look at the other."

After we finished our sandwiches, we followed his car to the building, parked in the back, and climbed the spiral metal staircase to the second level.

After all the run-down apartments we had already seen—many so close to the railroad tracks that they quaked with every train, night and day—this apartment was like an oasis in a desert.

The apartment was very small, but perfect for our needs. It had a long wall of floor-to-ceiling windows. When the drapes were open, the view of the main street was not much to behold, but the windows let in plenty of cheery light.

Its furnishings included two built-in sofas that turned into twin beds that slid together when the upholstery covers were removed, changing the living room into a bedroom. The living room was combined with the dining room and the kitchen in one large L-shaped open space. The only enclosed areas were the bathroom and a dressing room with mirrored closet doors. The upholstery, wall-to-wall carpeting, and drapes gave off a pleasant new-fabric smell. We went downstairs to sign the papers in our new landlord's office.

I knew very little about cooking, but John assured me he would help. He had saved all the menus that had been placed on the tables in the Academy dining hall so I would know how to put foods together for meals. He'd even assembled them in a loose-leaf notebook, hundreds of them for me to refer to.

During the remaining weeks of summer, I organized the kitchen and clipped recipes from magazines to begin experimenting. Mom Brucher sent some recipes to me that she said were John's favorites. John supervised the process if he was home, so I preferred to cook while he was at work. He would "help" me by centering the pots on the stove's burners—to avoid wasting gas—even if off-center by only a fraction of an inch. He told me not to make baked potatoes because "heating up the whole oven for just two potatoes is wasteful." He would pull out his notebook of Academy meals and encourage me to use it. But those meals were for large groups of hungry men, with each of the menus emphasizing meat and potatoes and consisting of seven or eight dishes—which was much more than we could ever eat and would take more time to cook than I would have at the end of my school day.

Early in our year in Chandler, John told me that he would bring one or two bachelors from his pilot training class home for dinner on Friday nights. "They have so few opportunities to get a home cooked meal," he explained.

When I started teaching again in the fall, I dreaded Fridays. After a tiring day in the classroom *and* bus duty after that, I'd still have to drive to the base commissary for the groceries I needed to prepare the dinner for John's friends. While I cooked, they had drinks and talked about flying in the living room. And even at the table, flying remained the topic. Occasionally, one of the bachelors would say something to include me in the conversation, but John always diverted the talk back to flying.

After dinner, as I did the dishes and cleaned the kitchen, the guys had more drinks, laughing and cursing in the living room. Since there was no place in our little apartment to get away, I had to sit and listen to them as they got progressively drunk and obnoxious.

I hated Fridays. John must have known, but simply didn't care.

I hadn't seen Mother since the "sliding glass door incident" in Santa Monica, the summer after I'd graduated from college. When I'd moved back to Colorado, we exchanged short notes that became gradually friendlier. When she mentioned coming to visit John and me, I was pleased but wary.

During Mother's three-day visit she stayed at a motel, since we had no spare room in our apartment. She spent her days with us, playing chess with John and talking about her work. These were the first meals I had ever cooked for Mother and I was anxious for the timing to work out so that all the dishes were ready at the same time.

"Dinner's ready," I called one evening, but I couldn't get them to leave the chess board. Dinner sat on the table, getting cold. I knew John had no idea of the trouble I'd gone to for the meal and the table setting to be just right, but Mother must have.

"John?" I called again, hoping to get his attention away from the board.

"Coming," he said. But neither he nor Mother made a move toward the food.

I continued to sit alone, with my elbows on the table and my hands supporting my chin. Eventually they did come. Neither of them said anything about the food or pretty table setting. They seemed so much alike, and with each of them I always had to acquiesce to keep the peace. The visit ended well and my correspondence with Mother seemed lighter and lengthier after that.

* * * * *

John did well in two of the three pilot training programs, the academic and the military, but he was struggling with the flying portion. Each evening, using the flashcards he handed me, I drilled him on the "bold face" emergency procedures.

Spin Recovery
Throttles – **IDLE**
Rudder and Ailerons – **NEUTRAL**
Stick – **ABRUPTLY FULL AFT AND HOLD**
Rudder – **ABRUPTLY APPLY FULL RUDDER OPPOSITE SPIN DIRECTION OPPOSITE TURN NEEDLE AND HOLD**
Stick – **ABRUPTLY APPLY FULL FORWARD ONE TURN AFTER APPLYING RUDDER**
Controls – **NEUTRAL AFTER SPINNING STOPS, RECOVER FROM DIVE**

I soon knew the procedures on those cards as well as he

did. Yet, when it came time for a flight check with an instructor pilot, John tensed and forgot the procedures. He kept getting "pink slips" for flight errors and almost washed out of the training class.

I often felt overwhelmed as I struggled to balance the new demands of marriage with my teaching duties. When John had a disappointing day at work, and I came home from school tired, things were tense between us.

One Friday, after a difficult flight, John was in our dressing room changing out of his flight suit. "Sally, come here!" he called. I left the pork chops I was preparing for dinner and went to see what he wanted. "What is this mess?" he asked irritably. "Some of your clothes are barely on the hangers and they're facing different directions. At the Academy, we were taught to have all clothes facing the same direction and that hangers should be two fingers apart." He demonstrated by placing two of his fingers between hangers on his side of the closet. They fit the gap perfectly. "It worked for me at the Academy and that's why I still do it. It only takes a little more effort, so I'd like you make that effort, too." As I nodded my head, I smelled the pork chops burning. *Oh no, all I need is a burned dinner.* I hurried back to the kitchen, grabbed the pan from the stove and managed to save the meal.

I had always been obsessively tidy and organized. How strange that John was calling me "messy" now! He was being too rigid, too regimented, and too bossy. He was behaving like a parent, like my mother telling me not to set the ironing board up in the living room.

I knew underneath this wasn't really about me, my clothes, or my closet. John had failed a flight checkride. I'd begun to understand his moods, his disillusionment. He needed to strike out at someone. He had always done well in everything, from high school through the Academy. Now

173

he thought that if I were a better wife and homemaker—a better woman—he could find the success he felt he deserved. He thought I was holding him down with my inadequacy. I knew he believed this. I was beginning to wonder if he was right. Tears brimmed in my eyes as I called him to the table.

I wasn't allowed to park my car in the school parking lot because it didn't have Arizona plates. John said that since we would only be in Chandler for a year, he didn't want to waste money buying them. Therefore, we would keep the Colorado plates and I would walk a mile to and from my school. In Arizona the temperature can get up to 120 degrees. The walk was very uncomfortable, especially in the afternoons. I never understood what really made John decide we must keep the Colorado plates, but because we had two incomes I didn't think it was a matter of money. Once again I felt a lack of love from him, or even mere concern for me.

One day the custodian at my school passed me as I headed to class and asked, "Don't you ever smile?" I was dumbfounded! I hadn't realized until that moment how unhappy I was. I couldn't remember ever feeling so defeated. I pondered the custodian's question for days. *Don't you ever smile? Don't you ever smile?*

"I'd like for us to see a counselor," I finally told John. "Something feels wrong and I'm not happy. I love you and I know we have a good marriage, but we're always upset with each other about one thing or another."

"You can go if you want, but I'm not going," he said. "It would look bad on my military record and could hurt my career."

So I started seeing a psychiatrist in Scottsdale on Saturday mornings. Her office was an hour's drive from our apartment and the expensive sessions took a large chunk of my salary, but I thought it would be worth it if I could learn how to make my marriage better and be happy again. After my appointment I would drive to visit my sister's family, just a short way from there, and play with her baby, Tammy, before heading home.

Dr. Martine, who'd been recommended by a friend, was a stylishly dressed woman in her fifties. Jewelry and silk scarves adorned her outfits. At the first few sessions, I felt comfortable with her. I sat in a chair across from her desk and answered questions she asked about my background and told her the reasons I thought I needed her help.

When I started telling her some difficulties John and I were having, she told me I was not being completely truthful, and added, "We won't get anywhere if you can't confide in me."

I didn't know what she was talking about. I *was* being truthful. I *was* confiding, and I wondered what would make her think otherwise. As I stared at her, waiting for her to explain, she adjusted the way she was sitting and, in the process, hiked her skirt and slip up inappropriately high, allowing the tops of her nylon stockings and garters to show. Then she stared back at me. I was stunned, but I just sat, not knowing what to do.

Several appointments later, Dr. Martine said, "Sally, I don't think we're getting anywhere this way, so I'd like you to lie on the couch over there, facing away from me. I think perhaps we can get at the underlying truths this way."

I settled myself on the couch with my head on a pillow and my feet crossed at the ankles. "Why did you do that?" she snapped.

"Do what?" I asked, startled.

"Why are you trying to close me out by crossing your legs?"

She was scaring me. I wanted to run out of her office,

but instead I could do nothing but uncross my ankles and lie there, frozen. Again she accused me of not sharing my thoughts, so I quickly thought of things to say—"I feel sad all the time. My neck and shoulders ache. I can't seem to please anyone."—just to get through to the end of the appointment.

Her office was one of many in the building that shared the same waiting area. There were marriage counselors, family counselors, psychologists and psychiatrists. I'd often noticed that other people in the waiting room—families and couples—were chatty and looked happy, as if *their* counselors were helping them. I wished I was seeing one of those counselors. I was scared of my psychiatrist. Was she as aggressive, accusing and insulting with her other patients as she was with me? She was respected and went on lecture tours. She was a *grandmother*! If only I was confident enough to tell her, "I'm not coming back anymore. I may see someone else." But I didn't have the courage to say it.

"If you ever feel like discontinuing our sessions, it's because we're finally starting to get somewhere and you're trying to avoid the answers," she said at our next session, as if she sensed my feelings. "You should press on no matter how uncomfortable it becomes." So I dismissed any thoughts of telling her I wasn't coming back.

As I lay on the couch during another session, she said, "What would you do if I came over and made a pass at you?"

I was horrified! All I could think to reply is, "I don't know." *She must be homosexual.*

"You know what you are?" she asked, without waiting for my response. "You're a lonely little onion in a petunia patch. I have another young patient who is a lonely little *petunia* in an *onion* patch, but that's not you!" I didn't know exactly what to make of this. *Was she saying I'm a*

horrible person surrounded by goodness? I didn't say anything. I just let it go, like I always let it go whenever John
did or said something hurtful. I let it go to avoid conflict or
upset.

I went home and told John about what was going on
and asked what I should do. He didn't know either. "Maybe
this is some form of therapy," he offered.

At my next session with Dr. Martine, I said, "When I
told John about what we discussed...." She angrily interrupted me.

"Don't you *ever* tell anyone what goes on in here," she
said. "That diminishes the effect of the therapy. Then you
have nothing to share when you come in. Don't you think I
know that when you lie on the couch without talking for
minutes at a time that you're having thoughts you aren't
sharing with me? I know you are!"

She was right, of course, but what I couldn't share with
her was my fear of *her*, that she wasn't reputable, that she
was some bizarre character with a hidden agenda, but I
wasn't sure. Because she ordered me not to talk with anyone about our sessions, I had no perspective.

"We aren't getting anywhere at this rate," Dr. Martine
said. "I want you to start coming in twice a week."

I told her I couldn't afford that. "Anyway," I added,
"John and I will be moving to our next assignment in a
couple of months. Do you think I should see someone else
when we get there?"

"That's up to you."

I'd wanted help in sorting through my marital difficulties, but I no longer trusted the one person I'd gone to for
help. I didn't have the confidence to stand up to Dr. Martine, and so I felt defeated. We had accomplished nothing. I
called the office secretary and cancelled further appointments. I also decided that when John and I moved to our

177

next assignment, I wouldn't seek further help.

* * * * *

John and I bought ten-speed bikes and would sometimes pedal around new housing areas in Chandler on the weekends. We'd stop at the A&W stand and drink a frosty mug of root beer at a picnic table. This was one of the few pleasant things I remember about life in Chandler and my first year of marriage.

In spite of all our difficulties, I believed we could have a good marriage. I thought John's drinking was at the root of all the discontent. If he didn't drink, we would be happy; he would do better in pilot training, be more thoughtful of me, and we would have the marriage I desperately wanted. When I cautiously suggested he cut back on the alcohol, he said he'd try—but his trying never lasted long.

I'd heard that the first year of marriage was the most difficult and that after the "adjustment period" each year got better. I counted on that being true. John had rallied in the flying phase of his training program and would be able to graduate with his class. That helped to reduce the level of tension at home and was a huge relief to both of us.

* * * * *

John had told me that if I ever heard about a flight accident, I was not to call and bother anyone on base. "Just stay at home." he said. "Someone from the base will call you if I'm involved in the accident." Since I was at school everyday and never heard the news, I never knew to be worried. But on a rare weekday off—the schools were closed for counselor conferences—I was headed out to shop at the Base Exchange and commissary when I heard on the car radio that a T-38 had crashed. The time and the aircraft matched up to John's flight. I drove straight to Base Headquarters and almost *ran* into the office of the base commander. "I heard about the T-38 that crashed," I said. "My husband, John Brucher...." I began to tremble. The commander stood up behind his desk and motioned me to a chair. I could feel my chin quiver and my eyes brim with tears. "I need to know if it was...him."

"Let me check." The commander said. He stepped out of the office, leaving me alone for several panicked minutes.

When he returned, he nodded grimly and said, "Yes, both the student and instructor pilots were killed, but it wasn't your husband."

The news had such an impact on me that I didn't know if I was steady enough to stand up.

"Are you okay?" the commander asked, helping me out of the chair and supporting me by my elbow as he walked me out to the lobby.

I abandoned my plan to shop on-base, drove home, and busied myself at the apartment as I waited for John to get home. I wondered which of the pilots had been killed. They had to have been husbands or bachelors I'd met.

When I heard the lock in the door turn, I ran to greet John. I explained the events of the day and told him how frightened I'd been. I stepped closer to him, reaching out for a hug. He blocked my arms and stepped away from me. "I'm disappointed in you, Sally," he said. "It was wrong of you to bother the commander. I *told* you not to! What if all the wives behaved like that? You should have driven home and waited for more news."

I didn't say anything. It was always easier for me just to let things go.

* * * * *

On a hot day in June of 1963, John graduated from pilot training. I wore a wide-brimmed straw hat and a navy blue linen suit as I pinned the wings on John's uniform. Because he had signed on for additional training to become a flight instructor, we would be staying on in Chandler for another six months. We didn't know yet where we'd be going after that, but since we would be moving in late November, I didn't apply for another year of teaching in Chandler. How relaxing to have my days free! I shopped and got together with some of the other wives whose husbands had stayed on for instructor training.

In November, when we went to my sister's home in Scottsdale for Thanksgiving dinner and to celebrate my twenty-fifth birthday, we knew our next assignment was Moody Air Force Base in Valdosta, Georgia.

"We'll miss you *so* much," Nan said. She looked sad and gave us hugs.

"We wish we'd been able to get together more often," John said, "but this last year-and-a-half has been so hectic."

Two-year-old Tammy, who had barely gotten to know her Aunt Sally and Uncle John, had dragged her toys and baby dolls into the kitchen to get some attention from the adults. "See my baby?" she said, holding one doll up for John's appraisal. He squatted to stroke Tammy's red hair and asked what she'd named the baby.

"Baby Kate," she said.

"That's a pretty name," John told her.

I started feeling sick just as dinner was on the table and Bob was pouring a sparkling wine to toast to my birthday, which had been just a few days earlier. I lay on Nan and Bob's bed with my arms wrapped around my middle, wondering what I could have eaten that upset my tummy so badly. Nan had gone to so much trouble to prepare a wonderful dinner to celebrate Thanksgiving, our new assignment, and my birthday, and I was curled up on the bed, feeling too queasy for a single bite.

Although I didn't know it when we left Chandler the following week, I was one month pregnant.

CHAPTER SIXTEEN

As we drove into Valdosta, a town about an hour north of Georgia's border with Florida, the tree lined streets and majestic century-old homes in the downtown area seemed to welcome us. Traffic was slow and pedestrians seemed to be in no hurry. We pulled into the first motel we saw, the Ashley Oaks.

The next morning, while having breakfast in the motel restaurant, we saw something on our plates we hadn't ordered. I poked at the white mound and asked John if it was rice or mashed potatoes. Neither seemed particularly appropriate for breakfast.

Taking a small taste, he said, "I don't think it's either."

The waitress, filling our coffee cups, noticed our puzzlement and said, "Oh, that's grits," her heavy southern accent stretching the word into two syllables. I'd heard the word *grits* before, but thought it was the word for a kind of pancake.

"You folks sure aren't "Georgia Crackers," she said, chuckling. John and I looked at each other and smiled, realizing we had much to learn while living in the South.

As we paid the cashier, we mentioned we were looking for a home to buy in the area. "There's a real estate office just down the street a block-and-a-half. If you turn right as you leave, you can't miss it," she said, pointing.

We sat down with the agent and explained that we were looking for a *furnished* home because we didn't own any furniture. "I'll compile a list of houses in your price range, though I doubt there are many that are furnished," he said. "If you can be here at nine tomorrow morning, we'll get started."

The next morning we learned that the only furnished house available wasn't in our price range, so the three of us spent the day looking at *un*furnished houses. Late that afternoon John and I decided we wanted to return to one we'd seen earlier in the day. It was an older three-bedroom house with a large, picket-fenced backyard that had many tall, slender trees. "I really like this one," I said, looking through the rooms again. The house was spotless, and the uncurtained picture window in the living room gave a view of the neighborhood. Sunshine spilled onto the oak floors.

"It's not only unfurnished," John said, "it doesn't even have appliances: no stove, refrigerator, washing machine, or dryer. Nothing!" I shrugged and smiled, and John took that to mean I still wanted to buy the house.

We arranged for our few belongings from Arizona to be delivered, including the only furniture we owned—a maple rocking chair we'd received as a wedding gift and the antique buggy wheel, converted into a glass topped coffee table that I'd bought at an antique shop in Chandler, and that was it.

Three days later, we rented a roll-away double bed and moved into the house. It looked bare, but the possibilities for decorating excited me. It was the start I'd waited for— my marriage to John, a home, and perhaps a family soon.

John hadn't met anyone on the base, so he was more involved than he might otherwise have been in getting settled. He went to Family Services on base to borrow some appliances until we could afford to buy our own. A couple of hours later he came in the door carrying an ice chest. "I got a Dutch oven, a two-burner hot plate, and this ice chest to use as a refrigerator," he said, setting the ice chest down on the kitchen's worn linoleum floor.

Two weeks after moving in, I went to a doctor at the base hospital. I'd had an upset stomach since Thanksgiving. The doctor checked me over and couldn't find anything wrong. He told me to give a urine sample to the lab, explaining that it was for a rabbit-test, to see if I was pregnant. I'd suspected I was pregnant, but it wasn't until the doctor ordered the test that it seemed like a real possibility. "I'll call you with the results sometime next week," he told me. I walked to the car with a spring in my step.

"Merry Christmas!" the man on the phone said. "This is Dr. Harmon. The rabbit test was positive."

"Yea!" I shouted into the phone. As soon as I hung up I started to laugh and dance around. I wrapped my arms around my middle and felt that all my dreams were coming true. We were going to be a family. It was a week before Christmas and this was the best gift ever.

John seemed nowhere near as thrilled. "I hope it's a boy," was all he said. I thought this lack of excitement was just a *guy thing,* that most men didn't express enthusiasm about starting a family.

During the early months of pregnancy, I couldn't stand to eat meat. Even smelling it nauseated me. So I made meals of grilled cheese sandwiches and homemade vegetable soup, macaroni and cheese, or sometimes just waffles and fruit. During that time, John ordered meat for lunch on-base.

As John began his instructor pilot duties, I settled in to decorate our new home. I bought an old, reconditioned sewing machine from the Singer store for fifteen dollars. It was called a *portable,* but it weighed a ton. Although I

185

hadn't sewn since taking home economics in junior high school, I managed to make curtains with beige and pastel sheets I purchased at the Base Exchange. I trimmed some of the curtains with rickrack, some with lace. Others I left plain.

John and I had a plan. To avoid going into debt we would allow ourselves only one major purchase each month. Because of all we would need to buy, we knew it would be a while before we could start saving money, but—however slowly—life would steadily become at least a little more comfortable and convenient.

The first month, we bought a refrigerator. It had a built-in automatic icemaker, which was a new feature in refrigerators; we didn't know anyone else who had one. We were so proud of our wonderful new appliance that we demonstrated its ice-making capability to everyone who came over.

The next month we bought a stove with a large oven. It made an amazing difference—for sixty days I'd had to crouch to use the borrowed portable appliances lined up on the warped floor, along the kitchen wall. I felt suddenly modern, competent, and proud, and my meal preparation became inspired. My aversion to meat had subsided and I now made chicken tetrazini, pork roast with homemade cinnamon applesauce, and lamb chops with scalloped potatoes.

But since each major purchase sapped our budget for the entire month, we still didn't have a dining set. John sat on the floor with his plate on the coffee table. Because I was pregnant, I got to sit in the rocking chair. I set the coffee table using candles and cloth napkins for every dinner.

I savored the feeling of settling in and starting our family. My shoulders no longer stayed hunched with tension, as they had in Chandler. I was relaxed and calm. Although

John wasn't the type to hold me and share his dreams, I felt we were closer to each other than we had ever been as we turned this house into a home and awaited our baby's arrival.

* * * * *

By my fourth month, I was suffering backaches due to my expanding middle and the lack of support from our sagging rented roll-away bed. So we bought a Thomasville pecan wood bedroom set in a country French design, which took our furniture fund for *two* months. It included two bed tables, a dresser, an armoire, and a king-size bed with a mattress firm enough to support my back.

Our clothes came out of the cardboard boxes at long last and were placed on shelves and in drawers of the dresser and armoire. I shopped at a discount store for linens and made throw pillows that matched the gold bedspread and the shades on the bed table lamps. With the lamps lit, the bedroom seemed to glow with soft golden light.

I hadn't bought any new clothes in almost two years— since John and I were married—because we'd had too many other expenses. But now my big tummy wouldn't fit into my clothes. I had the perfect excuse to shop for new clothes. At a maternity shop in town, I bought underwear, dresses, shorts and tops. Summer was on its way and Valdosta would be hot and humid during my last months of pregnancy. The new clothes made me feel fresh and pretty as I walked out to the front driveway to greet John when he pulled in from work each day.

We'd furnished the house by late spring, with the exception of the living room and the nursery. John's parents offered to pay for the nursery furniture, and told me to go ahead and pick out whatever I liked.

187

A week later, dreaming of our new baby, I sat in the newly furnished nursery and gazed at the Jenny Lind crib with its canopy top, the Humpty Dumpty lamp on the dresser, the small round table covered with a floor-length bleached muslin cloth with royal blue rickrack trim. I leaned back in the rocking chair, humming lullabies and rolling possible names around in my thoughts. My arms ached to snuggle this baby. I'd yearned to create my own family. Becoming a mother was going to be the most glorious happening of my life.

When I was six months pregnant, John told me he had to attend a two-month training course in Montgomery, Alabama. One of John's fellow instructor-pilots would also be going to Montgomery for the training. His pregnant wife, Jeanie, and I agreed she would move in with me while our husbands were gone.

With our husbands gone, Jeanie and I indulged our food cravings and laughed at our bulging bellies. We ate lunch at the drug store—hot dogs on grilled buns, topped with creamy coleslaw. Then we'd shop for little inexpensive baby items: diaper pins, rattles, bibs, cotton receiving blankets.

When our husbands returned from Montgomery, I was eight months pregnant. Almost immediately, I began hearing stories about John's infidelity from wives who'd gone along with their husbands to Montgomery. At get-togethers those wives laughed—half in embarrassment and half in sympathy—as they spoke of John coming on to women and leaving parties with them. *Why are they telling me these things?* I wondered. *Are they true?*

I didn't confront John. I feared he would deny the reports—and I wouldn't know if I could believe him. But if he *did* tell me they were true, what then? Would he be nonchalant about it and say, "So what?" Would he just ignore me? Would he stay away from home—or leave me entirely? I feared, worst of all, feeling unloved, abandoned.

My obstetrician said we couldn't make love during the last six weeks of my pregnancy. I worried that such abstinence would cause John to continue to turn elsewhere. I cuddled up to his back at night so he could feel the baby kick. He'd roll over to face me and place his hand on my belly. If the baby moved again, he'd exclaim, "I felt the little guy!" Oh, how I hoped it was the boy John wanted. He had missed so much of the pregnancy during the two months he'd been gone, but we were together now, and everything would be okay. To be a family we just needed to cling to each other.

Soon after John returned from Montgomery, he decided he wanted to visit Jake, a friend of his from the Academy who now lived with his wife in Panama City, Florida. It would be four hours of driving each way and we'd go during an upcoming three-day July 4th holiday weekend. Because of my pregnancy and my lack of trust in John, I didn't want to be away from him anymore. I didn't tell my obstetrician about this trip because I was afraid he would say I couldn't go.

At this point I wished John hadn't traded in the large, comfortable Chevy Impala for a tiny VW bug. The ride to Florida was rough for me. I felt every bump. I kept my arms folded under my big tummy to try to cushion the baby.

For much of the time we stayed with Jake and Caroline, I was stretched out on the guest room bed, resting. July in Florida was even hotter and more humid than it had been in Georgia. I couldn't find a position I could tolerate for long, so I was restless, hot, and sticky night and day. "Sally, do you feel like joining us for dinner or would you like a tray?" Caroline asked sweetly. I hoisted myself up from the bed to join them for most meals, but it was a great effort. I felt like

I had a house strapped in front of me.

"It doesn't seem very friendly for you to stay in here all the time," John said in a low voice. And that made me cry. Why couldn't he recognize that I was trying to be a good sport?—but at the same time I was embarrassed at my reclusiveness and eager to get home where it would be easier to deal with the physical discomfort.

* * * * *

The trip was miserable. I groaned whenever John slowed too quickly, hit a bump in the road, or even changed lanes abruptly. The little car rode as if it had no shocks.

Stepping into the comfort of my own home, I sighed deeply. I walked into the kitchen, leaned against the sink, and looked out the window at my peaceful backyard. As John came in from unloading the car, he called from the hallway, "What's for dinner?"

"I'm going to heat some soup," I called back.

I soon had a pot of canned clam chowder simmering on the stove and oyster crackers poured into a bowl. I was just starting to set the table when I felt an odd sensation: warm water running down my legs and puddling on the floor. I was wetting my pants and couldn't stop it!

I had heard the term *water breaking* and realized that must be what was happening to me, so I called the hospital and talked to a nurse. John stood nearby, waiting for me to tell him what the nurse said: "We'd like you to come into the hospital and let us check you."

"But I'm only eight months pregnant. My baby isn't due till next month."

"Yes, ma'am, however, once your water breaks, there's a chance of infection, so you do need to come in within the hour."

After I hung up, John asked, "What did she say?"

I told him we had to go to the hospital. "But the baby isn't due for a month," I added. "I'm scared, John." He helped me put the food away, and then I showered and shampooed and packed a small bag in case they kept me in the hospital. As John drove the familiar blacktop road to the base we were quiet, each of us lost in our own thoughts. I realized that the trip, so late in my pregnancy, had probably caused my water to break. I stretched my legs out as far as they could go in the floor of the car and leaned my head back. I now hated this wretched little car. I just wanted to lie down. I was totally exhausted—and worried about our baby.

When we arrived at the base hospital—an old wooden building, formerly a military barracks—John was barred from the labor room because my water breaking increased the risk of infection. I lay for hours, cold and lonely, on a narrow padded table in the labor room, which was actually just a small examining room. My contractions gradually increased in intensity. A nurse came in twice to see how much I had dilated, then quickly left. The second time, I held onto her and asked her not to leave. She smiled sympathetically, but said she had other women to attend to.

When at last it was time to be wheeled into the delivery room, I was grateful merely to have people around me. I knew John wouldn't be there with me. He'd told me that watching me give birth might make him faint—and *that* would cause him be taken off flying status.

I told the doctor I wanted to watch my baby being born, but a nurse took my glasses away and I couldn't see anything clearly in the slanted ceiling mirror. They buckled wide leather straps around my arms and legs to keep me in the proper birthing position, but when cramps started to knot up in my calves, I began to panic. The leg cramps hurt

191

more than the pains of labor. The doctor asked one assistant to massage my calves but to "stay out of the way as much as possible."

The delivery went quickly and I was told I had a son, just as John had wanted. I was allowed to hold my baby boy. That was my moment of fulfillment. I held him close and whispered his name: "John Nicholas Brucher, my Nick." Then they took him away to be weighed and measured.

Although not full-term, he weighed a healthy six pounds, fourteen ounces. He had blond hair, blue-green eyes, and olive skin. As I played with him, examined and admired him, I thought, *I know you're mine. Look here, your thumbs bend backward just as mine do. I love this mole on the inside of your wrist. What a beautiful baby you are!*

I cried every time they took him away to the nursery.

"You need your sleep," the nurses told me. "We'll take good care of him."

The young woman who shared the room with me had just had a baby girl. Her side of the room was filled with flowers, and her husband was there all the time, regardless of visiting hours. When John *did* visit, he was always late, and that made me sad. One time when I asked why so late, he explained, "I was at the stag bar at the officers club, sharing the news that I'd had a boy. They were making toasts to my son."

I wanted to share the joy with John. This was *our* time. I didn't care about his buddies in the stag bar. We were a family of three and that was all that should matter. I wanted either to shake some sense into John or cling to him and block out the world. But I was afraid if I said anything else, I would ruin the visit and he wouldn't want to come back at all the next day.

My roommate's husband took pictures of Nick. They're the only ones we have of him in the hospital. During the five days I was there, John never brought flowers. When he noticed all the bouquets my roommate had, he said, "Oh, did you want flowers?"

I shook my head. "No, I just want you and our baby."

* * * * *

I cradled Nick in my arms as John drove slowly and carefully home from the hospital. "You'll have to excuse the mess at home," John said. "I didn't have time to clean up. When I couldn't find things in the kitchen, I decided to just leave all the cabinets and drawers open so I could see where things were."

I thought he was kidding, so I smiled at him and turned my attention back to our sleeping son.

When we walked in the door, I couldn't believe it! Our home had never looked so awful. Not only were all the kitchen drawers and cabinets open, but all the dishes he'd used during the five days I was gone were piled in the sink and across the counter tops, caked with dried-on food. I felt a surge of disgust and disappointment. Tears ran down my cheeks as I clutched my son. I had wanted to bring him home to a special place, a home all clean and welcoming.

John quickly moved to push some drawers in and close cabinets, perhaps realizing for the first time how bad the kitchen looked. How had my super-meticulous husband allowed himself to become a slob?

Still holding Nick, I slowly surveyed the house: Dirty clothes strewn about, the bed unmade, a dirty cluttered bathroom with an overflowing wastebasket. I carried Nick into his nursery for the first time. "At least your room is clean," I whispered to him as I placed him gently in his crib and stood watching him for a minute to make sure he'd be okay. Then I went to the phone and called Jeanie, the friend who had lived with me while our husbands were gone. She'd already had her baby. "I just got home from the hospital and the house is a total wreck," I said, choking on a sob. I can't even prepare formula for the baby in such a disgusting kitchen." Then all she heard were sobs.

"Sally, calm down," she said. "I'll be right over. Just sit down and wait for me. Everything's going to be okay."

Jeanie and Carla, another friend and new mother, arrived just a few minutes later, after leaving their babies with Jeanie's husband. They took in the scene and nodded to each other with stiff, irritated smiles. I understood their irritation wasn't with me, but with the mess John had brought me home to.

They took a peek at sleeping Nick in the nursery. "He is so beautiful, Sally!" Jeanie said as Nick made a little sound in his sleep. Carla took my hand and squeezed it.

When we returned to the kitchen, Jeanie pointed to a chair and said, "You just sit there and visit with us." Then, without hesitation, they started to work. They scrubbed until the kitchen sparkled and then made a batch of formula that would tide me over for he rest of the day and night. I thanked them through tears, and then apologized for my crying.

"Hey, after my Shawn was born, my hormones were through the roof," Carla said. "This is a very emotional time for a woman, and then coming home to *this*...."

I didn't know where John had gone, but realized he must have been too embarrassed to show his face. "Is there anything else we can do to help?" Jeanie asked after they'd righted things in other parts of the house. I shook my head.

"Will you be all right?" Carla asked. I nodded, too teary to speak.

I tried to compose myself as I gave them both hugs. "I love you guys for doing this. I'll be fine. Thank you so much." They went back to the nursery to take another peek at Nick and then left.

When John arrived home, he steered clear of me. It was unusual for me to get mad, but as a protective new mother, I was plenty mad.

John seemed a bit wary of holding Nick and had only done so briefly, when I needed his help. One evening, after giving Nick a sponge bath in the kitchen sink, I zipped him into a new sleeper and carried him into the living room where John was reading the newspaper. I handed Nick to him and John looked down at his son with such a comical expression, as though he was holding a tiny alien. I couldn't help but laugh. My two guys were getting to know each other.

* * * * *

Mother had written to say she would take time off from work to come out to help when the baby arrived. I knew Mother loved babies, and I thought another visit from her might further thaw our relationship.

Because Nick surprised us by arriving early, Mother had to rearrange her time away from her job at Brookhaven Laboratory on Long Island, where she'd moved when she left Santa Monica. She arrived at our house full of enthusiasm and couldn't get her hands on Nick fast enough. He had this way of puckering up his lips when you talked to him, which Mother said made his mouth look like a little pink rosebud.

I welcomed her help. Nick had gotten his days and nights mixed up and I was tired most of the time. Mother slept on the sofa bed in the living room, with Nick in a portable crib next to her. At last I got a good night's sleep. The next morning she yawned at the breakfast table and said, "He's not only awake all night, but he wants to be entertained."

She gave Nick his first full bath—in the kitchen sink—and he showed he enjoyed it by splashing the warm water with his little frog-like arms and legs. I was amazed at how adept, relaxed, and confident Mother was with him.

In the evenings, John and Mother played chess.

Often during her stay, I could hardly believe I'd ever had difficult times with her or with John. Nick had brought us all together.

I was depressed when Mother had to leave. I wanted more of her company and instruction. I would be so lonely when she was gone. Simple things we did together as we talked—folding laundry or sipping tea—had felt comforting and reassuring.

When Mother was packed and ready to be taken to the airport, John loaded her suitcases into our car. Mother and I hugged carefully, with Nick in my arms, and she gazed lovingly down at him. She walked out the front door and stopped, glancing back before starting down the steps. *Please don't leave me,* I thought, for just the briefest moment. My inner plea was the same as when she'd left me as a three-year-old at boarding school. "Take good care of little Rosebud!" she said. The affection in her voice made my chin quiver.

CHAPTER SEVENTEEN

While out for a drive one day, John and I discovered a new housing development. It was located in a heavily wooded section of town, along the road to the base. We turned off that road into a cul-de-sac where only one house had been built. The other five lots were for sale. On a whim, we decided to follow the directional signs to the office. A flimsy cardboard sign out front said, "Forestwood Estates Office." As we walked in, a heavy woman in a loose frumpy dress who looked to be in her fifties approached us with no smile or greeting. "We'd like some information on buying a lot and building a home," John said. I took our squirming eight-month-old Nick from John's arms as he talked.

The woman launched into a sales pitch on the development's attractions. "We want it to look like an already established neighborhood," she said, "so we're cutting down as few trees as possible."

She told us a house could be built in two months and we could choose a lot, decide where the house would sit on the lot, choose the exterior brick color, the interior paint colors, the color of bathroom tile, and the flooring to be used throughout. It sounded exciting! But, buying a lot and building a house in Forestwood Estates would increase our monthly mortgage payment from $67 to $120.

"My name is Miss Jaynes," she finally said, without looking up. She splayed brochures of different floor plans on a coffee table. The buyer could choose from such fancy model names as Sturbridge, Charlottesville, or Madison. After taking one brochure of each floor plan, we thanked her and turned to leave the office. She walked to the door with us and suggested we look around at the available lots, all of which were marked with a red plastic strip on a stake stuck in the ground near the curb.

Outside, we noticed clothes hung to dry on a clothesline in the backyard of the office. Several pairs of very large bloomer-type knee-length panties were on the line. I mentioned how unprofessional that looked. John chuckled, saying the old biddy had probably been wearing a pair.

We drove back to the cul-de-sac and got out of the car to examine one of the lots there. We liked one particular lot because, if the house was positioned right, a large tree would provide shade where a back patio might be.

Another couple, friends of ours from the base, pulled in to look at lots on the same cul-de-sac. Guy and Marcie Butler had been living in a second-story apartment with their daughter, Amy, who was a little older than Nick. Marcie was pregnant with their second child.

"If we both build here, you and I can visit everyday while our children play," I told Marcie. Our husbands were both instructor pilots and had played tennis together. It seemed to all of us that we were meant to be neighbors.

We told them what we'd learned from Miss Jaynes and showed them the brochures. We made a snap decision right then. We drove back to the office—with the Butlers following in their car—to sign the papers that would make us new residents of Forestwood Estates.

"Are we over-extending ourselves financially?" I asked John in the car.

"We've already paid for our furniture and appliances and have no debt," he said, "so I think we can afford the extra $53 a month." We closed the deal and then went out to lunch with the Butlers to celebrate having new homes and being neighbors.

Two months later our white brick house and the Butler's red brick house were completed. We moved in when Nick was ten months old, and I discovered almost immediately that I was pregnant again. Marcie and I had even more in common now.

The next arrivals on the cul-de-sac were Colonel Will Dennison and his wife Claire, who built their house next door to ours. They had teenage children who baby-sat for us and the Butlers. As new houses were added to the circle, the cul-de-sac neighbors became close. We all worked at landscaping our yards while visiting with each other on the weekends.

I walked across the circle to Marcie's house one morning—we'd often get together for coffee after our husbands left for the base—and when she opened the door I smelled the bacon she'd cooked for Guy's breakfast. I couldn't go inside her house. I had the same aversion to meat during this pregnancy that I'd had when I was pregnant with Nick. We had to sit on the front steps to drink our coffee.

"Guy got upset with Amy for making too much noise when he was trying to watch TV last night," Marcie said, "so he packed up all her toys in boxes and put them in the attic to punish her. Now she doesn't have anything to play with." The punishment seemed excessive to both of us. Amy was only two. But I felt reassured to hear a friend agree that husbands could be unreasonable. I just wished mine wasn't so much more unreasonable than hers.

John's thoughtless and surly moods were beginning to permeate every area of our marriage. It irritated him that fourteen-month-old Nick wasn't able to do some small things that John thought he should be able to do. When Nick couldn't open a cupboard door that sometimes got stuck in the humid weather, or when Nick couldn't kick a soccer ball straight, John made him keep trying until he was in tears. "You're just being a baby," John would scold.

One morning John told me he'd invited a financial consultant to come by that evening to talk with him about insurance and investments. "If he arrives before I get home from work, don't let him in the house," he instructed. "It's not appropriate for you to have a man in the house when I'm not home."

"I hope you get home in plenty of time," I replied, "because it would be awkward for me not to invite him in."

John didn't get home before the man arrived; in fact, he wasn't home for another half-hour. I was sitting on the front step when the man pulled up in his shiny black car. He approached me wearing a dark suit and tie and carrying a briefcase. We shook hands as we introduced ourselves. I told him John hadn't gotten home yet, and when I asked if he'd like to sit outside on the brick stoop with me and wait for him, he seemed taken aback and hesitated for a moment to sit. "May I get you a Coke or a Fresca," I offered. We sat on the steps and sipped our drinks, but I felt completely humiliated by the situation.

"Your husband asked some very intelligent and insightful questions about investments," he said, after a long silence, "so I had to do some research before I could meet with him."

"I know he's eager to talk with you," I replied. "He should be here any minute."

When John *did* arrive, he cheerfully invited the man inside the house in a way that implied, *What in the world are you doing out here on the steps?* I was never included in conversations John had with other men, so when John gave me the nod, I excused myself to work on dinner and tend to Nick.

On Fridays, after flying, John would always go to the officers' stag bar to drink and talk flying with the other pilots. Many of the guys did this for an hour or two at the end of the work week and then headed home, but each week John stayed progressively later than the week before. Eventually, John would leave for work on Friday mornings and I wouldn't see him again until he arrived home, hung-over and disheveled, mid-morning on Saturdays. He'd be in no mood to hear a tirade from me, but I'd give him one. "After a full week of child care and housework with little stimulation, I *need* to be able to look forward to a start-of-the-weekend Friday night with you! I've been so distraught with worry that I called the highway patrol to see if there had been an accident involving our car! I was afraid you might have killed yourself—or someone else—after hours of drinking and then driving home....or who knows where else."

He'd tell me he'd been at the BOQ (Bachelor Officers' Quarters) "talking to the guys" and hadn't noticed the time. Finally, he just flatly said, "You can expect Friday to be my night out from now on." He held a hand up toward me to let me know there was no room for discussion on this.

I could never get any sleep on Friday nights even though I knew I'd be dragging in the morning when I had to get up early with Nick. I'd pace in front of the picture window, watching headlights go by, hoping one of the cars—our car—would slow and turn into the cul-de-sac.

One Saturday morning, the Butlers were already cutting and trimming the grass in their front yard by the time John arrived home. He was still wearing his flight suit from the day before. They stared at him, then at me. I was mortified!

I hadn't wanted anyone to know John did this.

Later that day Marcie told me, clenching her fists for emphasis, "I couldn't stand to be married to a man like that!" I was crushed. I needed her friendship, not her judgment. I avoided her for a long time after that, staying in the house or the backyard.

When couples went to the Officers' Club for dinner and drinks on the weekend, there were no charges at the on-base nursery as long as you picked your child up before midnight. For each minute after midnight, there was a twenty-five cent charge.

After dropping Nick off at the nursery one Saturday evening, we went to the O'Club. I was six months pregnant and was wearing a new black maternity cocktail dress and had my hair done up in curls on top of my head. I sat for hours at a table with some of our friends, but John stood at the bar all evening. I could see he was "talking flying" because of the way he moved his hands as he talked— swooping and banking them like two jets in formation. Other men brought over snacks for their wives—and for me—but John never came to the table.

As midnight approached, I walked to the bar. "John, it's almost midnight," I gently reminded him. "We need to get Nick or we'll be charged." Sloshing his drink as he set it down hard on the bar—either in irritation or drunkenness— he finally consented to leave.

On the drive home, I held Nick in my arms wrapped in a light cotton blanket. John was driving erratically and at one point he crossed the center line of the blacktop country road and was speeding toward oncoming headlights. I grabbed the steering wheel with my left hand to get us back into our lane. Instantly, John slammed his arm into my face, barely missing Nick. The blow knocked pins from my hair and curls tumbled down.

"You were on the wrong side of the road," I wailed, "and I was frightened."

"If you don't like the way I'm driving, you can just get out!" he yelled as he pulled off the road. I got out, holding Nick, who was still sleeping. Then John drove away. I stood at the edge of the blacktop road for a while, thinking he'd turn around and come back. The night was chilly. I had goose bumps on my bare arms and knew that Nick, wrapped only in his light blanket, must also be getting cold. Other cars occasionally zoomed by—people returning home from the officers club or men getting off from their late work shift. Their headlights washed across me. *They must wonder what in the world I'm doing out here.* I moved away from the pavement and hid behind a billboard. I didn't know what to do and I started crying.

Realizing at last that John wasn't coming back for us, I stepped out of hiding and moved closer to the road. A car pulled over. Warily, I peered in through the open passenger-side window. I saw two young, uniformed enlisted men illuminated by the dashboard lights. "Can we help you ma'am?" The one nearest me asked. "Are you having trouble?"

I knew I looked a mess. Strands of curly hair dangled in my eyes and my face was wet with tears. I might already have been showing a bruise where John had struck me. After I explained my predicament, the driver said, "We'll be glad to take you home, ma'am." The passenger got out of the car to help me into the back seat. I directed them to our house and when we got there I secretly hoped they'd take notice of our address and report the officer who lived there for abandoning his pregnant wife and child.

The house was dark. I panicked at the thought that John might have been so drunk that he'd crashed the car somewhere and perhaps been injured or killed. I turned on the hallway light. As I carried Nick toward the nursery, I passed our bedroom. Enough light spilled from the hallway into the dark room that I was able to see John in bed, already asleep. After I got Nick changed and settled in his crib, I went into the bedroom, careful not to awaken John. To calm myself down, I softly cooed to my unborn baby as I changed into my nightgown and slipped under the covers next to my drunken husband.

In the morning, neither of us said a word. I saw John take some aspirin after breakfast, and then he left the house. I didn't know where he'd be going on a Sunday. I stood before a mirror, remembering the events that had caused the half-circle of blue under my eye.

* * * * *

In my seventh month of pregnancy, John told me he had to attend another three-month school in Montgomery, Alabama. At first I thought he'd be leaving me again. Then I realized I would be going along. I wondered what another trip in late pregnancy might do.

"We can rent out our house to someone who's arriving at this base and needs more time to find a home of their own," John said. He told me there was a brand-new hospital at Maxwell Air Force Base, where I would have our baby. That was reassuring. Nick had been born in an old barracks hospital, but this baby would have a new, modern one.

Before leaving home, we made arrangements to rent a two-bedroom trailer at a mobile home park in Montgomery, near the base. After a long and tiring trip, we finally pulled up to the trailer park's office. We got the keys and drove slowly past the rows of trailers to look for it.

From the outside, the trailer looked smaller than its description. John went to unlock the door and I stayed in the car, not wanting to hoist myself out until I knew for sure it was the right one. He swung the door open and then just stood there on the metal step, looking in. I couldn't imagine what he was doing—why he didn't step inside or motion for me to join him?

He came back to the car frowning and shaking his head. He leaned down to my window and said, "The place is unbelievably filthy. I'll have to get some supplies and scrub the floors before you and Nick can go in."

John and I drove back to the park office so he could get some cleaning supplies. Then he parked the car in the shade of a tree near the trailer where I dozed off while Nick napped in the back seat.

After almost two hours of scrubbing on his hands and knees, John appeared at the trailer doorway and I carried Nick inside and looked around. The interior seemed even smaller than I'd anticipated from the outside. Every surface looked grimy. I couldn't start putting anything away until I cleaned the place. But at least the *floors* were spotless now. That was important to me, because Nick—at age one-and-a-half—still spent a lot of time on the floor.

Even two was a crowd in the little trailer, and my tummy was so big that when John and I met in the narrow hallway, one of us had to step into a room to allow the other to pass.

During my first obstetrics appointment at the new base hospital, I asked the doctor, "When should I tell my mother to plan time away from her job so she can come help with the baby?"

He advised me to have her arrive on my due date. "If you haven't gone into labor by then, I'll *induce* labor," he added.

Anticipating Mother's arrival, we borrowed a twin foldaway bed for her from Family Services and put it in Nick's room. At the Base Exchange, I bought a pretty blue-flowered comforter for her bed. January is cold, even in Alabama.

There were many parties for military students and their spouses, but I was uncomfortable most of the time now and tired easily. John insisted I go, but he was never willing to return to our trailer when I felt I needed to. I could usually find someone willing to take me home so John could stay at the party, but that embarrassed him. "You're always imposing on other people," he complained. "Can't you just sit somewhere and wait until the party breaks up?"

My due date came and went. Mother had just arrived when I went in to see my doctor, hoping he would induce labor. At the clinic, I was informed that my obstetrician was out of town giving a lecture, but that another doctor would see me. During the examination, I told him my doctor had planned to induce labor. He acknowledged my remark with a nod, but said nothing. I was prepared for a shot, but instead, without warning, he reached under the modesty sheet and inserted the fingers of both hands into me and manually stretched me into dilation. I screamed and pushed away from him on the examining table. "You can only scoot so far," he said coldly. The nurse looked shocked, but didn't say anything.

When I got back to the trailer, I cried as I told Mother about the ordeal and the cruel doctor.

"What can I get you to make you feel better?" she asked.

"I'd love a cup of tea," I said, shifting my position. I could barely sit because of the throbbing pain.

During the night, I went into labor. At first I wasn't sure it *was* labor. I moved out to the sofa in the living room to start timing the pains. Mother heard me and got up to see how I was doing. After an hour, she said, "Maybe I should get John. Your pains are getting closer together and it's a good drive to the hospital."

"I hate to disturb him if this is just false labor, because he has to make a seminar presentation today," I said, and then arched my back and groaned with another pain.

By dawn, I was in hard labor. John came out for breakfast and I told him the pains were ten minutes apart. "Geez," he said, just shaking the sleep off. "I'll get dressed and we'll head out."

As soon as we got to the hospital, the nurse sent me to the restroom to relieve myself before being prepped for the delivery. Never in my life had I felt so physically miserable. The pain from labor and from the tissue damage the doctor had caused with the manual dilation was so intense that I passed out on the restroom floor. A nurse found me several minutes later.

The delivery was excruciating. Nick's birth had been much easier—I was up and walking an hour after I delivered him. But, after this birth, I couldn't even sit up.

When we returned to our trailer five days later with our tiny Lee Whitfield Brucher, I was still in pain. I knew it wasn't caused by hemorrhoids, as the nurses had tried to explain, but from that substitute doctor's brutality. I had to take Darvon every three hours for two weeks before the pain let up. If Mother hadn't been there to lend a hand, I don't know how I would have managed.

Meanwhile, John was going out with his friends almost nightly. Sometimes one guy or another I'd never seen before would come to pick John up. This stranger would become a witness to the barrage of angry questions I'd fling at my husband: "Why can't you spend evenings at home with us? Why do you need to go out every night? Aren't we important to you?" When I got no response or reaction from John, I'd call him names, question his manhood, and scream at him, all to no avail. He and his friend wouldn't seem fazed, just impatient to get out of there. And that's what was most hurtful of all.

Mother never said anything. She stayed in the bedroom with the babies, keeping them distracted from the discord.

When Mother had to return to Long Island, I pleaded with her to stay. "I'll be so lonely," I said. "I'll never be able to take care of Nick and Whit by myself, and I won't have anyone to talk to."

"I wish I could stay and help for a few more days," she sympathized, "but I can't take anymore time off from my job."

In the evenings when I had both boys sleeping, I would sit and wonder what had happened. *Who is this person I have become? Who is this man I married?* I felt desperate and helpless. *What can I do?* Sometimes the old John showed through when he held me at night and we talked. I loved that John so. But by morning he was gone and this other John was here for the day. The glimpses of the man I loved grew fewer.

When Whit was six weeks old, we returned to Valdosta, to the house that now—after we'd been cramped in the trailer—seemed spacious and beautiful. The renters had left it clean and ready for us. My spirits lifted. Although John's excessive drinking and his Friday nights out continued, at least I now had friends and neighbors and my own home again.

Spring arrived and I bought a plastic wading pool for Nick to play in on the back patio. Whenever John and I talked, we avoided touchy topics. We made love often, and though it almost felt like our life was okay, it really wasn't. It didn't feel like we were a family. John didn't seem to care when one of the boys was sick, stuffy with a cold and running a high fever. He didn't play with them, bathe them,

or even seem aware of them. I tried to discuss this with
him, but he'd say, "They're just babies. Mothers take care
of babies. I'll spend time with them when they're old
enough to play ball." When John was home, he spent his
time staring at the chess board on the coffee table, figuring
out moves, oblivious to the family activity around him. He
was little more than a piece of furniture to clean around.

One Sunday afternoon, I was waiting for John to return
from a four-day training class in Montgomery. He'd said
he'd be home in time for us to go to our Sunday night Unitarian group meeting. I had freshly baked cookies to take
with us for the refreshment. The boys and I were dressed
and ready. When he came through the door—thirty minutes
later than I'd anticipated—he headed right for the bathroom
to get cleaned up. Trying to make use of the time, I started
unpacking his suitcase. While dropping the dirty laundry
into a pile on the floor, I saw a very obvious lipstick mark
on the collar of a white shirt. "What is lipstick doing on
your shirt?" I asked, walking to the open bathroom door
and holding the collar out to him. He glanced at it and then,
to my amazement, proceeded to tell me the story.

"I was at the O'Club having a few drinks one night
when a song came on I really liked, so I asked one of the
two women at the next table to dance. After a few dances,
she told me her friend had left without her and she didn't
have a way to get home, so I offered to take her. I walked
her to her front door to make sure she was safe, and in the
doorway she let her dress drop to the floor and was standing there in her slip. I went in and had sex with her, but realized I shouldn't have and got right up afterward, told her
she'd never see me again, and left."

John's explanation for the lipstick was delivered in a
matter-of-fact tone, as though he felt he'd handled the
situation with this woman well and expected me to say I

was proud of him.

I was in such a state of shock that I didn't talk to anyone at our church meeting. I'm sure our friends suspected we'd had a quarrel. But what we'd had seemed more like a disaster. I was stunned that he could have sex with another woman and then deliver the information to me so casually.

Part of me wanted to take the boys and leave John, yet I couldn't bear to break up our family. *Nothing matters as much as staying together. The boys can't be taken from their father. There has to be a way to work things out. Anyway, where would we go?*

On a Saturday morning, only four months after Whit was born, I became enraged at John about his Friday nights away from home.

"I deserve a night out and I don't want to hear about it anymore," he said, too calmly.

"How can I sleep when I know you're drinking and driving? It's so unfair!" I screamed. His calmness infuriated me. I reached out and grabbed what was close—what John most prized—a small factory model of the T-38 jet trainer, and smashed it to the floor.

John looked in disbelief at the pieces, and then at me. He stepped toward me and slapped my face, hard and repeatedly with both of his open hands. I ran to the wing chair in the den and drew my legs up, wrapped my arms around them, pressed my face against my knees, and cowered in that fetal position.

John followed me, and his fury had him breathing hard. His slaps turned to punches. My head and shins took the brunt of the battering. It went on for several minutes, until John had exhausted himself and walked off.

I couldn't catch my breath to even sob. I feared he would return. I sat trembling, and then felt a tender touch on my arm. I peered out and saw my little Nick. *Where have you been during all this?* He looked into my wet face and said in his barely understandable toddler talk, "Daddy still loves you, Mommy."

Moving like a zombie, my head and shins throbbing, I got out of the chair and walked to the phone to call Mother. I told her the boys and I were on our way. "I can't explain now, but I need to come," I said in a low voice. Then I called the airport and made flight reservations. I called a cab and quickly packed a few things, mostly baby necessities. I noticed John watching from the bedroom doorway, looking almost confused, as though he didn't know what had happened, but he said nothing.

My shins were already covered with fist-size bruises. My head was too sore to touch.

I had to make two trips out to the cab. The first was with two suitcases, a diaper bag and my purse. Next, I held Nick by the hand and carried Whit in his infant seat.

At the airport, I could barely manage. An airport employee helped me get everything up the escalator and to our gate. Whit cried nonstop on the plane, but I was so lost in a fog of pain and confusion that I was unable to soothe him. The flight seemed endless.

Mother didn't want to drive two hours to meet us at the La Guardia Airport, so we took the airport shuttle to Brookhaven, on the eastern end of Long Island. She met us at the shuttle stop and gave us quick hugs. Taking one of the suitcases while corralling Nick, she asked "Would you like to get a bite out or go to my place and have soup?"

"Mother, I can't make any decisions. My mind isn't working and I'm totally exhausted."

She drove us to her apartment where we hungrily ate her homemade vegetable soup. We got the boys bathed and ready for bed. Nick slept in Mother's room; I shared a room with Whit.

I felt such despair and sadness that I'm not sure how the week passed. I slowly filled Mother in on what had happened, and she advised, "If you get a divorce, you have every right to keep the boys."

Mother arranged for a babysitter one night, and we went to a stage play at a local theater-in-the-round. After the play we went to an Italian restaurant a half-block from the theatre where we sat in a booth and talked over dinner. With a smile playing on her face, she told me about a man she was dating, someone she had known professionally since they'd worked together in the late forties. John Mertie was a prominent geologist who worked for the U. S. Geological Survey. "I think we'll probably get married soon," she said almost shyly.

I focused on Mother's news and on my boys, and by the end of the week I was beginning to feel almost human again. But, whenever I tried to comb or brush my hair I was painfully reminded of the beating—my head was bruised and lumpy all over.

John phoned nightly:

"I love all three of you and I want us to be together again," he said.

"I bought a lullaby record for the boys, and I have a surprise for you," he said.

"Please come home," he finally begged.

I didn't trust that things would change, but the boys and I couldn't stay at Mother's indefinitely.

We returned to Valdosta, and for a while things seemed to be better. John even went for a couple of weeks without drinking, but soon gave in to the coaxing of his friends to "just have a couple." But it was never just a couple, so we were back in the same hopeless situation and I had no idea how to change it.

CHAPTER EIGHTEEN

In the summer of 1967, as the pilot training class that John was instructing neared its end, assignments to Vietnam started coming down for both students and instructors. At the first social gathering with spouses at the officers club after the pilots received their assignments, there was an undercurrent of anxiety. A couple of the wives, who believed the assignments their husbands had received were riskier than others, went from one pilot to another, pleading for someone to switch. They approached the bachelor officers first. I heard one of the wives say, "We have little children, and if something terrible should happen to you, God forbid, it wouldn't affect a whole family." He just moved away from her without saying anything. She moved on to the other unmarried pilots—apparently unaware that she was asking them to devalue their own lives—but got no takers. The husbands of these wives did nothing to stop them. Everyone understood the fear and stress provoking their panicky crusade.

John and I just watched. I didn't think it was possible to trade assignments. It seemed to me that *all* assignments in a war zone were dangerous.

John would be in a fighter squadron at Korat Air Base in Thailand, flying bombing missions in the F-105 Thunderchief over North Vietnam. The 105 was euphemistically known as the "Thud" because of the sound it was said to make when it impacted the ground. When the plane was new, it had a bad safety record, and though it had improved over time, the nickname stuck.

It would be more than a year before John was to leave for his tour of duty in Thailand. Prior to his departure date of September, 1968, he had to go through six months of training in the F-105, beginning in February, at McConnell Air Force Base in Wichita, Kansas.

"I got a one-year power of attorney for you," John told me one day. "It will become active on the day I leave for Vietnam. If you need to sell the car or make other decisions while I'm gone, you'll have the legal right to do those things. I also increased my life insurance so there would be enough money for you to stay home with Nick and Whit until they are both in school, should something happen to me." I felt he was being very caring to provide for us in these ways.

The thought of John in a war zone terrified me. But John's attitude seemed more an eager anticipation of a scary adventure.

At home, he was spending more time with Nick and Whit, but sometimes he didn't understand that at the ages of one-and-a-half and three, their abilities were limited. He would chide them for not kicking or throwing a ball better. One day he lifted them both into their red wagon and gave them a fast ride around our cul-de-sac. Whit fell out and his elbows and knees were skinned up and bleeding and he was wailing. I ran to Whit and picked him up, then scolded John: "They're too little for that! You've *got* to be more careful."

"You baby them too much," he replied. "They need to toughen up – and Whit needs to learn to hang on tighter. He threw up his hands and turned away. "I give up," he said.

I'd been pleased that John was spending time with the

boys, but I felt he was often too rough with them, which could cause them to get hurt even more seriously. *Is John right? Am I babying them too much?* I wondered. *Should I not interfere if playtime with their father gets too rough?*

* * * * *

During the summer and fall months our lives seemed slow-paced and routine. John's parents invited us to spend Christmas and all of January with them in Oregon, before we went on to Wichita.

As the holiday approached, I stayed busy sorting clothing and packing gifts we would take to Clatskanie, and clothing and household goods we would pack separately for Kansas. The Vietnam cloud hung over me, but I was determined to push it away and make this last interlude before John's departure a happy time.

Christmas with the Bruchers was relaxing for all of us. They kept a fire crackling in their living room fireplace, and good smells came from the kitchen.

The boys played with toys Mom had bought for them: Matchbox cars, Tonka trucks, and brightly colored plastic boats and ducks for splashing in the tub. Occasionally, Dad Brucher would get gruff with them in his own "affectionate" way. Once, he gave Whit a hard knuckle-rap on the head for getting into something off-limits. Whit, startled by this reprimand, started to scream. Mom scolded Dad and I grabbed Whit and angrily ran upstairs. *Dad's too rough, just like John*, I thought as I comforted Whit.

I watched through the window as Dad Brucher displayed the American flag from a bracket on the front porch each morning—standing there quietly for a moment, lost in private thought or prayer.

Friends, neighbors, and relatives from the area dropped

215

by from time to time to wish us all a Merry Christmas and stay for a toast "to good times ahead." Mom prepared delicious meals, and John kept going into the kitchen to dip a finger in a pot or steal a nibble before she shooed him out by flapping her apron at him, obviously flattered that he still loved her cooking.

One morning, as Mom and I were preparing breakfast, she paused before dropping more bread in the toaster and said, "I'll call on the weekends to see how you're doing, once John leaves."

John and I had overdone it on Christmas shopping. His parents were aghast at the pile of presents under the tree, spreading out across the living room floor. We spent the morning opening gifts and hauling off piles of wrapping. "We have never received so many presents," Mom said, beaming. "You shouldn't have done so much." I wished I could have done more to thank them for their love and kindness, and making us feel so welcome.

In the five years we'd been married, I'd worked on improving John's wardrobe. So, just as Mom set some steaming side dishes on trivets on the dining room table for Christmas dinner, John appeared wearing a new olive drab wool suit Mom had never seen. She just stood there smiling at him, tears brimming. Then, using the ruffle of her apron to daub her eyes, she said, "I've never seen you look so handsome, Johnny, not even in your uniform." Sniffling, she returned to the kitchen to carry out the turkey platter.

When we were all seated, we raised our glasses of wine and Dad offered a toast: "Here's to John's successful mission and to his safe return," Dad said, his voice cracking. We were all apprehensive about John's tour of duty, but—because we wanted to keep a festive spirit—we didn't discuss it at length.

January seemed to fly by. Mom cooked meals she knew

John loved. I cleaned up after her as we visited in the kitchen. The boys played catch outside and took walks with Grandpa. Evenings were spent watching the boys play and talking about our post-Vietnam plans.

All too soon we were back on the road and heading to Wichita. We were packed tightly in the VW Squareback we'd purchased just before leaving home, but the closeness was comforting to me. I didn't know what the future held for my family, but right now we were together in a safe cocoon.

* * * * *

Our unfurnished apartment in Wichita reminded me of the apartment we had back in Chandler, right after we got married. It was light and airy, with sliding glass doors that opened onto a long, narrow deck overlooking a grassy area that surrounded a fenced swimming pool. The apartment buildings formed a rectangle around the pool, and the parking lot was on the outside perimeter of the complex.

Trip and Carrie, another Air Force couple, were our downstairs neighbors. Trip was also a pilot in F-105 training for Vietnam. They had only been married a year and had no children. Their bedroom was directly under our boys' room. John and I worried that this would be a problem since our boys awoke at dawn and started playing with their heavy maple blocks on the oak floors, constructing roadways and bridges for their Matchbox cars. Collapsing structures would echo into the apartment below. When I apologized to Carrie for the awful racket and said we would buy a rug to muffle the noise, she said, "It's not a problem for us, Sally. After the first morning we got earplugs to wear to bed and now we don't hear a thing."

Whit had his second birthday shortly after we arrived

in Wichita. We invited Trip and Carrie up for cake and they brought Whit a two-foot long truck filled with plastic soldiers and military gear. Whit was more excited about this gift than anything else and played with it all day.

One month later, in March 1968, Trip was killed in a training mission. John and I stayed with Carrie through the night, mixing drinks and talking with her, until her mother arrived in the morning. Their apartment was vacated in two days. Trip's death changed John. He didn't share his feelings anymore and lost his cocky, invincible attitude.

John read to the boys every night, sitting between them on the orange tweed rental sofa, still wearing his flight suit after a day of flying. Nick and Whit—freshly bathed, blond hair tousled and damp, comfy in their pastel Dr. Denton footed pajamas—listened attentively. What a sight!

John reading to Nick and Whit – 1968

One night, after I'd tucked the boys into their beds, John said, "I have an idea, Sally. Why don't you shop for storybooks you think the boys would like and buy two of each book? That way I can read to them on tape and send it to you to play for them while they look at the other copy at home?"

"That's a great idea!" I said. I loved that he'd come up with it on his own.

The next time I went to the Base Exchange, I bought about a dozen soft cover and Golden books, two of each: *Billy and the Big Red Ball*, *Trucks Do a Big Job*, *The Mole Family*, and other early childhood books with colorful pictures.

John taught me how to operate the Wollensak tape player/recorder and how to use the large electric magnet he bought to erase each tape so it could be reused. He told me to be especially sure to do this with each tape he sent for *my* ears only, because he might be telling me things he didn't want anyone else to know.

John started coming home later during that summer in Wichita. I often walked around the apartment complex with the boys while we waited for him to get home. One day, to our surprise, we saw our car in the parking lot. "Daddy, Daddy!" the boys chanted, but we didn't see John anywhere. We headed back home, thinking we had missed him along the way, but he didn't come in the door for another hour. I wondered where he'd been, but I knew not to ask. *Don't imagine things*, I told myself, *this has to be a stress-free time.*

Sometimes John would go out for walks late in the evening after the boys were in bed, and I couldn't leave them to go with him. I was curious about this and tried to sound casual when I inquired. He dismissed my questions by saying, "I just need to clear my mind." I understood that he had a lot going on—leaving his family to go to war—but because of his nights out in Valdosta, I wasn't completely trusting.

One evening, after John left for one of his walks, I asked a neighbor to stay with the boys for an hour while I ran an errand. As I walked the dark grounds that warm spring night, everyone in the complex had their windows open. I could hear televisions going and children crying. I could smell dinners cooking and freshly popped popcorn. Suddenly, I was stopped by a voice—John's voice—coming from a lighted window in a basement apartment. I crouched in the dark to see who was with him. John was sitting in a chair across from a sofa on which a young woman lounged. From what little I could hear, they were having a philosophical conversation. Nothing obviously sexual was going on. If I moved closer, the light from the window would hit me, or the bushes in front of the window would rustle. *Who is she? How does he know her? He should be home with me, talking with me. He should be honest with me.* I couldn't keep lurking to see if anything would happen; I had to get back to relieve the babysitting neighbor. I walked back to the apartment feeling neglected and betrayed.

John arrived home almost an hour later. I didn't tell him I'd left the apartment. My mind filled with cautionary thoughts. *He'll be leaving soon to risk his life for our country. I mustn't quarrel with him. I can't be causing upsets.* My heart ached with unasked questions. I clung to him in bed that night, hoping he'd feel in his heart my claim on him, hoping he would need and love me in return.

* * * * *

We left Wichita in August to head home to Valdosta. We'd have another month together before John had to leave

220

for Thailand. That gave John enough time to teach me to operate the power lawn mower, instruct me on what to do if any of several household emergencies should arise, and fill me in on our investments and insurance policies. I had always written the checks for the monthly bills, so when John asked how much I would need each month to run the house, I added them up and told him it came to about $450. He made an allotment for that amount to go into our checking account each month. The rest of his pay—I didn't know how much—would go to John. (Later on, after John had flown off to the war, I realized I hadn't figured in clothes for me or the boys, gifts for family birthdays, or house and car maintenance and repair. So it became a struggle each month to make ends meet.)

Before John left, I got Nick enrolled in a nursery school for four-year-olds that met three mornings a week. That gave me a welcome break from my rambunctious Nick and allowed me some one-on-one time with my quieter, less demanding, two-year-old Whit.

On the day of John's departure, we drove solemnly to the Valdosta Airport. The boys didn't understand the length of time their daddy would be gone, how very far away Vietnam was, or the risk involved. During the past week we had tried to explain, without scaring them, so they'd know why Daddy wouldn't be coming home at night and wouldn't be reading to them on the sofa before bedtime. "Daddy is going far away, but he's going to think about us all the time," I'd told them. "He's going to protect America and we're very proud of him, aren't we?"

"Uh huh," both had said, nodding.

Now, as we waited for John's flight, I had to hold my emotions in check. The boys chased each other about the small airport.

When the flight was announced, I clung to John,

"Please be safe. We love you so much. Don't take any un-necessary risks." He had to unwrap my arms from his neck so that he could board the plane.

"I love you and the boys, Sally," he said, holding my hand before turning to leave.

"Wave bye-bye to Daddy, Nick and Whit," I told them.

They gave their funny little waves and said, "Bye, Daddy." Their perfect innocence tore at me.

Rain began to fall on the way home. Later, as I stood with the boys at the front window watching the steady driz-zle, I felt an inner chill and the same deep loneliness I'd experienced riding on the bus that took me from my foster home. If I didn't have the boys, my life would be empty. Looking down at them standing on either side of me, I pulled them close, feeling our lives would never be the same. We stood there, looking out at the rain and gray sky for a long time.

* * * * *

The first week after John left, I framed an 8x10 black-and-white photograph of him wearing his flight suit and standing by an F-105. I hung it low on the pale-blue wall in the boys' room, near their framed posters of aircraft and spacecraft. I wanted Daddy to stay fresh in their minds. For them, at ages two and four, a year would be a very long time.

Routine was what mattered; it would see us through. I played with the boys, ran errands with them, and taught them the colors, letters, and numbers. I fed them, read to them, and bathed them. I kept my days busy so time would speed by and John would be home again. But the house felt hollow, and I had nothing to look forward to at the end of each day. I worried constantly about John.

"Daddy is going to read to you now," I told the boys every night after they were ready for bed. They'd climb into the same gold wing-chair, sitting side by side, and I'd put the book on their laps so they could look at the pictures as they listened to another tape from John.

"Hi boys, can you say hi to Daddy?" John always began.

"Hi Daddy!" they'd say. My chin might quiver, but I'd keep smiling.

"This is the story of the big red ball. Do you see the ball on the cover? Can you put your finger on the ball?" And they would both touch the ball. "Now turn the page."

After they were in bed, I'd listen to the tapes John had sent for my ears only and then record tapes to send back to him. We sent each other a letter and four or five half-hour voice tapes every day, so I spent each evening "talking" to him. Together we counted his missions and the days left until his return. John sometimes felt disillusioned by what was going on over there. He told me that he had been sent out to bomb a small pick-up truck on a dirt road and felt the risk to him from hidden ground fire was too great for a bombing so inconsequential. "Erase this tape right after you finish listening to it, Sally. Always do that." He was intensely patriotic and worried that—in allowing himself to question such orders—he was being disloyal to his country.

After hours of listening to John's tapes, erasing them, and recording tapes to send back to him, I would go to bed and try to dream of happy times to come after the war, but I usually dreamt of nightmarish events: bombs exploding, planes blowing up mid-air, screams, wounded men on stretchers, Vietnamese yelling in their unfamiliar language. Sometimes I would dream that I was in the underground bomb shelter at St. Christopher's again, a little girl, swaying on the wooden benches.

I'd awaken in the mornings, still tired, to sounds of the boys in the kitchen. One morning Nick was pouring milk on Whit's cereal and had spilled some on the table. "Thanks for helping, Nick," I said, smoothing his tousled bangs. "You're a good boy."

"But I spilled," he said with a worried look.

"Well, get the cloth and wipe it up." And so another day without John would begin.

* * * * *

Our days were still largely focused on John's return, and many of our sentences began, "When Daddy comes home...."

Sometimes I became moody, wondering about what my relationship with John would be when we were together again. I believed his drinking was at the root of most of our problems, that if he stopped drinking he would be faithful and we would have the marriage we'd always hoped for. We discussed this on our tapes and John agreed to cut back on his drinking because he wanted our marriage to be better. I knew it was easy for him to be agreeable in these conversations, when he didn't need to take any immediate action, but in my heart I trusted that we would work everything out when he returned.

The days went by faster if I kept busy. I made clothes for myself and the boys. I mowed, weeded, edged, and raked the yard. I took the boys to YMCA swimming classes three times a week, and I always kept the house organized and clean. And once a week I'd drive the VW Squareback up on our front lawn, under the shade tree, to wash and wax it.

I surprised myself with my handiness when I sanded down the boys' rusted wagon and gave it a fresh coat of red

Rustoleum paint. I built a large plywood box for the boys' maple blocks and painted it light blue to match their room. I gathered all our family portraits, as far back as the great-grandparents on both John's side of the family and mine, and—over time, as I could afford it—had them framed. A portrait of John and me on our wedding day was at the center of the wall collage over our bed, with generations of family photos surrounding us.

I went to our church group and taught Sunday school. I joined the Waiting Wives, a group of Moody AFB women waiting for their husbands to return from Vietnam. I took the boys to the base nursery so I could work as a Red Cross volunteer at the base hospital two mornings a week.

My personality was slowly changing. I felt a need to be decisive and in charge. I could no longer afford to be dependent and compliant. I was becoming stronger and more confident, the way I had been when I moved away from Mother to go to college.

Since I had always loved expressing myself through my poetry, I decided to write a book of children's poems, at the rate of one poem for every mission John flew. He'd told me on a recent tape that a pilot with one hundred missions could come home even before his year of deployment was up. My book would have one hundred poems. Perhaps I could get it published and dedicate it to John.

In addition to the children's poems, I wrote poems that expressed my loneliness and love for John.

A poem I wrote on October 4, 1968 began:

It's October
A meadow of clover, a sea of mist,
It's been a month since I've been kissed.
A month with no touching, caressing has gone,
A month without my husband, John.....

For the Christmas holidays, the boys and I visited my sister's family in Chapel Hill, North Carolina, where she and Bob were getting master's degrees at the University of North Carolina. As we trekked across the snowy campus one afternoon, Whit stepped out of one of his expensive corrective shoes. We had to search snow banks for over an hour before we found it. We helped Nan, Bob, and Tam decorate their tree and helped prepare food to entertain their friends who dropped by for a holiday visit.

"Uncle Bob taught me how to shave," Nick said excitedly on Christmas morning, with shaving cream still in front of his ears. The toy shaving kit had been one of Nan and Bob's gifts to him.

My sister, who rarely mends, had saved of pile of mending for me to work on as we caught up with each other. The holiday with Nan and her family was just what the boys and I needed to get us through what might have been a lonely and depressing holiday.

* * * * *

By January of 1969, John had flown fifty-five missions. Like many of the pilots, he had a moss-green Australian bush hat on which he marked each of his missions. We were more than halfway through the countdown. The end was in sight. *When John comes home......we will be a family again, he will go to graduate school, we will move to a new place, and we will all be happy.* I smiled thinking of that.

John was due for his ten-day R&R (rest and relaxation). Most of the pilots' wives I knew were meeting their husbands in Hawaii for the R&R, either leaving children with grandparents or taking them along, but John wanted to come home to see the boys, knowing we couldn't all afford to fly to Hawaii.

I would have loved a trip to Hawaii. I wished for a break from mothering and a chance to get to know my husband again. I dreamed of drinking mai tais on a sunny beach lined with palm trees. But this was John's R&R, and if coming home would relax and restore him, that's what we'd do. I desperately wanted to make his too-brief stay everything he wanted it to be.

At the airport, John greeted us with hugs and kisses. "It's good to be home," he said. "The boys have grown so big!"

We went to a friend's party on a Saturday night and to the Unitarian Church group on Sunday night. We walked around our yard, and around the neighborhood holding the boys' hands and talking about how things had changed while he'd been gone.

"Those houses hadn't been built before I left," John said, pointing to a half-block of new homes. "I'm surprised so many people have For Sale signs out. I guess transfers to new assignments play a part in that."

At home, the boys wouldn't quit clinging to him. They showed him every toy, and shared every bit of little boy news.

"Guess what, Daddy," Nick said, tugging at John's hand and looking up at him, "Bryan's daddy went to the war, too. He *told* me!"

"And Daddy, and Daddy...." Whit said, wanting to chime in with some news but not able to think of anything as important as Nick's news.

When John and I were alone, I clung to him as much as the boys did. We snuggled on the sofa one evening, without speaking. But I smiled at the visions I had of being a closer family when the war was over, with John more involved. *Things will be so much better*. I leaned against his chest as he played some of his mood tapes on the Wollensak.

Whenever Rhapsody in Blue played, it reminded me of our dating days and how we'd looked forward to a life together.

Too soon, we had to take John to the airport. I didn't want to let him go. *It's not fair to allow him to come home and then take him away again.*

"Why do you have to go, Daddy?" Nick asked, confused and sad. I remembered myself at their age, asking Mother if she could stay at boarding school with me. I'd hoped my children wouldn't have to feel the insecurity of a parent leaving them. I wanted them to have a happy, normal childhood—a whole family. My heart ached, and I prayed John would come home safely to us once again.

This time the boys stayed close by John's side at the airport instead of running around. He picked them both up and hugged them. He held me for one last kiss. I closed my eyes and savored the moment.

Forty-five missions to go.

PART TWO

CHAPTER NINETEEN

The night seemed endless as I awaited word of John's rescue. I paced between the front window and the kitchen wall phone, willing it to ring. But each anxious hour passed without any news. *They're too busy rescuing him to call me.*

I went through the motions of our morning routine, trying not to let the boys see my anxiety. Luckily, Nick and Whit were eager to get back to their room to play with the toys Whit had received for his third birthday, just two days earlier. Once they finished their cereal, they raced each other down the hallway to start playing.

By mid-morning, my heart was pounding and beating irregularly. I wondered if I could be having a heart attack. *I need to stay calm. John will be okay. When they rescue him, they'll let him come home and we'll all hug and laugh, feel safe, and be grateful to be together as a family again.*

Shortly after noon, when the boys were playing in a neighbor's backyard, another navy blue Air Force car pulled into our driveway. As I watched through the front window, the officer—a colonel—stepped out of the car and came up the walk. *John has been rescued!* As the officer reached the front door, I held my breath in anticipation and flung the door open. *Oh my God, he's not smiling! I can't bear it.*

I moved aside without saying anything and he stepped into the living room. He motioned toward the sofa for me to sit down. He sat across from me on the other sofa and placed some papers on the coffee table. He folded his hands in his lap, and simply looked at me. All the lines in his face drooped downward. When he finally spoke, his voice was so soft that I had to lean toward him to catch every word: "The rescue team saw only a limp parachute in the tree where Captain Brucher landed. There was no electronic signal from his equipment to identify his location. There was enemy ground fire in the area, so the rescue aircraft couldn't land. It is assumed that your husband was captured, but since we don't know this for sure, he will continue to be listed as Missing in Action."

I was silent.

In my mind I pictured John hiding in the brush, listening to the foreign-speaking enemy closing in on him, afraid any movement he made would attract them. I wanted the rescue chopper to land, fighting back the enemy with their own fire, and find John.

The colonel said I needn't worry about finances. "Captain Brucher made sure that you and your children would be taken care of in this event, Mrs. Brucher." He said that in the next day or two an Air Force finance officer would call to set up a time to come to the house to explain the details. "Your Air Force family is available to help in any way we can."

I seemed to have lost the ability to function, or even think. I felt as though I needed someone to take me by the hand and say, "Do this, Sally," and, "Now do that."

The officer stood and asked me if I would like him to stay while I made calls to friends and family—the Air Force would pay for any long distance charges, he said. But I wanted to be alone. Although I managed to see him to the door, I couldn't bring myself to thank him for delivering the news. Before stepping outside, he turned to me and briefly placed his hand on my shoulder. Then turned away and walked to his car.

As I slowly closed the door, my skin began to tingle from my scalp to my feet, as if my whole body had gone numb and was now regaining sensation. I shuddered as the latch clicked.

Mother was the first person I called. I wanted her to take emergency leave from her job and fly out immediately to be with me, to hold and comfort me and help me think clearly in my time of devastation. I was just her child again and I needed her love and support.

"Sally, is that you?" she barely recognized my quivery voice.

"Mom, John's plane was shot down and he's missing." Tears ran down my face. "He landed in his parachute in North Vietnam, alive, but now they can't find him."

There was a long pause on her end before she said, "I'd be a hypocrite if I said I cared, because I never liked him."

The words sliced through me. Suddenly, the receiver was too heavy to hold anymore and I hung up without saying goodbye. I stood there as though I was frozen in ice. The tingling sensation increased. I felt electrified.

Then it dawned on me; Mother didn't like John because he had beaten me, and I'd had to flee to her house with the boys to get away from him.

But I need you! I wanted to scream. I had always yearned for my mother's love. *Why couldn't she be here...for me?*

That call was the last contact I had with Mother for twenty years. Yet, my aching need for her was always there.

Still standing at the beige wall phone in the kitchen, I

realized that I had to be strong. Life must go on. The words I'd said to myself as a little girl in boarding school returned to me: *I am my family. Wherever I go, my family will go. I will never leave me.*

I didn't *have* a good mother, but I would *be* a good mother, and I would give my boys everything *I* had always wished for, telling them again and again that I love them and am proud of them. But I didn't know how to tell them about their father.

John was alive on the ground, they had radio contact with him. It's just a technicality that he's listed as MIA. He had to have been captured and taken to a prison camp. He will come home when the war is over, my inner voice assured me. *That's what I must tell the boys.*

When Nick and Whit got home, I sat them next to each other on the sofa and got down on my knees in front of them, reaching an arm around each of them.

"Boys, you know that Daddy has been away flying his jet in the war." They nodded, wide-eyed. "Daddy's jet crashed yesterday, but he got out okay in a parachute. The rescue men can't find him yet, but they're still looking. When they find him, they'll bring him home." As I said the word *home*, I almost lost it. I needed to cry, to scream, to protest!

The boys seemed unsure how to react. Was this good or bad news? I smiled and hugged them both and said cheerily, "So, we'll just stay busy and wait for them to find him, okay?" I told them they could go play while I prepared their lunch. They slid off the sofa and did a little hop-skip down the hallway. "And just because I love you so much," I called after them, "I'm going to fix something special."

A particular song always seemed stuck in my head during that time and no matter what I was doing around the house, I hummed or sang it. *Give Me a Kiss to Build a*

Dream. I sang it to Nick as he rode on top of the Electrolux vacuum cleaner. I sang it as I mowed the grass. And I hummed it that day as I prepared lunch for the boys— veggie sticks and chicken strips they could dip into a creamy salad dressing. I wondered what Nick and Whit were saying to each other when I wasn't with them. I was glad they had each other.

* * * * *

We were big news in the small town of Valdosta. A photographer from the *Valdosta Times* snapped some shots when I had the boys at their YMCA swimming lessons. Our pictures were in the newspaper along with John's.

In conferences I had with the boys' preschool teachers, I told them what was going on and asked them to watch for signs of distress. They told me that the other children had heard bits of news from their parents and repeated it to Nick and Whit:

"I know your Daddy got kilt."

"My mom said his airplane crashed and the bad men kilt him."

"He's just lost!" Nick said. "They're gonna find him and bring him home."

I knew these children weren't being mean; they were just sharing their information. But such comments were hurtful to my sons. They made Nick aggressive and Whit withdrawn.

"Daddy will come home when the war is over," I reassured them. It was a bold statement to make when I couldn't know for sure, but I felt the uncertainty of the situation was too much to expect such young children to understand.

When I watched President Nixon speak on the evening news, the boys knew to be very quiet because, as Nick told Whit, "Mommy is finding out when the war will be over and when Daddy will come home."

Two weeks after John's plane was shot down, an Air Force pickup truck delivered all of John's belongings to the house, in two large boxes. My neighbor, Piper, took the boys to her house to play with her girls and prepared their lunch. "Take all the time you need, Sally," she said. "The boys will be fine. I'll keep them busy till I hear from you."

I sat on the sofa for a while, looking at the boxes in front of me. I wanted to tear back the flaps, but I was afraid. Something seemed wrong. *John needs these clothes and belongings. What will he wear? They should be with him.*

I pulled the wide packaging tape from one box and hesitantly folded back the flaps. I took a deep breath as I looked in. *Calm, stay calm.* I lifted some of the folded clothing onto my lap. *Yes, these are John's things.* I pulled a white cotton undershirt from the pile and shook out its folds. I held it to my face and breathed in the smell. It had been laundered, but I could still detect the aftershave John wore, Old Spice. I remembered the undershirt's cotton-softness against John's chest. It brought his vivid presence to me. I could feel *him.* I cried into the t-shirt the wettest, saddest tears I'd ever cried.

For days after the boxes arrived, I could barely sleep or eat. I went through life in zombie mode. One morning, after taking the boys to nursery school, I stretched out on the sofa; lying there, I lost track of time. I don't know whether I slept or not; I only know John came to me. He wore the cotton undershirt and when he held me I could smell the Old Spice. I melted against him as he tenderly yet passion-ately made love to me. I felt his sweat, his strength, his need. When I so desperately needed someone to be there for me, John had come. It was too real to have been a dream.

* * * * *

There was one other MIA wife in town. Elizabeth was twenty-three and had been married to her husband for a very short time before he left for Vietnam. They had no children. Unlike John, her husband was not seen—or heard from in radio transmission from the ground—after his jet exploded in mid-air. But Elizabeth wasn't at all short on hope. She and I passed hours together talking about the future when our husbands were home again. "We'll start a family right away," she said, as though he'd be back any day.

Elizabeth and I would occasionally be called to the base to sit in a small, dimly lit room with some officers to view the latest news video of American prisoners being paraded or dragged through the streets of Hanoi, or being tortured. Elizabeth and I leaned close to the video to see the men's faces. "Let us know if you think you recognize one of them," an officer always told us, "and we'll freeze that frame so you can get a closer look."

Only rarely did one of us say, "Stop the film!" Then, with our faces close to the screen, we'd both stare at the captive's face in hope of recognition, but then shake our heads.

Because Elizabeth had no children and had moved in with her parents after her husband went MIA, she had the time and money to shop for clothes, have her hair and nails done, buy a new car, and come and go as she pleased. She usually came to visit without calling first, and always looked like a fashion plate. She would find me in old clothes washing the car, playing with the boys in the sprinkler, preparing a meal, or mowing the grass with the Silent Scott push mower while sweat dripped off me.

I continued to attend the Waiting Wives group. The membership grew as the war went on. More than ever I needed the companionship it offered. So, I was stunned when a wife in the group called one day to say I was no longer welcome.

"There was a young wife at the last meeting who just joined the group," she said, "and she was quite shaken to learn that your husband's plane had been shot down and that he's listed as MIA. She has been depressed and crying frequently since the meeting."

She went on to say, "Since your situation is so different from ours, the Waiting Wives feel it's not appropriate for you to attend future meetings." She paused before adding, "It is, after all, a social group for wives of men in Vietnam who *are* returning home at the end of their tour of duty. We want to keep the group upbeat and positive, and that's difficult to do with you present as a constant reminder of what could happen." Then she wished me well and we hung up.

One of my last lifelines had been cut. I was hurt by the exclusion. I couldn't form a POW/MIA wives' group because there were just two of us in Valdosta.

That spring and summer of 1969, I kept busy with yard work, an activity I'd always loved. I went to the local nursery and bought clay pots, potting soil, and bright red petunias to put in the window boxes on the front of our white brick house.

Piper cared for the boys when I needed a break. She knitted cardigan sweaters for Nick and Whit while they played with her daughters, Tracy and Nita. And now and then Piper and her husband, Steve, would invite me over for a cookout. At one of them, I laughingly mentioned that

Nick had become such a good climber. Although he was only four years old, he sometimes playfully hid from me in the high branches of our backyard tree. Steve immediately suggested that we build a tree house in that tree for all the kids to play in. "If you pay for the supplies," he said, "I'll come up with a design and build it." I loved the idea.

There was hammering from morning till evening that went on for days. We'd all take turns carrying cold drinks and snacks out to Steve. He'd laugh and take a break to talk to the kids about what he'd do next and when it would be completed. When I thanked Steve for being so generous, he said, "I'll be leaving for Vietnam soon, and I while I'm gone I would want someone to help my family."

The boys said they wanted to help me paint the tree house. They chose glossy red enamel. We put on our oldest clothes and went to work. By the time we finished, we were so paint-spattered that we could only point at each other and laugh.

Steve left for Vietnam a few months later and in less than a month after his departure his plane was hit by enemy fire. Steve didn't make it out alive. His little girls were three and five years old.

Since I was no longer making conversation tapes for John, I spent my evenings organizing a letter-writing campaign to help the POW/MIA cause. Once or twice a week, I'd invite a group of friends or neighbors to meet at my house. The letters informed people about the POW/MIA situation, told how many men were currently captive or missing, and asked the recipients to voice their concern by contacting our government representatives, whose contact information was listed below. We sent out as many letters as we could, using the slim Valdosta phone book for names and addresses.

We'd chat as we stuffed envelopes. I usually served

homemade almond or lemon cookies and glasses of Fresca with an orange slice floating in each glass. For me, a "social occasion" was anytime I was with adults. I needed adult conversation to help me stay sane and focused.

Sometimes we went around town together, distributing bumper stickers to various locations—"Remember our POW/MIA."

* * * * *

All during the months John had been missing, I kept in close contact with his parents by phone and letter. They had as much faith as I did that their son would be coming home after the war. It helped to share our optimism.

When Mom Brucher called one day, she asked, "What do you think of the idea of Dad and me coming to Valdosta for the winter?" She said they'd be glad to escape winter in Oregon and would like to help me care for Nick and Whit.

"How soon can you come?" I responded.

The boys would love having Grandma and Grandpa near us, and I wanted their company and help, too. At Mom's request, I found a very small furnished apartment for them, less than a mile from our house.

Welcoming them at the airport made the boys and me happier than we'd been in months. We had family now.

We took Mom and Dad to lease a car, and then lead the way to their apartment, which I'd already stocked with some food and drink, including a bottle of Bacardi rum, some limes, and Cokes for the Cuba Libres Mom always enjoyed in the evening. I told them I had a dinner planned. "We'll drive over after we get cleaned up, unpacked, and rested a bit," Mom said. We kept giving each other quick hugs because it felt so good to be together—all the people who loved John.

Now the Bruchers became regular babysitters for Nick and Whit whenever I had to be out in the evening at a church event or stuffing envelopes at someone else's house for the letter-writing campaign. When someone in my church group invited me to a New Year's Eve party, Mom and Dad fussed over me before I went and complimented me on how I looked. I felt loved, as if I was *their* daughter.

Sometimes they'd stay the night after babysitting. Mom would read to the boys before their bedtime, just as John had done. Then she and Dad would sleep on the sofa bed. The boys would run out to them in the morning, rousing them much earlier than their usual wake-up time. After the commotion of breakfast at our house, Mom and Dad were always happy to return to their own quiet apartment.

Dad assembled a train set in the boys' room with tracks, signs, shrubbery, and electrical lights and signals. Nick and Whit were a bit young to operate the trains without getting them derailed, but it was a good Grandpa activity.

Nick was a happy, energetic boy. He was motion without thought. When he played with his brother, with his friends, with his schoolmates, someone usually got hurt. Nick didn't mean to injure people; he just couldn't always control his boundless energy.

Whit suffered many injuries as a result of Nick careening around without paying attention. "How do you deal with that day in and day out?" friends asked.

"I'm used to it," I'd reply. "Nick has always been this way."

I corralled Nick when I could, but I couldn't prevent problems from arising. When he was at his friends' homes, he'd trample their flowers, toss game pieces about like confetti and jump on their beds, which he was never allowed to do at home. He was a terror on his tricycle, wagon, or feet.

Nick took so much of my attention that Whit, my

milder boy, started mimicking his brother's wild-child behavior.

My favorite time of day always came at the very end, when I could look at my little boys sleeping. With their damp blond hair peeking out from under the covers, they looked peaceful and angelic. In the quiet, I talked to John's sons in a voice they couldn't hear, telling them that although I hoped their daddy would come home to us, I just couldn't be certain. Tears clouded my vision and my heart broke for all of us. They had become my life and all its meaning. Sometimes my need for comfort and closeness was so great that I would awaken them, and I would tell them I was sorry I'd had to scold them that day for some misbehavior. I would hug them and tell them I loved them. And as I held their warm sleepy bodies, they would respond with a barely audible, "I love you, too, Mommy."

CHAPTER TWENTY

Almost two years after John's plane went down, the base wing commander contacted me with an offer to arrange for my boys to spend some time with a male officer. It would be a "big brother" type arrangement. I responded enthusiastically. The boys were now four and six, old enough to be away from me. The commander sent down a request for an officer to volunteer to devote occasional hours to "the two young sons of an Air Force captain who is Missing in Action." Captain Greg Mann responded to the request and called me to make arrangements to meet the boys and take them on an outing.

One Saturday a month, Greg came to the house to pick up Nick and Whit early in the morning, spend the day with them, and—in the late afternoon—return two very dirty, tired, and happy little boys. They went hiking, fishing, and did other *guy things*. After each such day to myself, I felt refreshed and renewed and eagerly awaited their return. The boys exploded with excited chatter the moment they were in the door.

One time, they went fishing but didn't catch any fish, so they came back with a five-gallon bucket of water lilies. As Greg left, I thanked him again for giving his time to make them happy. "They're great little guys," he said. "I'm glad to help."

All through dinner Nick and Whit filled me in on their day, both talking at the same time.

"And Captain Mann had fishing poles for us..." Whit said before Nick interrupted.

"They were really neat ones you wind up!"

"But we didn't catch any fish, so we brought you the flowers," Whit glanced at me to see if I'd fully appreciated the surprise.

Through their bath time I was still getting their nonstop accounts of adventure, even as fatigue began to catch up with them. They fell asleep before I finished the bedtime story. Their happiness amazed me. It sprang from something I couldn't give them— the chance to enjoy time with an adult male for the first time in over two years.

As it turned out, however, the boys would have only five of these monthly outings with Greg before the boys and I moved to New Mexico to live near my sister and her husband, who had now resettled in Albuquerque.

"Bob will be a good male role model in the boy's lives," Nan had said. I'd been getting similar advice—that I should move from Valdosta and live closer to family— from many people who cared about us, including John's friends and members of our church group. I'd been tempted by the idea, but delayed action on it because I thought John would want to return to the familiarity of our home in Valdosta, the place he'd surely yearned for since he'd been gone.

Go or stay? It was such a dilemma that I lost my appetite and started losing weight rapidly. I also experienced flutters in my chest, as though hundreds of wildly flapping butterflies were trapped inside. I wished there was a door in my chest that I could open to release them. The sensation was so unnerving that I saw a doctor.

"What you are experiencing is called tachycardia and

it's brought on by stress," said the Air Force doctor, who didn't know me or my situation. "It's not a serious condition, but you need to find a way to eliminate some of the stress from your life if you're going to get relief."

That's when I decided to heed all the advice I'd been given and began making plans for the move. I talked to a realtor and to a base attorney about selling the house. I learned from them that because my power of attorney had already expired and the house was in John's name, it would have to be auctioned off on the courthouse steps. Fortunately, I wouldn't have to be present for the sale.

A base representative told me the Air Force would make arrangements to ship our household goods and our car to Albuquerque, and send the boys and me there on a commercial flight. And after we were settled in a new home, the Air Force would fly the boys and me to Oregon for a short visit with John's parents before school started.

I still wasn't convinced that moving was the right thing to do, but I did know that my nerves were shot and that I couldn't lose any more weight. I was almost down to one hundred pounds, which was what I weighed when I left my foster home as a nine-year-old.

The day before we were to leave, the movers packed up and loaded our household goods into the moving van. I had cleaned each room as it was emptied.

Greg Mann's wife, Lynn, called to invite us to have dinner at their home that night. We would get to meet Greg and Lynn's baby daughter, Michelle. It was Nick's seventh birthday, so Lynn suggested I bring a cake for dessert. When the boys and I arrived, Greg left to pick up take-out barbecue ribs and brisket while I visited with Lynn and the boys played with Michelle. That evening of relaxed conversation at their home was a pleasant distraction from the thought of boarding a plane to leave, perhaps forever, the place where I'd lived longer than anywhere else.

After that dinner, the boys and I stayed in a motel close to the airport. Our flight was early the next morning, so I arranged for a wake-up call and scheduled a cab ride to the airport. As I lay in the motel bed waiting for sleep to come, sadness overwhelmed me. Although I'd lived in Valdosta for more than seven years, and the boys had lived here all their lives, no one had offered to see us off; no one would shed a tear at our departure or just wave goodbye. We would be gone as though we'd never been here.

I was awakened the next morning by a knock on the door. I leaped from the bed, thinking it must be the cab, and that we had missed the wake-up call. I asked who it was as I looked through the peephole—and saw Greg.

"I couldn't just let a cab take you to the airport," he explained through the door. I was touched by his kindness—and the boys were delighted to hear that their friend, Captain Mann, had arrived. He waited in his car while I called to cancel the cab and the boys and I hurried to get dressed and packed up.

On the ride to the airport I felt oddly relaxed. Greg would see us off and my brother-in-law would be at the airport to meet us. I was relieved to have such support. The boys asked Greg if he would come visit them.

"That would be nice," Greg answered, vaguely.

After checking our luggage inside the airport terminal, we walked outside to board the plane. We each gave Greg a quick hug before climbing the steps to board the plane that warm July morning. Greg stayed and waved as our plane rolled away. The boys waved back through the porthole window.

* * * * *

We arrived in Albuquerque on July 8th, 1971, one day after Nick's seventh birthday and almost three years after John left for Vietnam.

Bob met us at the airport and took us to his and Nan's home near the Old Town section of Albuquerque. It was a house made of adobe—dry blocks of mud reinforced with straw—and had a rounded kiva fireplace in the dining room, brick floors throughout, and vigas (logs) supporting the ceiling. The house oozed warmth and charm.

Nan was in Germany with her daughter Tammy for the summer, both studying the language. I would fill in for her with cooking and cleaning, until the boys and I found a house of our own.

The next morning I met with Karen Garmin, a real estate agent Bob knew. She was a fiftyish woman and all business. She asked personal financial questions to determine what price range house I could afford. When I told her what I had coming in monthly and what I had in savings, she said we could afford a house in the $40,000 price range. I was stunned. That was higher than either of us expected and was definitely above the average price for a house in Albuquerque.

The following day, Karen picked us up, prepared to drop the boys off at Kiddie Corral, a daycare facility.

"Will they have toys?" Nick asked on the way there. I understood his anxiety—he and Whit were dealing with so many rapid changes.

"They'll have toys and there will be lots of kids to play with and you'll have snacks," Karen assured them. The boys were poking each other and wrestling around in the back seat as she was driving. She wasn't used to having children in her car and was eager unload my squirming boys with their nonstop questions so we could get on with house-hunting.

All of the houses Karen had lined up for viewing were in the northeast part of the city, which she said was the nicest area, but they were too far from Nan and Bob's home. After all, I'd moved to Albuquerque to be close to family. Plus, these houses lacked the charm of the adobe construction I had loved at first sight. They were houses you would see anywhere in the country. Nothing appealed to me. By the end of the day, Karen seemed perplexed. I hadn't said anything positive about any of the houses we'd walked through. "Okay, we'll try again tomorrow," she said.

The next day went the same. I began to feel guilty about seeming to be impossible to please. Karen was getting impatient. "You know, you can *change* wallpaper, paint, and carpeting," she said as we left the last house. I realized I hadn't been explicit enough. So, before picking the boys up from daycare, we sat in the car talking about what was really important to me in a house. I told her I wanted to live in the southwest part of the city so I could be near Nan and Bob, and I wanted my house to have the same charm as theirs. Karen nodded in understanding, relieved to know what hadn't been working.

On the third day, after dropping the boys off at daycare, Karen turned to me and said, "We're going to try something else. There's a house just coming on the market that hasn't been shown or even listed yet. It will be our first stop."

She took me to the Los Altos subdivision in the southwest part of the city, not far from my sister's home. Los Altos consisted of several streets of adobe houses that had been built by Leon Watson, an adobe home builder in Albuquerque since the 1920s. Mr. Watson lived in the house directly across the street from the house Karen wanted me to see. When we stepped inside, I knew instantly that it was just what I was looking for. The floors were all burnt-red bricks. The kitchen, accented with colorful Mexican tile, was large enough for a table and chairs, and there was even a dishwasher, which I'd never had before. Just like our house in Valdosta, this one had three bedrooms and two baths, so our furniture would easily fit. "This is it, Karen!" I said, clapping my hands. "This is our home."

"Well, finally!" she said, but with a friendly smile, clearly pleased that I was satisfied.

Within hours, the papers were drawn up and I closed the deal with my signature. I felt powerful, but scared. In the back of my mind, I still had qualms about the move. But the boys were counting on me. I couldn't worry about whether John would approve of my decisions. I was doing the best I could and second-guessing myself wouldn't help.

The boys were quick to make friends in our new neighborhood that summer. They were out riding bikes and playing ball with the other kids, and all of them were trooping in and out of our house, getting popsicles and drinks. I loved it. I kept homemade cookies out for them and often made popcorn.

When the school year started, all the neighborhood children met right in front of our house to catch the school bus. Nick was beginning first grade at Larrazolo Elementary School and Whit was entering kindergarten. I had mixed feelings when I saw my boys off that first day. I'd hovered over them for years, and now both would be in someone else's care. Yet, it meant a new freedom for me, hours to spend however I wanted.

On Wednesday mornings, I'd go to Nan's house right after getting the boys off to school. It was our day to run errands together and have lunch at the drugstore a couple of blocks from her house at the edge of Albuquerque's Old Town. Nan and I enjoyed being with each other, and though it seemed we looked at everything in life from a different perspective, we were interested in each other's views. Nan had been wounded more than I by our childhood. Having been older by four years, she had been closer to our father. The hurt of losing him had never gone away. Nan was more interested in intellectual pursuits—reading books on philosophy, visiting art galleries. I was more of a homemaker and more patient with children. Nan had a bohemian style of dress and home décor. I had more traditional tastes. She tended to be less scheduled. I was nervous without a schedule. Since my days in junior high school, I'd made daily lists of things to accomplish.

Nan knew what time I would be arriving on Wednesday mornings, yet I always found her in bed. It usually took some coaxing to get her up and dressed for our day together. Nan's bed had always been a haven for her, her retreat when life became too stressful. At times, she'd stay in bed all day, only getting up for food or to use the bathroom.

One morning when I arrived, Nan was less motivated than usual to get going. "Mmm, I'm so warm and cozy," she said as she rolled over, avoiding the sun coming in the window.

"C'mon, Nan," I said, tugging at her covers, "we can get some coffee at the drugstore." She rolled out eventually and pulled on some clothes. Despite her initial reluctance, we had a fun day together.

On Sundays, after the boys and I went to the Unitarian Church, we'd go by to visit Nan and her family. Ten-year-old Tamara was much too grown up to be a playmate with Nick and Whit, but she would get them involved in some activity before taking off to play with her friends. Tam had beautiful red hair, long and wavy. She was slender and tall, and mature beyond her years. She joined adult conversations, giving her opinions without any qualms.

I'd frequently invite Nan and her family to our house for spaghetti or lasagna dinners. To help us settle in, Bob would do handyman tasks whenever they visited. Sometimes Tam spent the night and she and I would do girl stuff together, maybe brush each others hair or trade manicures. I was becoming ever more convinced that I had made the right decision. Moving here to be near family *was* good for all of us. I was more relaxed than I had been in a long time. We had needed this fresh beginning. I didn't know what the future would bring, but I still believed John would be coming home. When President Nixon spoke on the news, I listened for any indication that the conflict in Vietnam was coming to an end.

Nan and Bob had a cocktail party where I met many of their friends. As some of them invited me to their own parties, my social circle gradually expanded. I started reciprocating with once-a-month dinners for three or four couples I'd met at Nan's, in the neighborhood, or at church. When I hosted these parties, I allowed the boys to greet everyone, but only if they promised to stay in their room during the rest of the evening and come out only briefly at their bedtime to say goodnight to everyone. I would roll the TV into their bedroom and carry a special dinner back to them on a tray. They felt they were having their own party.

* * * * *

Four months after we moved into our house, my sister's husband, a city planner, was offered an opportunity to move to Texas for a higher-paying job in San Antonio. Nan didn't want to leave. "My sister just moved here," she told him. "I don't think it's right to move away and leave her. And I don't want to leave this house. I love this house, Bob!" But he convinced her they would get a house she

251

liked just as well, and promised he would buy whatever new appliances and furniture she wanted. He told her he would do everything he possibly could to see to it that the boys and I were completely settled into our home before they moved.

It was December 1971. In spite of the approaching holiday, I found it difficult to feel any joy. I understood Bob's need to move up in his career, but I couldn't help feeling I was being abandoned after struggling with my decision to move from Valdosta specifically to be near family.

One morning, after seeing the boys off to school, I put the Christmas tree up, and spent the day decorating it. That afternoon, as I was hanging the last few ornaments, the tree started to lean. When I tried to push it upright, the tree came completely loose from the stand and fell into my arms. To prevent the fragile ornaments we had collected over the years from being broken, I held the tree with one hand, pulled off all the ornaments I could reach with the other hand, and tossed them onto the sofa. Then I lowered the tree gently to the floor, sat beside it, and cried; I cried about leaving Valdosta, about Nan and Bob moving away, about feeling lost and lonely. I had only recently become convinced that moving here was the right thing to do. Now the boys and I would still have no family, and we wouldn't even have long-time friends. I felt pitiable as I sat there by the toppled tree.

I'd washed my face and calmed down by the time the boys got home from school, but they immediately noticed the tree lying on its side with tangles of tinsel, and then my tear-reddened eyes. When they asked me what had happened, I just told them I was sad about the tree falling over. "We'll go get Mr. Watson. He'll help," Nick said.

Leon Watson, the older gentleman across the street who

had designed and built all the adobe homes in the neighborhood, had already helped the boys repair their bikes and he'd come to my rescue when I backed the car into one of the posts that supported the carport.

"What we have here is a stand that's too small for your tree," he said. "Give me a few minutes and I'll build you a larger one."

The boys were proud to have saved the day. "I told you he'd help," Nick said.

* * * * *

Nan's family moved to San Antonio shortly after Christmas. As I faced the reality of their absence, the blues set in. Each day I felt more remote, seeming to function on auto-pilot. I was often still in my nightgown, sitting on the side of my bed, when the boys got home from school. *Where did all those hours go?* Sometimes I forgot to prepare dinner for the boys. "We're hungry," Nick said, one evening, after finding me in the dark yard pulling weeds. *Dinner. What time is it?* I felt confused. *It's almost the boys' bedtime and they haven't eaten. I'll make popcorn.*

I drastically lost weight and my clothes hung on me. Mr. Watson watched from his house as I watered trees in the front yard well past dark. He sometimes checked to see if I was okay. He asked me to call him Leon. I'd heard from neighbors that he referred to me as "the pretty little widow." I resented that. I was *not* a widow.

Depression took over. I wasn't adequately caring for the boys and they were getting into mischief in the neighborhood and neighbors were complaining. I wasn't tending to chores or meals. The roof leaked. Hours, even days, seemed to escape me.

On a morning after the boys had prepared their own

bowls of cereal and gotten themselves off to school, I sat on the side of my bed and thought, *I'm lost and I need help.*

I called the Kirtland Air Force Base hospital and asked to speak to a psychiatrist. While I waited to be connected to the mental health clinic, I remembered my sessions with Dr. Martine during my first year of marriage, how she had ridiculed me and seemed to despise me. I was tempted to hang up, but just then someone at the clinic answered the phone.

"I'm the wife of a pilot who has been missing in action for four years and I'm falling apart," I told him. "I can't take care of my boys anymore. Is there someone who can help me?"

"Our clinic is full right now," he said, "so you'll have to get outside help." He went on to inform me that my military insurance would cover the cost, and then gave me five names from which to choose.

I selected a psychiatrist named Dr. Alan Hovda from the middle of the list and called his office. After I briefly described my problem to the receptionist, she transferred me to the doctor's desk phone, so I went through the explanation again.

"Could you come in next Monday?" he asked.

"This afternoon wouldn't be too soon." I was almost begging. He must have detected the desperation in my voice, because he set a time for the following day. After hanging up, I cried in relief. *Someone's going to help me!*

* * * * *

The waiting room was small but decorated tastefully with stained glass lamps, Oriental rugs, and classic furnishings. The lighting was low and restful.

Dr. Hovda was about forty-five and had a stocky build.

He was wearing a suit, white shirt, and tie—looking professional—like someone I could rely on. He leaned back in the chair behind his desk and said, "Tell me what's going on in your life right now and how you're coping." He kept an understanding smile on his face as I explained my problem.

I told him that I worried about the boys because I wasn't caring for them properly, that I felt I was lost in depression and wasn't functioning well in any area. "My Dad died in a mental institution," I confessed, "so maybe I've inherited his illness." My eyes brimmed with tears at that point, so I stopped talking and just listened as he responded:

"You haven't inherited any mental illness from your father, Sally. You are a normal, healthy woman with a situational problem that you can neither change nor handle alone. I will be here for you and we'll handle it together."

I put a hand over my mouth and tears flowed as I felt the burden lifted.

My weekly visits to Dr. Hovda were life-saving. Sometimes I'd cry through the visits and sometimes we'd laugh together. Whenever I voiced my concerns about the boys, he assured me they'd be okay. "Children are more resilient than you think," he said. "Youth seems to allow them to roll with the punches. Just think of your own survival day to day."

With his encouragement, I became active in the community. I started taking tennis lessons and joined the alumni chapter of Alpha Phi, my college sorority. I joined the American Association of University Women (AAUW) and attended its monthly meetings. I signed up with the University of New Mexico's Continuing Education program for a yoga class and later for a creative writing class. In these and other ways I began to get acquainted with the city and the people of Albuquerque. I anxiously learned my way around the city by using the freeway system and even found my way to Kirtland Air Force Base, where I was entitled to shop. With the boys both in school, I felt free to explore.

I joined the local group of POW/MIA wives and was asked to make a community service television announcement: "My name is Sally Brucher and I am the mother of two young boys, ages five and seven, whose father is missing in action in North Vietnam." Then I urged viewers to contact our government representatives to ask them to put pressure on the North Vietnamese government to release information on the POWs they held captive.

I joined the Unitarian Church in Albuquerque. I enjoyed the services as well as the coffee and social hour afterward, which was always enlivened by the arrival of Nick and Whit and other children from the Sunday school classes.

At first, I felt the church was supportive and welcoming. But this was the Vietnam era and the Unitarian church was becoming political, actively protesting against U. S. involvement in the conflict. At times I felt some members of the congregation were antagonistic toward me because I was a military dependent.

Once, for example, I tried to provide flowers for the altar in John's name and to have the church bulletin say, "The flowers this Sunday are to honor John Brucher, who is Missing in Action in Vietnam." The minister was agreeable to the flowers when I spoke with him, but later I was informed by the church secretary that they would neither print the dedication in the Sunday bulletin nor mention it in the service, "because of the church's disapproval of U. S. involvement in the war." I was crushed that my church would put its political leanings before its concern for a member of the congregation. When I was a little girl, my mother had memorialized my dad by giving flowers to the Unitarian Church she attended, and I still had a copy of *that* Sunday bulletin. I wanted my boys to also have a keepsake bulletin honoring their daddy.

I looked at the church differently after that. We slowly withdrew from the church until we were not attending at all. Instead, I used that time on Sunday mornings to sit on the living room sofa between the boys and read poetry, to talk to them about values I wanted them to have, and to speak of all things spiritual and beautiful in our lives and in our world. That would remain our Sunday morning ritual for many years.

CHAPTER TWENTY-ONE

M iss Griego, Nick's first-grade teacher, called to ask if I would meet with her. I assumed it was a routine conference and that all the parents were being scheduled. Nick's move into first grade had seemed smooth. When he brought his first report card home, he had all "Excellents." No behavior problems were checked and there was no note from Miss Griego.

When I arrived at the school, I was directed to the principal's office, which puzzled me. Mr. Sandoval, the middle-aged principal, and Miss Griego, a twenty-something first-year teacher, stood to greet me as I entered the office. After we'd all settled into chairs, Mr. Sandoval nodded to Miss Griego to begin.

"Mrs. Brucher, I felt you should know that Nick is very disruptive in the classroom," she said. "He disturbs the other children and rarely settles down to get any work done. When he tries to do the assignment, it is done poorly, or he is unable to do it at all." Her words seemed rehearsed, and her eyes flitted nervously between the principal and me as she spoke.

I was stunned. "Why didn't his report card reflect these problems?" I asked. The principal took over then. He asked for my cooperation and said that by encouraging Nick at home I could help him avoid further problems at school.

They rambled on, ignoring my stammering attempts to ask questions. After only five minutes, Mr. Sandoval stood, followed by Miss Griego, so I stood also. Mr. Sandoval held out his hand and said, "Thank you for meeting with us today, Mrs. Brucher. Miss Griego and I have other things to attend to now, but I know we can count on your help in resolving your son's problems." My questions hadn't been answered, yet I was being dismissed.

I walked out to my car and sat in it with my hands at the top of the steering wheel, staring ahead for a minute before I let my head fall forward onto my arms. *Why wasn't I notified about Nick's behavior problems before being called in for that calculated attack?*

I drove straight to a store that sold school supplies and bought a set of eleven-by-fourteen inch flashcards. Each of the cards had a colorful, boldfaced upper and lower case letter on one side and, on the other side, a picture of something that began with that letter. You could flip **M m** and see a picture of a monkey, or flip **B b** and see a picture of a book.

"The Letter Game" became our evening routine. Our two sofas faced each other, with the coffee table in between, and the boys sat across from me. As I held up each card, they eagerly competed to name the letter first. The game made it fun for them to learn the letters and the letter sounds. Before long, they were calling out the letters in billboards and commercial signs as we rode in the car, and if they recognized the advertising, they could change the sounds into words. This discovery was exciting and enlightening for them, and empowering for me. I was a *teacher*. They *would* learn, if not in the classroom, then at home.

One evening, I asked Nick if he was behaving in the classroom, if he was getting along with the other children and his teacher, and if he had trouble with his school work. "I'm doing okay," he said, with no elaboration.

Nick continued to get perfect grades on his report cards. There was never a note from the teacher about his progress, or lack of it. Whenever I called her, Miss Griego cheerily dismissed my concerns about Nick's progress, which seemed bizarre—as though she had never called me in to discuss Nick's problems and she didn't have any idea what I was talking about. Nick didn't miss a single day of school that year and was the only child in the school to receive the "Perfect Attendance" award.

* * * * *

I'd dreamed of having another child—a little girl— when John came home. Because that wouldn't be possible for the indefinite future, I called the Department of Human Services in the spring of 1972, to find out how to become a foster parent. I was told that since mine was a one-parent home, only a child less than a year old could be placed with me. The department's position was that children older than one year needed both parents in the home. That was okay with me—I would enjoy caring for and cuddling a baby. And by taking in a foster child, I could repay the love shown to me in my childhood foster home.

A social worker came to interview me and assess the home environment. She asked if there were any sorts of children I would prefer *not* to have in my home.

"If an abused child is placed in my home and later taken away to be placed back with the abusive parents, it would be very painful for me," I told her. "I'd rather not get involved with that."

"I think this would be a good temporary home for a baby," she said as she prepared to leave. "We'll see to it that the papers are in order for you to be a foster parent, and then we'll have to wait for a baby who needs your care. You'll be hearing from us."

One Friday morning in July, I received a call from Human Services. They had a baby for me! "We'll wait until the end of the day to deliver her to you," the woman said, "so you will have the whole day to prepare for her arrival." *Her! We're getting a girl!*

It was almost five o'clock when a man and woman arrived, setting an infant carrier down in our living room. The boys and I peeked in. Our baby girl was sleeping.

The man handed me his card—which identified him as Burk Coonz, Social Worker—and told me I could call him at his office on Monday with any questions I might have.

It wasn't until they'd driven away that I gasped, "We don't know her name!" The boys looked startled, so I added, gazing down at the baby, "but...she looks like a Theresa to me."

The boys glanced at each other, and then Whit said, "She looks like a ladybug to me." We all laughed, and that was it. We had our Ladybug.

When I called Burk at Social Services on Monday I learned that her name was Juanita and she was four months old. Because her seventeen-year-old mother was addicted to drugs, Juanita was a high risk baby. I would have to take her in for monthly check-ups to track her progress.

I received an allowance to help cover Juanita's needs, but it wasn't nearly enough for everything I bought for our chubby-cheeked Ladybug: bonnets and dresses, embroidered sweaters and lacy socks, beaded leather moccasin booties, rattles and a soft baby doll.

Once a month, Burk came by to pick up Juanita to take her to the Social Services office for a supervised visit with her mother, Silvie. On one occasion, the visit was canceled because Silvie was in jail on a drug possession charge. When Silvie *did* see her daughter, she had to have been comforted by the sight of her healthy, clean, and happy infant. I sent along photographs of Juanita for Silvie to keep.

As Juanita grew to be a toddler, pulling herself up on furniture and trying to walk, the boys would station themselves on either side of her and coax her to take a few steps. As she toddled along between them, they clapped and cheered.

While out in the back yard, I overheard Nick ask one of his friends, whose mother was pregnant, "Don't you hope your baby will be as cute as Ladybug?"

"I hope it is," the friend said.

I wrote poems about our "Angel on Loan," put them to music and sang them to Juanita, this baby we had all come to love. I told Burk I wanted to adopt her if Silvie's parental rights were severed, but he reminded me I'd been required to sign a form that I would never try to adopt her. Although the department encouraged adoptions, I surmised it just didn't want to lose its foster homes.

Juanita and I saw the boys off in the mornings with kisses, and then she'd watch *Captain Kangaroo* on TV in the quiet house as I went about my morning tasks. After her nap, we ran errands together in town or shopped for groceries on-base, taking time out to put a dime in the mechanical bouncy horse for Juanita to ride. We were always home before the boys arrived on the school bus. Juanita greeted them with squeals, hugs, and kisses. She kissed all their friends getting off the bus, too. For her, each afternoon was like a grand reunion.

* * * * *

263

Shortly after Nick started third grade, he lost his bouncy step and happy disposition. He didn't like himself or anyone else. This child, who had always been happy-go-lucky, now seemed depressed. I decided to visit his classroom unannounced in hopes of finding an explanation.

I bypassed the office and went straight to the portable building that was Nick's classroom. I knocked and quickly stepped inside. The teacher, a stern-faced older lady, was pointing at Nick who was sitting at a lone desk in the center of a circle of desks occupied by the other students. She'd had the other children's attention until they all looked over at me. She hurried over—her wrinkled face reddening—and stammered something.

Nick got up and ran to me, grasping my hand. "Why is Nick's desk the only one inside the circle?" I asked the teacher.

"Some children just aren't bright enough to learn and can't do the work," she said in a husky voice. "We have to keep an eye on him."

I couldn't make sense of it, but she offered no further explanation. Without saying a word, I gave Nick's hand a tug and we left the room.

"You will never have to go back to that classroom again," I told him as we walked across the school yard. Instantly his bounce was back.

I cringed to think what Nick must have been going through in school. I knew he was smart and eager to learn and—before school had started weeks ago—happy. *What was wrong?* And then it dawned on me that Nick might have dyslexia, the same learning disability I had dealt with most of my life. *How could I have been so distracted not to see it?* I knew now what dyslexia was. If my son had it, I would deal with it. I hated to think he had already endured some of the same humiliation and shame I'd experienced.

We entered another portable building where the principal had his office. The secretary told me Mr. Sandoval was free and we could go on in. Nick and I stood across from his desk while I told him what I had witnessed in the classroom. "Nick is a very bright boy who happens to have dyslexia, a learning disability," I said, giving him my presumed diagnosis. "I won't take any action against the teacher since she's retiring at the end of the year, but Nick won't be going back into that classroom."

Mr. Sandoval said, showing irritation, that he would look into placing Nick with another teacher and would set up a meeting with all of us soon. I couldn't tell if his irritation was with me or with the old teacher.

Nick and I stopped at The Soda Straw ice cream parlor on the way home. As we sat at the little round table with our dishes of ice cream, Nick's loving gaze and sweet smile told me he was grateful I had saved him.

Mr. Sandoval called me the next morning to say Nick would be transferred to Miss Connors's class. He suggested we all meet in her classroom after school the next day, so Nick and I could meet her and ask questions.

Miss Connors was young and energetic, but with several years of teaching experience. She assured me that I had nothing to worry about. She was familiar with dyslexia and would encourage Nick and work with him individually for as long as it took for him to grasp the material.

After two weeks in her class, Nick told me, "I love Miss Connors."

* * * * *

In January 1973, four years after John's plane was shot down, I heard on the evening news that the Paris Peace Accord had been signed, ending American combat in Vietnam.

American POWs in North Vietnam were to be released from the prison camps in the following months. The military received the names of those prisoners, but I was informed that John's name wasn't among them. I thought it was simply an error. I still believed John was coming home. He *had* to be alive. They'd had voice contact with him from the ground after he ejected from his plane.

Local news reporters began calling my home night and day to see if I had received word that my husband would be returned. The calls soon became so disruptive that I got an unlisted number.

When I received a call the next day from yet another reporter, I asked how she'd gotten my number. She said she'd told the information operator it was an emergency, that she had news of my husband. "I saw your husband's serial number on the list," she told me. "So he'll be among those being repatriated. I didn't know if you had received word yet."

This confirmed that John *would* be coming home. But how odd to be notified by a reporter! As soon as I got off the line, I called my POW/MIA contact in Washington, D.C., to whom I had always directed my questions. He assured me that John *wasn't* on the list and that he didn't know how the reporter could have gotten such erroneous information.

The families of the soon-to-be repatriated POWs were being flown to Clark Air Force Base in the Philippines. No one notified us. No one made arrangements for us to be there. I felt forgotten.

In March of 1973, when the TV news was covering "Operation Homecoming," the boys and I sat on the floor in front of our television and watched every detail. The crowds. The families of the POWs at the front of the crowd. The children clinging to their mothers. The C-141 aircraft, dubbed the "Hanoi Taxi," arriving with its precious human cargo—the final delivery of returning POWs.

The door to the plane opened. Steps lowered to the tarmac. I held my breath. The boys and I almost had our noses pressed to the TV screen. The first man appeared. Was it John coming out? Was it Daddy? We couldn't tell. He came down the steps, saluted, shook hands with an officer, stepped away from the plane and walked toward the crowd. A woman and two children ran toward him. He embraced his wife, then swept his children into his arms.

Not John.

As the scene was repeated over and over and over, we examined each face. Too soon the aircraft was empty. The happy families dispersed.

Where was John?

I felt my face contort with anguish, tears silently flowing. The boys looked at me with bewilderment. I whispered, "I'm sorry."

* * * * *

Weeks later, the school counselor called me. "Mrs. Brucher, Nick is having a great deal of difficulty at school," he began. "He doesn't seem to know where he is. He gets up in the middle of class and does cartwheels down the aisle and sometimes looks out the windows, seemingly lost. He needs help and it's more help than I've been trained to give. I think you should find a child psychiatrist for him."

By then, I had been seeing Dr. Hovda weekly for over a year. When I told him what the school counselor had said, he referred me to a child psychiatrist named Dr. Heber Hudson. "He'll be someone you can talk to about what you're feeling," I told Nick. "You can talk to him about anything."

Nick was so excited about having a special adult he could talk to that he even bragged to his friends: "I get to go to a psychiatrist!"

Nick soon felt Dr. Hudson was his good friend. They would do things together—go shopping for office toys, build model ships, work on puzzles—with Nick talking to his *friend* all the while.

Tests arranged by Dr. Hudson showed Nick to be hyperactive as well as dyslexic. This revelation explained the wild behavior that had added to Nick's difficulty in school. In addition, Dr. Hudson told me, Nick had experienced a break from reality and had withdrawn into himself when the POWs came home without his daddy. He wanted to put Nick on a drug called Ritalin for his hyperactivity, but I was wary of possible unknown or long-term side effects.

"If I'm right, it will settle him down, allowing him to concentrate, follow directions, and do better in school and other activities," he said. "If I'm wrong, and Nick isn't hyperactive, he will literally bounce off the ceiling on this medication. We'll know within days, if not hours, if this is the appropriate treatment."

I decided I was willing to give it a try.

Ritalin made a night-to-day change in Nick. For the first time in his life, he worked on a puzzle for almost an hour. He played normally with other children without anyone getting injured. He quietly read a book, ate meals without acting up, and talked sensibly.

Dr. Hudson's intervention had turned Nick around. During the next year, Nick moved ahead three grade levels in his schoolwork due to his ability to concentrate on assignments. With continuing therapy, he was coming out of the depression and learning how to cope with his disabilities. He'd become the most wonderful son, brother, friend, and student he had ever been.

* * * * *

To heal from the past four years, the boys and I had to let go of the hope that John would come home. It was difficult to have to accept that we might never know what happened to him. He was still listed as Missing in Action, but in our hearts, the hope we'd held onto was gone.

That summer of 1973, I received an official letter from the Air Force informing me that John's "case" had been reviewed. All of the repatriated POWs had been interviewed extensively and had been shown photographs of the servicemen still listed as MIA. None of the returnees had seen John or heard his name mentioned while they were in prison camp. The letter said the review had determined there was "no information to indicate that Captain Brucher had been taken captive." The review had also concluded that because there had been ground fire in the area where John went down, it was entirely possible that enemy soldiers or villagers had killed and buried him in an unmarked site.

"Do you have any reservations about a change of status to Killed in Action for Captain Brucher?" they asked. They gave a phone number for me to call a Major Gruber with my response.

"I have no objection to a status change," I told him, "*if* you feel all avenues of investigation have been exhausted." There had to be an end. It was almost five years since John had left for Vietnam.

Major Gruber told me it would take two or three more months for the status change to be official. In the meantime, the investigation would remain open, should any new evidence be discovered. He asked that I send a letter for John's file, stating that I concurred with the Air Force findings and agreed with the status change. I was also asked to have the two psychiatrists send letters for the file,

269

assessing our current health situation and any impact the status change might have on us.

My psychiatrist, Dr. Hovda, and Nick's psychiatrist, Dr. Hudson, each wrote a letter.

Dr. Hovda: "She has a Situational Depressive Reaction which is directly related to her husband being listed as Missing in Action since February 1969. Since the release of the prisoners of war from Vietnam, her husband is still being listed as Missing in Action, and it is my understanding that this status may continue for several more years. For medical reasons, I consider it therapeutic for her and her children to be able to reconstruct their lives without carrying the uncertain hope of the husband and father returning."

Dr. Hudson: "A good deal of the boy's anxiety stems from an unresolved mourning for his lost father. The prolonged delay of mourning appears to be directly contributing to his current anxiety and dysfunction. It would therefore be extremely helpful in the treatment of his condition if a firm, fixed decision could be made about his father's status. It would be helpful if his father could be declared permanently deceased."

The status change became official in November. Although it closed a painful chapter in our lives, it was still pitifully sad. John would never be home for us to hold and love. He would never see his boys grow into men. I finally had to accept that—at thirty-two years of age—John had given his life on foreign soil, fighting for democracy.

The Air Force offered assistance in arranging a memorial service for John. I decided I wanted it to be at the Air Force Academy, where he had run with the deer as a cadet. I knew his spirit would be free to run there forever.

* * * * *

Nick was in such a fragile state that I worried how he would handle the occasion. I decided to leave both boys in Albuquerque with a friend when I flew to Colorado for the memorial service. I didn't tell them where I was going, just that I had some business and would be back in two days.

The Academy's magnificent chapel with its skyward spires was filled with cadets in uniform. While waiting for the service to begin, I looked at the program I'd been handed. When I turned it over to the back, there was John's picture. I gasped and people turned to look at me. *This is John. This is the man we've lost. This is the patriot, the fighter for democracy, the hero, the father, and the husband I'd so loved.*

Just before the end of the beautiful service, an officer folded the United States flag neatly into a triangle and, with a formal bow, he handed it to me. I struggled not to lose control. I knew John would have wanted me to be strong.

As those attending the service moved outside, there was a fly-over of planes in the "missing man formation." It had a wrenching impact on me. My hand flew to my mouth as the planes thundered overhead. The slot where the aircraft was missing was a reminder of how much John loved to fly, how much it was a part of him, and that the poem, "High Flight," by Gillespie Magee was his favorite.

"Oh, I have slipped the surly bonds of earth
And danced the skies on laughter-silvered wings;
Sunward I've climbed, and joined the tumbling mirth
Of sun-split clouds...."

I said goodbye to John and left my love with him on that windy site where we had been joined in marriage. The boys and I would now begin to heal—and look to the future.

CHAPTER TWENTY-TWO

Ｄ uring the first holiday season after I moved to Albuquerque, I'd received a Christmas card from Greg and Lynn Mann with a printed greeting in it, but no news. By spring, I'd learned from mutual friends that they had separated. Lynn took Michelle to live with her parents in Decatur, Illinois, and Greg left Valdosta shortly after that for an assignment to the Pentagon. Their divorce became final in late 1972.

In April, Greg sent a card with a note to the boys:

"Hey, Nick and Whit, I hope you are enjoying New Mexico. I miss fishing with you guys. I hope you're being good boys for your mom.

Your friend,
Captain Mann"

On the back of the card, he added a message to me: "I have a cross-country training flight into Kirtland Air Force Base toward the end of the month. I'll be there just one night, but I'd like to stop by to say hello, and maybe take you and the boys out to dinner, if that's okay."

When Greg arrived at the house, the boys ran to open the door and were immediately all over him. He greeted

Nick and Whit—now seven and eight—as old buddies, giving them hugs and playful punches. Then we introduced our newest family member to him. Juanita had just learned to walk, and with the boy's encouragement, she toddled to him, arms raised to be lifted. After the enthusiastic greeting, the boys calmed down and Greg and I stood in the kitchen, drinking wine and catching up on each other's news: the divorce, the job at the Pentagon, the POW's return. After the boys showed Greg their room and shared samples of their school work, Greg took us all out to Pancho's for Mexican food.

The evening ended too soon. Although I hadn't really gotten to know Greg in Valdosta, it now felt as if Greg and I were old friends enjoying a reunion. Perhaps the boys' enthusiasm was contagious. When we got back to the house, Juanita was asleep in the car and had to be carried to her crib, but the boys were still wound up and wouldn't let go of Greg until he promised to visit again.

"I'll try to get another trip out here," he told them, "but I have to go back to my job in Washington now."

By summer of 1973, Greg had completed his assignment at the Pentagon and was assigned to Kirtland AFB as a test pilot in the F-4 with the Special Weapons Test Center. He moved to Albuquerque almost two years after the boys and I had moved here, and one year after Juanita had joined our family.

Our activities included Greg more and more frequently. I introduced him to the city and to my friends. He was tall—six-foot-three—with hair almost black and eyes a clear, pale blue. He had a calm, confident demeanor. In his company, I felt unburdened and I had a new enthusiasm for life.

We hiked in the Sandia mountains and walked the streets of Old Town, Juanita riding happily on Greg's shoulders. We went to movies, ate at pizza restaurants, and picnicked in parks.

One weekend we all went to Santa Fe for the day and were seated for lunch on the restaurant's patio. Greg and I were chatting when Whit suddenly pointed at a bird splashing and flapping in the fountain at the center of the patio and said, "Look at that, Daddy!" My eyes met Greg's and we silently agreed not to correct him. It was an awkward moment. *Is he a friend, or is there more?* I wondered. *It feels like so much more.*

As we were walking out of the restaurant, Greg was ahead of me with Juanita and one of the boys when the waitress ran up behind me, saying, "Ma'am, your husband left his pipe on the table." I thanked her, but I was so glad Greg hadn't heard. There had been enough awkward moments for one day.

One evening I left the boys and Juanita with a babysitter while Greg and I took the aerial tram to the top of the Sandia Mountains to have dinner at High Finance restaurant. While waiting for our food, we had Manhattan cocktails. We clicked glasses and Greg said, "To our future!" *Does he mean our futures as separate people or a future together?* My face flushed with the thought.

After dinner, Greg and I walked out on the deck that overlooked the city. It was chilly even in August at that altitude, over 10,000 feet, and Greg put his arms around me. The sparkling lights of the city spread across the Rio Grande Valley a mile below us.

"I want you in my life always," he said. "When the time is right for both of us, I want us to be married. Will you marry me, Sally?"

Two tears slipped down my cheeks as I nodded.

"I love you and want to spend my life making you happy," he said, with tears welling in his own eyes.

I clung to him as thoughts ran wildly through my head.

This is happening so fast, but I know I love him. I couldn't fathom such happiness lasting for a *lifetime.*

We spent most of the next three months together, feeling more and more like a couple—and a family. In November, Greg moved in with us. "Living together" wasn't a common arrangement at the time, so we tried to keep it under wraps, which was almost impossible to do in a small, close neighborhood.

Every minute of life had become glorious, as if the five year cloud that had dimmed my hope of ever finding happiness had now suddenly lifted. Like the Velveteen Rabbit of my boys' bedtime stories, I had come to life because someone, at last, loved me *enough.*

* * * * *

On Christmas Eve, everyone in the neighborhood outlined the houses with hundreds of luminarias along the roof lines, outdoor walls, driveways, and street curbs. Each was a flickering candle set in an anchoring bed of sand inside a brown paper lunch bag. By dusk, all the houses had to have their inside lights turned off, or have the windows darkened. No electric lights were to outshine the glowing luminarias. A seemingly endless line of cars and tour buses drove through our neighborhood's narrow streets with their headlights turned off, so passengers could best appreciate the enchanted glow of our annual—one-night-only—Christmas Eve wonderland scene.

We walked through the neighborhood in our holiday clothing—Juanita and I both wearing long dresses—and stopped at parties being held in several different homes. Neighbors cooed over our cherubic Juanita. In our small community, they'd watched over our "angel on loan" as she grew from infant to toddler.

The neighbors had always been kind to our boys, but wary of them. Over the years, Nick and Whit had put fire-crackers in mailboxes, climbed on neighbors' walls and roofs, thrown dirt clods at the stuccoed sides of the adobe houses, and careened their bikes across lawns and through flower beds.

In spite of all those pranks, our patient neighbors would just shake their heads. "Lord, save us!" they'd say, or, "How can a sweet young woman like you have two such naughty boys?" But on this Christmas Eve, the boys were dressed up, behaving well, and looking almost angelic as we proudly walked the streets of our neighborhood, glowing with the *Feliz Navidad* spirit of our family's first New Mexican Christmas together.

That winter, we went skiing at Purgatory, in Colorado, and stayed in a condominium near the lodge. To baby-sit for two-year-old Juanita while the rest of us took ski lessons, we brought along a thirteen-year-old neighbor girl named Maria. She was round-faced and had waist-long blond braids. She was always cheerful except when disciplining the boys. Then she was stern and in control, and the boys seemed to respect that.

The guys took to skiing quickly, leaving me behind to fall helplessly into snow drifts. Sometimes I just gave up and sat in the lodge with Maria and Juanita and drank hot apple cider. Through a wall of windows, I could watch my rosy cheeked boys swooshing down the final run and coming to impressively controlled stops at the bottom of the ski slope.

Seeing the boys laugh as they interacted with Greg made it so easy for me to be happy again. Our lives were filled with adventure, caring, and love. Each of us had experienced heartbreak and loss, but we'd come together and created a whole from the broken pieces of our lives.

* * * * *

Greg and I "eloped" to Santa Fe while the boys were in school. We were married by the Justice of the Peace in a civil ceremony. Two deputy sheriffs were our witnesses.

We had considered having friends and neighbors over for a small champagne reception in the backyard to celebrate our new beginning, but there was still an unsettled edge in our lives. Greg had been divorced for just a little over a year, and John's official status had been changed to Killed in Action only four months earlier. So we told no one, not even Greg's parents, when we went from living together to being married. It was simply an evolution.

Just as he had in Valdosta, Greg sometimes took the boys on adventures—without Juanita and me—that lifted the weight of the past years from them and allowed them to laugh and be lighthearted boys.

With the arrival of spring, we bought a big, bright-orange nylon tent and other camping equipment, and all five of us spent days in the Jemez Mountains. We'd camp near a stream to have water for washing. The boys used pieces of tree bark as little boats and—keeping themselves out of the cold water—chased along as their small crafts drifted downstream, bumping into rocks and spinning in erratic eddies.

Greg taught Nick and Whit camping safety and responsibility: "Always leave a camp site cleaner than you found it." "Set up a good fire site with lots of rock to contain the fire." "Set up your tent a safe distance from the flying sparks," Each boy wore a leather shoelace around his neck with a whistle hanging from it in case he wandered too far. Greg recruited their help in cooking over the campfire. Nick gathered firewood and Whit became the "King of French toast." We roasted marshmallows at night as Greg told ghost stories, scaring us all into our tent.

We bought life jackets that summer, and a six-man raft to float on the Rio Grande. Sometimes we'd drive to southwest Colorado to raft the rapids of the Pine and Animas Rivers. At the end of each day, we camped in the hills overlooking the city of Durango.

We sometimes camped in rain and in wind so strong we were sure our tent would blow over. I thought camping was wonderful because we were all snuggled in together as a family—and also because Greg and the boys did all the cooking and cleaning. I crawled out of my sleeping bag each morning to be greeted with a warm, wet cloth to wash my face, and a hot cup of coffee to drink by the fire.

* * * * *

With my marriage to Greg came a large extended family of Texans. Greg was the eldest of H. C. and Wilma Mann's six children. Greg's youngest sister, Amy, was younger than either of our boys. Greg's grandmother, Rosie Sullivan Alexander, was known to everyone as "Mama." She was in her eighties, yet still kept her own home and went fishing whenever she got the chance.

We attended regular reunions of the "Mann Clan" in Texas, usually on South Padre Island, where we rented condos. We fished and crabbed, played on the beach and in the condo pool, and took boat rides. One afternoon, Juanita tossed one of her tennis shoes off the dock and into the water while we were crabbing, to stir up a little excitement when she thought the attention on her was inadequate.

On most of those beach evenings, we'd cook up a "mess" of fish, play board games, and make s'mores from graham crackers, marshmallows, and Hershey bars heated in the condo oven.

Nick, Whit, and Amy hung out as a trio, walking along the water's edge, feeding seagulls, and playing in the sand. Amy was eight, Whit nine, and Nick ten when these reunions began. As years passed, these children remained close summer companions.

Wilma and I would walk on the beach and have long conversations about her having Amy so late in life. "I thought I was in menopause," she said, "but what a blessing Amy has been!" She shared her worries, her views on religion, and her joys with me, and quickly became so much more than a mother-in-law. Being welcomed as a new member of Greg's large family gave me a feeling of belonging I'd never known.

* * * * *

Greg and I had many adjustments to make: Who would discipline the boys? Who would manage the money? What roles should each of us play in this new partnership? Out of necessity, I had become very independent over the five years I raised the boys alone. Now there needed to be a sharing, and neither Greg nor I was sure how to go about it. The boys were still young enough to adjust to Greg as the head of the family, so—since I was such a softy—I encouraged him to take the lead on discipline. I would manage the monthly bills. He would take charge of investments. I would handle routine family-living tasks such as laundry, meals, housecleaning, and supervising the boys' homework. He would plan our recreational activities, including weekends and vacations. Our division of labor worked well, largely because we were all so grateful to be a family.

Greg, a clever handyman, began work on enclosing our carport to create a family room. He became involved in our subdivision's homeowners association and was soon elected president, which made him feel fully integrated into the neighborhood.

* * * * *

One night while Greg and I were talking about all the changes in our lives, he said he wanted to adopt the boys rather than just be their stepfather. We gathered Greg's divorce papers, our marriage license, the boys' birth certificates, and John's death certificate. With the boys and Juanita in tow, we went to our first appointment with an attorney.

The attorney said that he would like to talk to the boys alone. Greg and I agreed and carried Juanita out of his office into the empty reception area. The boys came out after about ten minutes, smiling and seemingly pleased with themselves. The attorney was chuckling from the doorway as he motioned for Greg and me to come back in.

"Your boys are delightful!" the attorney told us. "I asked them if they were sure they wanted to have Greg for their father. 'Yes!' they both practically shouted. Then they didn't stop talking for a minute: 'You've got to let him be our dad!' 'He takes us camping and fishing and hiking!' 'And sometimes he takes us rafting!' 'He's gotta be our dad!' 'We really, really like him!' "

We laughed with the attorney, delighted by the impression Nick and Whit had made on him. "Adoptions are the more pleasant duties of my profession," he told us. "I see too much of the other side of the coin, and this matter brightens my day."

By the end of a series of meetings, and then a court hearing before a judge, the boys were officially declared Nick and Whit Mann.

I told John's parents I'd remarried but I didn't have the

heart to tell them Greg had adopted their grandsons. I didn't want them to feel they'd lose the boys. Nick and Whit loved their grandparents. But then, in one of my letters to the Bruchers, I enclosed a news-clipping about Nick making a touchdown for his Pee Wee Football team. "Nick Mann ran with the ball....," the clipping said. It wasn't until the letter was already in the mail that I realized what I'd done.

Would they be hurt? I fretted until a return letter arrived: "We think it is wonderful that you have come together as a family. Congratulations!"

CHAPTER TWENTY-THREE

G reg and I were eager to add to our family, and by mid-summer of 1974 I was pregnant. We shared our news with everyone, and the boys announced it in the neighborhood and in their classrooms.

"We don't want another brother," Whit told us. "We want a sister!"

Since the sex of the baby couldn't be determined in advance, I worried that the boys wouldn't bond with a baby boy. So I started cutting appealing pictures of boy babies—wrapped in blue blankets or dressed in blue clothes—from baby magazines and putting them on the refrigerator door. I added a sign that said, "Maybe I'm a boy!"

Greg and I decided that if the baby *was* a boy we'd name him Peter. But we couldn't decide between Julia and Sarah, if she was a girl. Nick liked Julie. Whit liked Sarah. Nothing was ever easy with them.

During a phone conversation with Mama, Greg's grandmother, I asked her which name she favored.

"I like Alexa," she said.

Greg, who was talking on an extension line, looked at me. We nodded to each other. "We like it, too," he said.

After the call ended we told the boys the name Mama had suggested, but of course they didn't agree with Mama or each other and an argument erupted between them.

"Julie is a cuter name," Nick said, leaning into Whit's face.

"It is not!" Whit shot back. "Sarah is prettier!

"Stop!" Greg said firmly. The boys both stopped, looked at me, and sheepishly walked off to their room.

Greg spoiled me shamelessly, satisfying my every craving, no matter the time of night. One night, when I was already in bed, he brought a tray down and placed it on my lap. It had everything on it that I had been hungry for: vanilla ice cream, saltine crackers, grape juice. Although I had gained only seventeen pounds when carrying Nick, and twenty-three pounds when carrying Whit, I put on forty-five pounds with this pregnancy. Because I had always gained weight when I was happy, I decided this pregnancy was the happiest time in my life.

Shortly before dinnertime on February 4th, six days after my due date had come and gone, I began to feel contractions, mild and irregular at first. Greg told me not to worry about preparing dinner. Instead, he ordered pizza and told me to sit at the kitchen table and time the pains while we waited for Alexa or Peter to arrive. A little later, as Juanita and the boys chewed on their slices of pepperoni pizza, they watched for my face to contort with the next contraction. As each pain began, Juanita's little face would scrunch up, too, making me laugh through the contraction. By the time they'd finished the pizza, I was feeling increasingly intense pain every five minutes. Greg called Maria over to baby-sit, and as soon as she arrived, he and I headed for the base hospital.

At each of my monthly obstetric appointments, I'd seen a different midwife, and one of them was scheduled to deliver our baby. However, when I was examined by a midwife at the hospital that night, she determined that our baby was in a breech position and breech deliveries weren't done by midwives. Two midwives attempted to turn the baby for a head-first birth, but weren't successful, and at that point, they called a doctor in. He ordered the operating room be prepared for a cesarean delivery. But before the preparations could be completed, our baby decided it was time to make her appearance. So Alexa Sullivan Mann arrived, bottom first at 8:30 that night—less than a half-hour after we got to the hospital. Even the doctor seemed surprised. He said he had never seen such a fast breech delivery.

Alexa, who weighed seven-and-a-half pounds, was handed to me briefly and then whisked away, crying, for her APGAR test, which is performed immediately after birth and uses factors such as pulse, respiration, and muscle tone to evaluate a newborn's condition. I worried that she might not be healthy because of my age, 36, and the fact that she had been delivered in the breech position—both indicators of possible problems.

"If there are any problems with her, I want to be told first," I told the doctor. "I don't want to see you whisper to my husband or hear the nurses talking about any problems. I want you to come directly to me and explain what's going on." He promised he would, and soon reported back to me that Alexa was robust and healthy with an APGAR score of 9-10, with 10 being the highest possible score.

I'd missed dinner—hadn't even had a bite of the pizza—and now that I knew all was well, I was starving. Even though it was past the dinner hour, the hospital kitchen prepared a little supper and Greg kept me company as I ate. We called the boys to tell them they had a sister and they cheered at the news.

A week after we arrived home with our baby, my good friend and neighbor Karen gave a baby shower, inviting the whole neighborhood. We felt as though our small community was rejoicing with us. By the time Greg and I arrived with tiny Alexa, Karen's home was filled to capacity with about forty neighborhood women and some of their husbands. Gifts were piled high, and everyone watched as I unwrapped and held up each item to be admired: handmade dolls, blankets, sweaters, booties, and music boxes that played lullabies. Each gift was a treasure from a friend who had been there for me over the years, offering kindness and concern in times of loneliness and heartbreak—and now in celebration of our happy family and new baby.

Our "Lexie" made us feel complete.

* * * * *

One month after Alexa was born, we celebrated Juanita's third birthday with a party. A week after that, Greg received orders for his next assignment at Wright Patterson Air Force Base, just outside of Dayton, Ohio, where he would attend graduate school at the Air Force Institute of Technology. We'd be moving in two months.

Juanita was my first concern. It seemed ridiculous now, that when I first took Juanita as a foster child I had been required to sign papers agreeing I would never attempt to adopt her. She had been with us for three years, ever since she was four months old. She was our Ladybug and a part of our family.

"You don't give a family member away," I said when I called Burk, the counselor who had always worked with us.

"That's the way the foster care program is set up," he said. "It wouldn't be in your best interest to try to fight it. We will see to it that Juanita is placed in another good Albuquerque foster home." I talked to his supervisor and others at the New Mexico Department of Health and Human Services. I couldn't comprehend how the department could

286

do this to a tiny child who had only ever known us as her family. Juanita had already taken on the role of Alexa's big sister: alerting us when she cried, stroking her hair, choosing what she would wear, and giving her gentle hugs and kisses. Feeling defeated after making no progress with my calls, I slumped down on the side of my bed, next to Juanita and Alexa. Juanita was wearing her white t-shirt with a blue Cookie Monster on it, her hair in braids tied with royal blue ribbons. To give her up seemed inconceivable!

My mind went back to the loss and isolation I'd felt when I had to leave my foster family. I wondered if our little Ladybug would ever come galloping back to us. *Have we given her enough love and security to see her through whatever lies ahead?*

Two neighboring families each said they were willing to become Juanita's new foster family. I asked Burk to please request that the department consider these homes so that Juanita could stay in her same neighborhood and be watched over by the same caring neighbors. After home inspections and interviews, one of these homes *was* selected. Juanita would be placed in this home, but only after a slow transition. First she went on outings with her new family. Then she was comfortably moving between our home and theirs, spending several consecutive nights with them—and then every night.

Juanita lived with that family for the next three years before her biological mother's parental rights were severed and Juanita was adopted by a family from outside the neighborhood.

* * * * *

After the moving company had taken away our furniture and most of our other possessions, Greg sat on the dining-room floor in our empty house and leaned back against the wall. The boys were out in the neighborhood, saying goodbye to their friends, and the house was quiet. He looked around at the brick floors, the adobe walls, the bright Mexican tile in the kitchen, and out toward the addition he'd put on the house. "I'm going to miss this house," he said. "There is a feeling of warmth and comfort here." Minutes turned into an hour as he reminisced about the times we'd shared as a family in this house and in the neighborhood. I listened to him as I cleaned empty cabinets and drawers, sharing his thoughts and wondering if any other house would ever feel so much like home.

We left Albuquerque in late May of 1975 in a red, VW bus we'd named Chubby. We towed a packed-to-bursting U-Haul trailer. Chubby had no air conditioning, so we had to keep all its windows open and let the wind whip at us as we snailed across the hot miles.

Early the next morning, as we were coming up on Amarillo in the panhandle of Texas, we heard tornado warnings on a local radio station. We were on open highway when Greg looked in the rearview mirror and saw a dark funnel cloud a few miles behind us. At first, it looked like it might be gaining on us. We watched, hoping it would veer off in another direction, but it stayed on course with the freeway. We had planned on covering some distance before stopping for breakfast and before the day got hot. Instead, we decided this would be a good time to move out of the funnel's path. We pulled off into a little town and found a restaurant in the one-block "downtown" area. The mom-and-pop place was filled with aromas of homemade biscuits and gravy, bacon, and coffee. We were suddenly ravenous and in no hurry to get back on the road. Alexa slept in her carrier as we ate huge country breakfasts and listened in on conversations around us about the latest tornado warnings.

After breakfast, we drove on through Oklahoma, Missouri, and Illinois and didn't get bogged down in traffic until Indiana, when we encountered backups caused by the crowds attending the Indianapolis 500 car race.

When we arrived in Fairborn, Ohio—a suburb of Dayton—we pulled into a Holiday Inn to spend a night or two until Greg could arrange temporary lodging for us at Wright-Patterson AFB, where we could stay until we found a house. Within minutes after we arrived, all sweaty and windblown, the boys found their bathing suits and were jumping into the motel pool.

We spent the next several days with a real estate agent, looking at houses. Fairborn was a tidy town with wide streets, two-story houses with shutters, two-car garages, and manicured yards. We found the picture-perfect home on Sartell Drive in the Rona Hills subdivision. It looked like all the other houses on the street, but this one sat on a one-acre lot with most of that acreage in its park-like back yard.

When the truck with our furniture arrived on moving-in day, neighbor children watched from side yards, and neighbor ladies brought homemade goodies and introduced themselves. They pointed to their houses and said, "Anything you need, you just knock on the door."

Our new home had four bedrooms and three bathrooms. The boys shared the largest bedroom so Greg could use the smallest one for a study where he could close the door and escape family distractions to read and do the required work for his classes. A sunny front bedroom became Alexa's nursery. The house seemed large until all our furniture was arranged inside—and then it seemed to have shrunk. The family room and dining room were much smaller than we were used to in our old house.

The backyard provided our entertainment. An awning

covered the patio just outside the sliding glass doors. From the edge of the patio, the terraced yard was landscaped on four levels that sloped gradually uphill, each level defined by a low rock wall. Flowers of many varieties, surrounded by grass that needed mowing, bordered the rock walls. A flagstone path wound to the farthest point of the yard, where the boundary fence was hidden by trees. Birds chirped and sang in our paradise of private outdoor living. Seeing it the first time had reminded me of Mom's tour of the yard at my foster home almost thirty years earlier.

The boys spent most of that summer in the yard, enjoying the Slip n' Slide water game, sprinkler jumping, and Frisbee tossing. They pitched a tent out there and invited new friends to overnight campouts. We ate our dinners at the redwood picnic table on the patio. On rainy days I often sat under the awning with a book and read the afternoon away. There was something to be said for leaving the desert behind.

At the end of the summer, the boys would attend Black Lane Elementary School, just a short walking distance from the house. Nick would be in fifth grade and Whit in fourth. I went to the school to register the boys and spoke with Nick's teacher about his dyslexia. It was reassuring to hear her say, "My son has always dealt with dyslexia, too. So I understand and will do everything I can to help him." Nick would be in good hands.

* * * * *

In the summer of 1976, a year after we'd moved to Ohio, we received a call from Greg's former mother-in-law who told us that Lynn, his first wife, was ill and in need of surgery. Could five-year-old Michelle, Greg and Lynn's daughter, come live with us for the indefinite period of time it would take Lynn to recover from the surgery? "Of course she can!" Greg said.

Greg drove to Illinois to pick Michelle up with all her clothing, toys, books, and anything else she wanted to bring that would fit in our car. It was good for them to have the quiet drive back to visit with each other before arriving at our noisy, busy home.

Michelle was Lynn's only child, and the two of them had lived alone for the three-and-a-half years since the divorce. Now she was suddenly one of four children, and having to share the attention was an adjustment for her. She felt insecure and wanted the exclusive attention of her daddy. Everything was new to Michelle, and she showed some signs of anxiety and distress.

I felt certain her attitude would improve after she started school in a few weeks. We all just needed to be patient and understanding with our new little family member. At Lynn's request, Michelle went to Bible school that summer and I also got her into a neighborhood Camp Fire Girls group.

In the fall, Nick and Whit joined a Pee Wee football team—the Fairborn Flyers. Alexa, Michelle and I went to their practices, and Greg and I went to their games to cheer them on. Every night I soaked their muddy yellow-and-white uniforms in Biz "stain fighter" and then washed them in detergent so they'd be ready for the next day's grime.

As winter moved in, the house hummed with activity. To lose the extra baby weight I'd gained, I jumped rope in the garage for half an hour every day. Greg escaped to his study in the evenings.

The boys and Michelle walked to and from school together each day. And each evening they sat at the kitchen table, sharing the events of their day and working on their homework as I prepared dinner. As a first grader, Michelle didn't have much homework, but she felt like a big kid sitting there with the boys with school papers in front of her. "Dinner's ready, Greg!" I'd call upstairs to Greg, and he would come down so the six of us could share our day over dinner.

The winter of 1976-77 was the coldest in Ohio's history. In January, the temperature dipped to a record-breaking minus twenty-one degrees—with the wind chill factor, it was fifty below. Total snowfall that winter was over 37 inches—with January alone accounting for 20 inches of snow—making it the second snowiest winter in Ohio history. Through most of the winter there was at least a foot of snow on the ground, and drifts much deeper.

Dayton's *Journal Herald* printed "Survival Certificates" for those who managed to shiver through Dayton's record cold spell. Warnings were broadcast: "Don't let your children or pets out. They can fall on the ice and freeze to death before they are found." Parents, however, were required to get out in the frigid temperatures to shovel the sidewalks in front of their houses for the postman. Dressed for the Arctic, I was out there each morning, shoveling the night's snowfall, cheeks burning with the cold.

Greg took the children to school, but Alexa and I rarely got out. At times it seemed oppressive to remain inside with four children and a husband trying to study. My cabin fever reached a peak when I discovered Greg had gone out in the car to get gas without inviting me to go along.

On days that were above freezing, even if temperatures climbed only into the low forties, the neighbors were out washing their cars, waving to each other and calling out, "Beautiful day!" Greg built an igloo in our front yard and in the backyard the boys made a snowman and an R-rated snow woman, her chest adorned with two pink marbles.

We braved a blizzard in mid-December to cut down our own Christmas tree in a forest an hour's drive from our home. The cold was almost too painful that day, and Michelle cried as I clung to her mittened hand, helping her through the deep snowdrifts. The difficult trek back to the car, with Greg carrying Alexa while also dragging the tree, was almost our undoing. From the front seat of Chubby, the VW bus, I looked back into the cargo space our four children now shared with the sparsely needled, slightly crooked tree. Rosy-cheeked in their heavy coats and pants, scarves, hats, mittens, and boots—all squished between the branches—they looked like a *Saturday Evening Post* cover by Norman Rockwell. There wasn't a smile among them, just frozen silence.

The next day we decorated the tree, had warm apple cider and homemade ginger-raisin cookies, and talked about our tree-cutting adventure.

"I saw a duck by the frozen pond that couldn't walk," Nick said. "He acted mad when I went near him."

"I saw him, too," Whit said. "I think he was supposed to fly away before it got cold."

"I don't want to get Christmas trees anymore," Michelle said, chewing on her cookie. Nick and Whit agreed they didn't want to either.

"Next year can we just buy a tree?" Nick asked.

* * * * *

The welcome sight of tiny crocuses popping up to bloom through the dwindling remains of snow in out backyard was the first sign of spring awakening in 1977. I walked outside in my nightgown one morning with two-year-old Alexa tagging behind, just as happy as I was to be free of the confines of the house. I raised my arms in sheer joy and sang, "Oh, What a Beautiful Morning." Despite all the losses in my first thirty years of life, I felt whole, healed, happy, and so very blessed on that glorious morning.

Our family of six, December 1976

On Mother's Day that May, Greg made reservations for a midday dinner for the six of us at Derr Road Inn. The restaurant was a converted country estate located amid many acres of rolling hills. From our big round table on a glassed-in side porch, we gazed out in appreciation of spring's offering of grass, flowers, and newly leafed-out trees. We were dressed in our best clothes, and before we'd left home Greg and I had stressed the need for manners and politeness. Nick was twelve by then, Whit was eleven, Michelle was six, and Alexa was two. As we waited for our food to arrive, they were behaving beautifully and talking softly.

After placing a plate in front of each of us, the waitress stood back, looking at us for a moment. I assumed she was wondering if there was anything else we needed, until she moved behind me, leaned over, and spoke close to my ear—but loudly enough that we all could hear: "You have a beautiful family, Mother."

I took in a deep breath, and felt myself fill with pride. I smiled at the children, so well-mannered, so lovely, and then at Greg.

Three-year-old Sally, still inside of me, had found her family at last.

EPILOGUE

I n 1979, an Air Force assignment brought us back to Albuquerque. Greg and I had an adobe home built in the foothills of the Sandia Mountains, where we still live. Our children are grown and scattered across the country, but every other year Nick, Whit, Michelle, Alexa, and Juanita return to our Albuquerque home with their spouses and children to celebrate Christmas together as a family.

* * * * *

My sister, Nan, is the only one who has shared my life from the beginning until now. We have visited each other frequently over the years, and talk regularly by email now. We see life differently, yet appreciate each other's views. Nan is more unconventional, and I am more traditional. Nan has more intellectual interests and pursuits, and I am more the nurturing mother and grandmother. We refer to each other affectionately as "Nanny Goat" and "Sally-mannder"—sisters through both troubled and joyful times!

* * * * *

Mother died in May of 1999 at the age of ninety-three, having outlived her second husband, from whom she was estranged. She'd spent her final years in a retirement community in Santa Barbara, California, taking daily strolls with the aid of a wheeled-walker, reading library books, and writing short stories. I'd called her weekly and visited her once or twice a year. She died in her apartment one evening, with a library book on her lap and a vodka tonic and plate of cheese and crackers on the table next to her. She left her estate to the Salvation Army and her body to medical research. She had no friends; there was no funeral or memorial service.

Greg and I hiked into the Sandia Mountains on a morning shortly afterward and sat on a sun-warmed boulder. I couldn't bring myself to talk about Mother. The unrelenting and unresolved problems in our relationship weighed too heavily on me. Greg understood. Instead, we talked of life and death in general and of the importance of family.

* * * * *

Reflections on my marriage to John are complicated. I don't know whether John and I would ever have been able to make our marriage work if he had returned from Vietnam. Growing up, I'd always felt there was a void in my life that having a family would one day fill. John was handsome, intelligent, and he told me he loved me. I'd loved him, too, and I accepted his proposal. I was young and eager to start a family with him. Although he was an admirable man in many ways, he had inner demons that frightened me. In the sixties in Valdosta, I was unaware of any groups that could help me, such as Alcoholics Anonymous, Al-Anon, child care centers, shelters for battered women, or other sources of assistance. I had no family close by to lean on for advice and comfort and I temporarily lost my way, my courage, and my confidence.

John was a hero to his country. I tell my story with the hope it doesn't malign his character or diminish his sacrifice. He was a patriot through and through.

* * * * *

Greg will retire soon and looks forward to having more time to pursue his many hobbies and interests. His coming into my life was the turning point. He made my dreams come true.

* * * * *

Once our children were all in school, I returned to teaching for twenty-three years, until I retired in 1997. I'd found what I had always searched for—security and the closeness and love of family. I have dealt with my *lot in life* and discovered an inner strength and peace along the way.

CPSIA information can be obtained at www.ICGtesting.com
Printed in the USA
LVOW041232140912

298843LV00001B/2/P